Comparative Legislative Studies

Malcolm E. Jewell, Editor

R·E·F·O·R·M

IN THE

HOUSE OF COMMONS

The Select Committee System

MICHAEL JOGERST

THE UNIVERSITY PRESS OF KENTUCKY

Editorial and Sales Offices: Lexington, Kentucky 40508–4008

Library of Congress Cataloging-in-Publication Data

Jogerst, Michael A., 1959–
    Reform in the House of Commons : the select committee system /
Michael Jogerst.
        p.   cm. — (Comparative legislative studies)
    Includes bibliographical references and index.
    ISBN: 978-0-8131-5303-2
    1. Great Britain.   Parliament.   House of Commons—Committees.
2. Great Britain.   Parliament.   House of Commons—Reform.   3. Party
discipline—Great Britain.   I. Title.   II. Series.
JN679.J64   1993
328.41'07658—dc20   92-22420

Contents

Tables and Figures

Tables

Figures

Acknowledgments

Researching, writing, and completing a book that required over a hundred interviews in a country not one's own usually requires the advice, help, and encouragement of a number of people. This case is no exception.

A number of colleagues have helped me with their comments and suggestions for transforming my original, often vague, ideas into this final project. I especially want to thank James Christoph, Larry Dodd, Marjorie Hershey, Norman Furniss, and Freddie Diamant for their contributions and criticisms early on in this project. And special recognition is deserved for Vince della Sala, who continues to challenge my understanding of legislative politics and whose contributions to this field have shaped my own scholarship.

I also want to thank the fellows and students of Nuffield College, Oxford, and in particular Vincent Wright and David Butler, for providing me with the resources and facilities to complete such a major part of this research. David and Vincent were particularly helpful in keeping me on track and getting me over those inevitable hurdles one finds when doing research in a country not one's own.

This book also would not have been possible without the generous help of the Fulbright Commission and the patience of many members of Parliament and House of Commons staff who agreed to be interviewed and so willingly gave of their time to answer my endless questions. They deserve special thanks.

I am indebted to Mark Ruggeberg and Bob Brooks. They make life easier and the burdens lighter.

I am also grateful to the University Press of Kentucky for making an interesting manuscript into a publishable one. In particular, I want to thank Malcolm Jewell, the series editor, for his comments and those of the reviewers chosen by him.

Finally, I want to dedicate this book to Ted and Joyce. And they know why.

1

Introduction

Since the Reform Act of 1867, parliamentary government in Great Britain has steadily yielded to the primacy of party government. Members of Parliament were first and foremost members of a political party, and their behavior and attitudes were guided by this constraint. Parliamentary politics were understood in terms of front- and backbenchers, leaders and followers, policy-makers and policy-ratifiers. Through this tight nexus of party dominance, Parliament's purpose seemed to be to ratify what had been decided elsewhere. The leaders of the largest party in the House of Commons returned at the last general election became the nation's executive branch, retained their legislative seats in the House, organized the majority party in the legislature, and dominated the proceedings, timetable, and agenda of the House. Perhaps Parliament was sovereign, but the cabinet had become supreme.

This accepted notion of party and executive control over the House of Commons has served to inhibit closer scrutiny of the internal political changes in the 1960s and 1970s, changes that coincided with the creation of a new committee system for the House of Commons. In the House, nascent committees were created in the mid-1960s to investigate politically safe policy domains, such as agriculture or science and technology. When committee members actually undertook parliamentary inquiries into executive policies, the majority party in power had them abolished. But during the 1960s and particularly the 1970s, the cracks in party solidarity began to appear. As Norton (1975; 1978; 1980b) has so ably demonstrated, backbenchers were rebelling in greater numbers on more occasions and with more effect than had been the case since the introduction of party government into the House in 1867. Outside the House, voters were deserting the two major parties at the polls, decreasing their partisanship and loyalty to Labour and Conservatives, and showing up in smaller and smaller numbers on polling days (Crewe, 1985). And despite the traditional notion of national parties contesting national elections based on national manifestos, local constituents increasingly expected their local MP to serve his or her constituency, even if that meant voting against the party's leaders and campaign promises (Cain et al., 1987).

American political scientists generally embraced this pre-1970 view of parliamentary government (APSA, 1950; Kirkpatrick, 1971) and lamented its passing when they became cognizant of the changes taking place (Epstein, 1980). The Westminster Model had provided order, efficiency, and strong government at a time when American political institutions were challenged by constitutional and policy struggles between the legislature and the executive as well as a politically unaccountable Supreme Court whose decisions increasingly changed the laws of the land and challenged its social fabric. Parliamentary sovereignty in Britain, however, had bestowed all such questions and issues on one democratic institution: the "Mother of Parliaments." The executive was drawn from the legislature and constitutionally accountable to it. Laws and government policies could not be declared unconstitutional precisely because they were Acts of Parliament and had been subject to parliamentary assent and legitimacy. There was no judicial review left to another institution comprised of politically appointed jurors-for-life. Democracy, efficiency, and accountability. These were the watchwords, the marvelous attributes of the Westminster Model.

Of course, from an institutional and constitutional perspective, the differences between the American Congressional Model and the British Westminster Model are fairly stark. Nevertheless, supporters of the British polity would also still bemoan continental parliamentary governments for their (perceived) gross shortcomings. Britain's European counterparts appeared to be a hodgepodge of ignoble proceedings and practices. Governments were more often than not forged by coalitions of several parties, the largest of which may have received not more than a third of the vote in the previous election, e.g. Italy. These countries were subject to continued government crises and collapse; the French Fourth Republic had twenty-seven separate governments in twelve years before the regime itself collapsed in 1958. France's written constitution provided for a strong legislature, but the multiparty system it engendered created representation of many parties in the National Assembly, most of which were not cohesive and were plagued with internal fractions and fissures. In theory the legislature could be a strong policy-influencing body, but its powers were exercised primarily negatively—to block parliamentary reforms and topple governments. Electoral systems based on proportional representation widely used in various forms on the Continent seemed to remove the voters from their "representative." The party lists presented to German voters, for example, seemed to remove the important democratic link between the citizen and his or her representative. To whom would one petition for redress of grievances? While party had indeed come to predominate in Great Britain, its parliamentary system, unlike those on the Continent or the Congressional Model in the United States nevertheless continued to facilitate democracy, efficiency, and stability.

In 1979, the newly elected Conservative government under the leadership of Margaret Thatcher introduced legislation into the House of Commons to establish a comprehensive select committee system. Several members of Parliament (MPs), including the Leader of the House, Norman St. John-Stevas, greeted the proposals as "the greatest parliamentary reform of the twentieth century." New committees whose task it is to monitor the executive were subsequently established. Backbenchers, those MPs who do not hold government or Opposition leadership positions, alone are eligible to sit on these committees. Unlike previous committee experiments, then, these reforms were designed specifically to remove party leaders from, and their institutionalized influence on, investigatory committees.

The British House of Commons is currently working under this new committee system and has been doing so since 1979. This new system, proposed by a Special Procedure Committee report (HC 588-I,II, 1977/78), is composed of fourteen departmentally-related committees. (Scottish Affairs was not reconstituted following the 1987 election, reducing the number to thirteen). These committees and their members are to monitor and scrutinize corresponding government departments. Party loyalty, however, suggests that MPs would continue to be reluctant to criticize party leaders and to assert Parliament's constitutional role of scrutiny and accountability. The Procedure Committee's report is all the more pathbreaking precisely because of what is expected of members of Parliament. For the proposed committee system to be successful, members' attitudes about their jobs, about Parliament, and about committee service necessarily had to differ sharply from the assumptions predicated in previous Procedure Committee reports that continued to advocate the subservient status of Parliament and backbenchers in the Westminster Model.

To understand fully the implications of this new system for Parliament and its members, this study recognizes two important parliamentary features characteristic of legislative dynamics in Great

Britain. On the one hand, one must recognize the traditional role of backbench MPs, which remains consistent with the "textbook" image of representation and government in Great Britain. On the other hand, one must also be aware of Parliament's institutional role in governing and/or formulating policy vis-à-vis the executive and question whether the theory is indeed consistent with practice. In short, I suggest that the theory and realities of the roles of Commons and of backbench MPs within it have met serious challenges in the past two decades. The subsequent committee reforms in particular can thus be seen as recognizing contemporary realities while at the same time adjusting to the expressed goals and desires of many backbenchers, thereby extending both the formal and the informal role and capacities of Parliament.

Comparative Legislative Change

From a comparative perspective, the calls for reform were not unique to Britain, nor should one presume that strong parties in other legislative settings prohibit parliamentary influence. Throughout the Old Commonwealth, Britain's former colonies, including Canada, Australia, and New Zealand, adopted similar legislative reforms in the late 1970s and early 1980s. The Westminster Model had come under reform worldwide. In Ireland, however, the select committees established by Fine Gael to monitor the executive were summarily dismissed in 1988 when Fiana Fail returned to power. After fifty years in Opposition, Fine Gael, under the leadership of Garret FitzGerald, sponsored a number of reforms for the Dail, notably select committees. With Ireland the exception to the rule, the 1970s were also a watershed era for a variety of "types" of parliamentary legislatures in Europe (Norton, 1990).

In the case of Italy, for example, Furlong (1990) argues that Parliament undeniably has power and influence in policy making and that rather than talk of the decline in Parliament in Italy, it is more appropriate to understand the constitutional impasse in which government and Parliament find themselves because they have been unable to develop a stable and effective working relationship. Specific parliamentary reforms in 1971 further allowed parties and deputies outside the *pentapartito* (the five-party coalition) access to the organization of parliamentary time. Article 23 of the new rules also transferred effective power over the legislative agenda to the Conference of Party Group Leaders (the *capigruppo*). Moreover, there must be unanimous support for the agenda within the *capigruppo*. This means that even the minor groups in Parliament have a say over what will be discussed in the chamber. The 1971 reforms marked a clear recognition that the government, or its majority in Parliament, does not have the power to determine the legislature's activities, unlike the situation in Great Britain. As Della Sala (1990) has pointed out, these provisions are important because the government does not have any legal or constitutional guarantee of priority passage for its legislation. All legislative proposals are considered equal, governments do not have the power of closure, and there are no limits on the areas allowed to be introduced by private members. And because governments in Italy do not have an electoral mandate to carry out a policy program, they do not have the political leverage to pressure Parliament to consider their legislative proposals. Like governments in Fourth Republic France, those in Italy cannot exert effective leadership on the legislative agenda.

The 1971 reforms in Italy also diffused power not only between legislature and executive but also within Parliament. As Della Sala notes (1990, 7), committees act as important gatekeepers in that they may decide which legislation will be scrutinized and which bills will not. This is much different from the pre-1971 situation in which the effective gatekeepers were the committee chairpersons who, more often than not, simply carried out decisions taken by the governing majority (Leonardi et al., 1978). Moreover, 80 percent of the legislation passed in Italy never reaches the full chamber for a vote; in many policy areas and under a variety of circumstances, parliamentary committees alone have the constitutional right to approve or reject legislation.

Recent legislative scholarship suggests that parliaments are declining and thus rejects this revanchist theme of the 1970s. The German Bundestag may quite possibly be reactive, but it is certainly not a powerless legislature. In spite of party discipline, the government does not normally have the capacity to impose its will on the legislature, let alone on the coalition's parliamentary parties, or *fraktionen* (Saalfeld, 1990). Despite the number of left/right and confessional/secular parties in the Netherlands, and despite the possible erosion of consociational democracy, developments over the past two decades suggest that parliamentary influence upon national policy making has actually increased (Gladdish, 1990). And since Sweden introduced a unicameral Riksdag and a revised electoral system in 1971, small specialist committees, minority governments, and votes of no confidence have emerged. As a consequence, Arter (1990) suggests, the Riksdag has strengthened itself as a policy-influencing assembly. Even in France, where the president legally and constitutionally possesses seemingly more power vis-à-vis the National Assembly compared to that of any other European democracy, the legislature cannot be said to be in decline (Frears, 1990). Fitzgerald (1990) too notes in his study on the Finance Committee in the French National Assembly that despite the intentionally constrained role of the parliament in the Fifth Republic, careerists in the legislature have been responsible for asserting its one basic monopoly, the legitimate right to make laws, and these deputies have continued to find power potential in parliament. He concludes: "In contrast to the modernization theorists who predicted the constant decline of legislative bodies everywhere, the recent years of French experience show that their best days may lie ahead" (Fitzgerald, 1990, 26).

Careers in the House of Commons

From a comparative perspective, the reforms introduced in Britain were consistent with parliamentary developments elsewhere in Europe, although this seems to be overlooked by many parliamentary scholars. Notwithstanding, these proposals were absolutely path-breaking for the British Parliament, not least of all because the Procedure Committee's report placed high expectations on the proposed departmentally-related select committees. They were to be "the eyes and the ears" of the House in its relation with government departments. Committee members hoped the result would be greater participation in the parliamentary process by backbenchers and improved information access for MPs. For the institution, this also meant increased accountability of the executive to the legislature and a reassertion of the role of the House in policy influence and evaluation. To achieve these desired aims, the onus of responsibility would fall to members of the new committees. Although the necessary institutional structures were created, they would remain relatively ineffectual without a corresponding interest, dedication, and will among their members. For the new system to be successful, the backbenchers would need to possess attitudes commensurate with those expected and anticipated in the Procedure Committee's report.

These reforms and active MPs would not necessarily be welcome news to all parliamentary actors and institutions involved in the national policy process. Backbench specialization through committee work could very well undermine the authority relationship inherent in party government. Specialization would result in diffusion of authority, authority that up until recently has been monopolized by party leaders. The norms of the House of Commons reflect the values of the most important and powerful actors in Parliament and have served to support the heretofore existing distribution of power and status quo. David Judge's research (1981) indicates that as long as backbenchers remain convinced that their political careers should be oriented to the attainment of executive office, then they will continue to conform to those norms most likely to secure this goal. Attaining executive office or achieving influence in the legislature, however, were not considered the primary goals or duties of many MPs. The notion of amateur, part-time "legislator" fit well with the Westminster Model, in which politics and policies are dominated by the respective party elites supported by loyal backbenchers. Contrary to this perception of the role of MPs, Norton (1975, 1978, 1980b) indicates that members have proved increasingly unwilling to be used as lobby fodder. Instead, they have proved willing to rebel against party leaders. Norton posits that rather than becoming an accepted and entrenched characteristic of parliamentary government in Great Britain, frontbench dominance and prerogatives have eroded during the past two decades.

Of course, as long as executive office is the only available career goal and as long as party loyalty is the only avenue or career ladder to pursue, MPs are subject to the logical demand of pursuing those "choices" that ultimately serve to legitimate party government and the authority-hierarchical relationship. Should alternative career opportunities and structures be created in Parliament, party loyalty and party unity would diminish in importance as means of achieving career goals. My research (Jogerst, 1991) suggests that select committees can indeed be viewed as alternative "career structures," allowing MPs to specialize and therefore removing them, to a degree, from the dictates of party leaders. Second, as several MPs have commented in debates and testimony, committee posts grant backbenchers more active and rewarding participation in the governing process than would be possible through years of service as mere loyal party men and women. Third, committee service can also guarantee *parliamentary* careers to those persons for whom the call to executive office will never come. Finally, whereas backbenchers achieve a degree of freedom in policy influence with party leaders in Opposition but not when in power, the creation of departmental select committees could provide the structural prerequisites necessary to maintain a sense of continuity in backbench influence over the executive, whether it be a Labour or a Conservative government.

Research and Organization

In 1979, Lees and Shaw, commenting on the state of comparative legislative committee research, could write with confidence: "When one searches for published material on committees in legislatures other than the American Congress, one becomes aware of a grotesque imbalance of systematic information. Knowledge on this subject is specific to only a few countries, and such non-American literature as exists is often legal and formalistic" (Lees and Shaw, 1979, 5).

Virtually all the existing literature on the new select committees in Britain also remains descriptive. Englefield and Drewry, for example, have produced works highlighting committee assignments, the number of reports issued, the costs of committee proceedings, lists of witnesses, and the number of pages printed per committee per year. It is unclear, however, why and how this information is important or compelling to the understanding of contemporary parliamentary politics. Second, such works lack any theoretical framework and do not suggest what, if any, ramifications exist based on their assembled information.

The fundamental question that academics, when asked, remain unable to answer is why members of Parliament wanted to establish these committees and why they chose to serve on them. These questions can usefully be addressed through survey research and personal interviews. During the 1986–87 parliamentary session, I conducted interviews in Great Britain with over one-hundred members of Parliament, committee clerks, and House of Commons staff. Three panels of MPs were used for this research project. Group A consisted of those members who had remained with the committees since 1979. Group B was a statistically-drawn random sample of MPs who had served on the committees but had left their posts. Group C was a statistically-drawn random sample of all MPs, front- and backbench, who had never served on one of the Select Committees.

Dividing the interviewees into three groups was important for a number of reasons. First, I wished to avoid skewing my results by relying solely on the attitudes of committee members. My questions on members' attitudes toward parliamentary service and particularly on the role and importance of the select committees would likely reflect biased perceptions if I relied on Groups A and B alone. It would be extremely misleading to suggest that Conservative or Labour MPs shared a common attitude about executive-legislative relations, committee importance, or Parliament as a debating forum if the subject sample consisted solely of committee members.

Second, since I maintained that members sought committee assignments to pursue individual goals that could be realized through rewarding committee service, it was necessary to interview members who resigned their committee assignments as well. Why did some members stay and other move on? Did members who left their committees find committee service frustrating, or did they perceive it as a "stepping stone" in their legislative careers? Is it then fair to suggest that committee members from Group A are less likely to be concerned about frontbench positions than those in Group B? If Group B MPs do indeed view committee service as a means to end, i.e., frontbench posts, are they less likely to pursue vigorously the inquiries and questions that may be critical of their party leaders? The answers to these questions are important in understanding potential select committee influence and highlighting the degree to which committee service is rewarding and satisfies members' goals.

Third, the inclusion of Groups B and C allowed me to include frontbench MPs, some of whom were promoted to those positions subsequent to their committee service. Others from Group C were frontbench MPs who had not served on select committees. In order to extend the influence of committee recommendations and reports, responsive, or at the very least nonhostile, ministers and frontbench spokesmen are crucial. Are select committees considered an irritant by members of the frontbench, and do the perceptions of committees' utility seem to alter when one has moved from a committee post to an official government or Opposition position? These questions, and their possible implications for Parliament, are addressed in later chapters.

The survey questionnaire I prepared was divided into two parts and is presented as Appendix A. The first part was subdivided further into three sections consisting of ope-ended questions. Section One asked members about their attitudes toward their jobs as MPs. The second section focused on their attitudes toward Parliament as an institution and its role vis-à-vis the executive. The third and longest section required members to answer several questions about the select committees created in 1979. Some questions were amended slightly to ensure that they were appropriate for the member interviewed. For example, question 27 for MPs in Group A read, "Does your committee assignment have any link to your constituency interests?" while members in Group B were asked, "Did your committee assignment have any link to your constituency interests?" And members of Group C, who had not served on committees, were asked, "Do you think there is any link between select committee members and their constituencies' interests?" Instances in which amended questions were presented to the three groups of MPs are clearly noted throughout the text.

Part two of the interviews consisted of closed-ended questions. These questions were typed on index cards and handed to the interviewees. As Appendix A illustrates, these questions ranged from asking members to rank the tasks best performed by Parliament to describing their own ideological positions within their parties.

All member of Parliament were assured in writing and immediately prior to the interview that their identity would remain anonymous and their statements "nonattributable." Some members indicated that what they had to say was clearly "on the record" and did not object to being quoted (indeed, encouraged it). Where this was the case, I have attributed particular quotes to their sources. In all other cases, however, anonymity has been maintained.

Before beginning each interview, I asked the member if he or she would allow our interview to be tape recorded in order to ensure an accurate and precise account of his or her views and statements. It also meant that I was not encumbered by the need to write as quickly as words were spoken. Every member agreed to be recorded, and the interviews averaged slightly more than an hour in length. In order to preserve the precise context of members' responses and to present both contextual and statistical analysis, all taped interviews were subsequently transcribed verbatim.

Once I had transcribed all the interviews, each open-ended question was coded for further statistical analysis. The coding of some questions was straightforward. For example, question 8 asked members, "Do you consider yourself a specialist in any particular policy area?" The answers were either yes or no. For other questions, however, members' responses were coded into as many different categories as there were response types. For example, I asked members in question 41, "In what ways would the select committees you would like to see a generation from now differ from those of today?" There were six different response categories for this question, and they were coded accordingly.

I also constructed individual "characteristic profiles" for each member interviewed. These profiles included a number of variables that would prove useful when identifying which "types" of MPs tended to share certain attitudes. These variables, which were also useful in subsequent analysis, were: (1) party, (2) sex, (3) age, (4) education, (5) occupation prior to Parliament, (6) year first elected to Parliament, (7) number of years in Parliament, (8) percentage of the vote in the last election, (9) percentage of the majority in the last election, (10) committee assignment, (11) other committee assignments, (12) length of time on the select committee, and (13) background or expertise in the committee topic.

In this book I assert that members' attitudes on parliamentary service are not only incompatible with (and indeed may undermine) the traditional interpretation of the Westminster Model, but constitute a significant change from those commonly shared—or presumed to be shared—by their predecessors. Longitudinal comparisons are best made when either the subjects remain constant or the variables subject to evaluation can be observed, measured, and tested with precision from one era to another. Although the research design used for the purposes of this research can be replicated and used in future studies, the lack of previous academic work on British parliamentary committees based on attitudinal survey research poses obvious difficulties.

These difficulties notwithstanding, useful and reliable comparisons can nevertheless be made. Suggestions for reforming the House of Commons have been made for decades, many of them funnelled through the Select Committee on Procedure. The importance of identifying these reforms rests not in describing what they were but rather in discovering why they were proposed, who supported them, and what their implications were for parliamentary influence.

If indeed there has been an attitudinal shift among MPs concerning their perceived roles in Parliament and the role of Parliament as well, I would expect this change to be reflected in the arguments, testimony, reports, and recommendations of successive Procedure Committees. As I point out in the following chapters, Procedure Committee members began to press for increased parliamentary assertiveness in the early 1960s, especially after Labour's victory in 1964. In particular, committee members questioned the control exercised by the government over the affairs and proceedings of the House. This marked a significant departure from the interpretations of parliamentary-executive relationships offered by previous Procedure Committees.

Both of these approaches are useful and appropriate in analyzing attitudinal change and institutional assertion. Robert McKenzie used a similar approach when he wrote *British Political Parties* (1964). As with Jennings's reliance on biographies, memoirs, and conference reports, McKenzie had to face the problem of the relevance of the past to the present. McKenzie examined the contemporary situation by interviewing current politicians "to find whether they really thought as their predecessors had done and recognized the same customs" (Butler, 1958, 46). Although much of the American congressional literature focuses on aggregate voting scores, contextual analysis has also made significant contributions. In his American Political Science Association presidential address, Richard Fenno noted that "observation is a crucial part in understanding and theorizing about legislative politics. It has an important role in political science" (Fenno, 1986, 5).

This research, then, is designed to move away from the descriptive, sometimes anecdotal, analysis of legislative politics in Great Britain. It examines the establishment and dynamics of party government in Britain, relies on comparisons of past and present committee proceedings, and uses survey research methods to order, arrange, and otherwise quantify members' attitudes.

These research methods allow me to present my argument that contemporary members of Parliament are indeed more likely to be "professional" legislators than were their predecessors. Colin Mellors suggested that the criteria for distinguishing professionals from amateurs can take the form of either counting electoral victories or measuring the duration of parliamentary service (Mellors, 1978, 82). In his study of British MPs, Philip Buck chose the former approach and claimed that "on the occasion of his third election a contestant loses amateur standing and becomes a professional" (Buck, 1963, 78). Donald Matthews (1984), on the other hand, favored the "length of service" approach in his study of American senators' political career patterns. For him, the demarcation between amateur and professional was ten or more years in public service.

Both of these approaches define professional status as a consequence of length of tenure in a legislature. The assumption, of course, is that seeking reelection and continued membership signify an individual's commitment to a legislative career. Buck further points out that between 1918 and 1959 more than 70 percent of all government posts and 98 percent of all cabinet ministries were held by MPs who had achieved professional status (Buck, 1963, 81) This definition, however, is inappropriate and misleading for my purposes. I make a distinction between the notion of MP as "gentleman amateur" (the textbook image) and that of the professional legislator who wants to pursue an activist role in Parliament. Therefore, I characterize a "professional MP" as one whose own role orientation in Parliament and attitudes toward the role of Parliament depart significantly from the traditional understanding of British MPs. In contrast to amateur MPs, the professional legislator would reflect the following characteristics:

1. Desires an active role in influencing or forming national policies.

2. Supports parliamentary reforms that give backbenchers and private members increased participation in Parliament.

3. Seeks opportunities to focus on and specialize in particular policy areas.

4. Rejects the assumption that they can be used as "lobby fodder" by party leaders.

5. Possesses identifiable goals that are pursued and satisfied in Parliament.

6. Considers the job of an MP as full-time and supports as well as uses increased resources to be able to accommodate the burdens imposed by increased legislative-related activities.

On Buck's and Matthews's definitions, however, a member of Parliament who had less than ten years' experience or fewer than three consecutive election victories would be considered an amateur without necessarily possessing the characteristics outlined above. It seems that Buck and Matthews are primarily concerned with legislators' ability to or interest in maintaining a position in a legislature. I suggest that it is more appropriate to understand how and why legislators define their jobs and the likely implications this has for legislative politics. Whether members have been in the House for three sessions or three elections is less important than the attitudes they share and the behavior they display during that time.

Select committees are a useful unit of analysis in addressing the issues and questions highlighted above. If Parliament is indeed a reactive legislature whose role has been reduced to rubber-stamping government-sponsored legislation, how can one explain the pressures to create committees to monitor government departments? Committee members often criticize party leaders' policies and propose alternative policy options. Promotion to the frontbench, however, is usually predicated upon demonstrated party loyalty. If members of

Parliament seek committee assignments as first rungs on the ministerial ladder, this apparent contradiction must be explained. On the other hand, if MPs do not envision advancement to the frontbench for themselves, one needs to explain why, unlike members in the past, they are not content to leave policy formation exclusively in the hands of party leaders and to enjoy the relatively burden-free and easy life which welcomes them on the backbench. I suggest that members are not willing to absolve themselves of the duty to fulfill Parliament's constitutional role of scrutiny and accountability. They do not seek to devolve policy formation to party leaders in order to pursue extraparliamentary interests and duties. They want to be knowledgeable and informed during debates and policy discussions and to participate in them; therefore, they seek ways to acquire specialization and expertise. They recognize the cost and benefits of national policies for their constituencies and seek means to pursue their constituencies' interests. For many, the call to the frontbench will never come, or has come and will not be repeated. These members, nevertheless, want to lead active careers in Parliament. The select committees created in 1979 provide the opportunity for them to fulfill these desires.

Organization

The following chapters are organized under two broad sections. Section one, comprised of chapters 2 through 5, examines the dynamics of party government and the associated constraints imposed on the development of parliamentary select committees. Section two, comprised of chapters 6 through 9, highlights the development of the current committee system and presents the results of my survey research.

Party domination of a parliamentary legislature should not be considered a natural or necessary phenomenon. Influential roles for members and committees with broad powers are not incompatible with parliamentary government, as the workings of the German Bundestag and the Canadian House of Commons show. Chapter 2 explains the consequences of party control in Britain over the attitudes and behavior of MPs and why party dominance ensured executive control of the legislature's power and agenda-setting capacities. The important point to be made here is not merely that party government did emerge in Britain. Rather, it is imperative to explain why the Opposition frontbench and generally the backbenchers of the major parties acquiesced in abdicating parliamentary powers and prerogatives to the executive.

Once this newly-defined relationship between the legislature and the executive became entrenched through formal procedures and informal norms, fulfilling the House's constitutional role of making the executive accountable was virtually impossible, even for the few who may have believed this still was Parliament's role and wanted to uphold it. I suggest, then, that today the only viable means of breaking the mold of executive control is the creation of alternative "role routes" in the House: alternative parliamentary avenues for influence and activism for backbenchers.

Given the influence of political parties over the organization of the House of Commons between 1867 and 1979, few parliamentary committees seemed necessary. In particular, development of policy proposals was monopolized by the leaders of the majority party, not by select or standing committees. Chapter 3 discusses the early use of committees in the Commons and the limited room for maneuver they had in monitoring the executive in any meaningful way. Committees were hampered by executive domination of the legislature through formal rules and party discipline, members' commonly shared attitudes about their parliamentary roles, which reinforced their subservient status, and the apparent development of a constitutional doctrine prohibiting Parliament from questioning government ministers and their policies in a committee forum. A number of scholars and politicians have lamented this "decline of Parliament," but I suggest that this perceived "decline" in truth reflected a normative concern with the current state of parliamentary influence in comparison to the constitutional and theoretical powers that the institution possessed.

With the high turnover in membership following the 1964 general election, the new parliamentary entrants pressed the Wilson government to ensure that members would have the opportunity to influence policy decisions. Chapter 4 demonstrates that the ensuing Crossman Reforms served as a catalyst for further and more comprehensive committee reform proposals. And I argue that this did not occur simply because MPs were given a taste of power and wanted more. Instead the government grossly miscalculated the degree to which members of its own party would use their committee posts to develop bipartisan, "parliamentary views" on a policy issue and willingly criticize party leaders and their policies. The ensuing row between the Labour frontbench and the Labour backbench was transformed into an institutional confrontation pitting a heavy-handed and duplicitous executive against a sovereign legislature invoking its constitutional powers. It is one of the great legislative challenges to executive ascendancy in the twentieth century that complacency and obsession with the "decline of legislatures" leitmotif have caused legislative scholars to overlook and ignore.

In subsequent governments, both Labour and Conservative leaders recognized that calls for committee reforms could no longer be avoided. They could, however, appear sympathetic to members' demands by accepting some Procedure Committee recommendations, but only those recommendations that would be beneficial to the governments of the day. In this respect, governments continued the tradition so clearly pursued in the decades following the introduction of party government of supporting parliamentary reforms that were in the best interest of the executive. In concluding section one, chapter 5 focuses on the 1977–78 Select Committee on Procedure report that recommended the creation of a comprehensive system of select committees to monitor all executive departments. Implementing the committee's proposals could have far-ranging consequences for legislative-executive relations and the role to be played by backbenchers in the policy process. Most members, including the newly chosen Conservative prime minister, failed to appreciate these possibilities—essentially because they failed to appreciate how much the attitudes and backgrounds of fellow members had changed. The views presented in testimony, the breadth of the Procedure Committee's investigation, the changed perception of executive-legislative relations, and the final recommendations represented a sharp departure from the proceedings and reports of previous procedure committees. This change in the nature of this committee's report compared to previous ones was facilitated by a corresponding change in members' attitudes about their obligations and roles as MPs and the duties that Parliament as an institution *should* be performing.

If indeed this attitudinal shift has occurred, one should find that members' attitudes on a variety of job- and parliamentary-related questions differ from those commonly assumed to have been held by their predecessors. In chapter 6 I present the evidence collected from my survey research. This chapter argues that backbenchers do indeed want opportunities to be active in the legislature and disagree sharply with frontbenchers who argue that enough opportunities already exist. There are also sharp differences between what members spend their time and energies doing in Parliament and what they would like to be doing. This gap between their preferred and actual roles serves to create frustration and impatience among members.

For some, the solution is either to reform Parliament and make it "backbench-friendly" or to recognize and accept finally the institutional and party constraints of the House and abandon any intentions of a career in public service at the national level.

Members who seek more involvement in the policy process must have the structural avenues necessary to secure their goals. That MPs are discouraged by their present job orientations in Parliament may also suggest that they are dissatisfied with the current institutional capacities and procedures of Parliament. Indeed, the evidence presented in chapter 7 suggests that a gap also exists between those tasks Parliament performs best and the tasks members state it should be performing. Furthermore, it appears that members do indeed have different career goals and have structured corresponding avenues to secure these goals.

When members spoke of their goals in Parliament, their jobs as MPs, and the role of the legislature in national politics, select committees were often identified as forming crucial components in all three of these facets of parliamentary life and legislative reform. Chapter 8, then, focuses on their attitudes toward select committees, addressing why some members chose committee service and others did not, why some committee members remained on and others left their respective committees, and which goals they hoped to pursue on their committees. Where applicable, comparisons are made between those who selected committee service and those who did not. Because the Procedure Committee in 1978 expressed a desire for a normative subculture to develop among committee members, comparisons between the two groups highlight the differences and similarities in their attitudes toward select committees specifically and parliament generally.

This study makes clear that in the Westminster Model, the duties and tasks of a committee member differ substantially from those associated with chamber-related activities. Committee members need to specialize in a subject area, whereas on the floor of the House an MP may be expected to move adroitly from one subject to another as debate progresses. In debate, an MP's oratorical skills are crucial; in committee they are pointless. Questions raised in chamber serve to score debating points or embarrass the Opposition. In committee they are probing, sustained and nonconfrontational.

Chapter 9 addresses the qualities and skills that MPs assume are important to be effective committee members, how members define their committee jobs, and how they perceive the role of select committees. Members have found committee service rewarding, especially through access to information and opportunities for specialization. They benefit personally and professionally, but they also emphasize that parliamentary government benefits from select committee activity. Select committee service may not be attractive to all members of Parliament, but even non-committee members recognize the role these committees have played in the House and their potential for development.

Far from being "wound up" by the government, as was the case just twenty years ago, and with consistently high attendance rates and low annual turnover, these select committees appear to be a prominent feature of the parliamentary landscape and have served both Parliament as an institution and its members individually.

2

Party Government in a Parliamentary Forum

The introduction of a comprehensive system of committees whose task it is to monitor and scrutinize the executive breaks with parliamentary tradition and practice, given the primacy of party government. Members of Parliament and political scientists have long noted the underlying foundations and practices necessary to support and sustain the Westminster Model. Most important among these characteristics are a strong two-party system, party cohesion and loyalty both in and out of Parliament, large numbers of amateurs or part-time backbenchers who primarily leave day-to-day governing and policy making to a small leadership elite, and party interests that are to take precedence over local or parochial interests in an MP's vote in a division and his or her behavior on the floor of the House. Indeed, while in this view the chamber was seen as the primary arena for debating policy, the House has come to have little impact on influencing the nature of a particular policy or the outcome of the ensuing vote.

But Parliament was not always vastly overshadowed by the whims and power of the executive. Nor was the floor of the House a mere "talking shop where Members speak past each other," knowing their speeches will largely be futile attempts to exercise policy input or alteration. While the House of Commons and some form of parliamentary government have been in existence for centuries, those characteristics attributed to the Westminster Model are of relatively recent origin, beginning in the mid- to late nineteenth century with the introduction of party government into the parliamentary equation.

This chapter offers an analysis of the role party dominance plays in parliamentary processes and reforms in the House of Commons. I examine both the reasons for reform and how they came about. This examination is important in understanding longitudinal shifts in members' behavior and attitudes as well as in comparing institutional changes. Having established a historical and institutional framework from which to proceed, I will in my next chapter examine in greater detail the calls for reform from the late 1950s to the early 1970s and early experiments with departmentally-related select committees. And I will demonstrate in the following chapters that the nature of reform proposals and debates changed as members' attitudes about the role of Parliament and select committees changed.

Constitutional Powers and Parliamentary Practice

Both scholars and members of Parliament note the "Golden Age" of Parliament, a period in the mid-nineteenth century when the legislature was comprised of relatively independent legislators, when the chamber was undoubtedly the locus of power, and before party government had firmly superimposed itself on parliamentary government. But the era of independent legislative action and parliamentary supremacy passed out of existence certainly by the turn of the century, and contributors to the prevailing "Decline of Parliament" thesis in the 1960s appeared to be primarily comparing the reality of Parliament's role in Great Britain with the idealized institution of a century previous. Moreover, a common omission in this literature is the impact of political parties in organizing parliamentary functions and processes. The evidence offered by many authors to describe decline or decay could easily be seen as a phenomenon naturally accompanying the introduction and subsequent maintenance of party government. Party dominance of Parliament relied upon and was sustained by tight party discipline, institutional hierarchy defined by intraparty positions, members pledged to support national party manifestos but elected by local constituencies, and the majority party's (executive) monopoly of expertise and information coupled with control of the timetable and debates of the legislature. Nevertheless, the issues raised by these academics, civil servants, MPs, and journalists were important in setting the parliamentary reform agenda during the first Wilson government in particular. Their contribution, arguments, and implications will be examined more thoroughly in chapters 3 and 4, where I address the "Crossman Reforms."

The challenge facing many legislative scholars, particularly those concerned with an institution as enduring as the British House of

Commons, is one of appreciating routinized procedures and institutional norms. Many parliamentary customs and practices represent responses to political and social phenomena of decades past. The problem is not merely one of deciding if the way in which a situation was handled in the days before politicians were professionals and suffrage was universal will influence the way in which it will be handled in the present era of rigid parties and a mass electorate. As David Butler adds, so many political customs have such intricate roots in the distant past that "a clear exposition even of obsolescent precedents can be an invaluable aid to the understanding of current practices" (Butler, 1958, 45–46).

Chief among the political customs from the distant past that shape and direct contemporary politics is the organization of legislative activity by political parties. Indeed, party is central to an understanding of the House of Commons in the twentieth century—its composition, procedure, and output, as well as the voting behavior of MPs and their activity on and off the floor of the House. Formally, political parties are unofficial bodies and as such are not recognized as part of the constitutional structure; they are, however, at the heart of British politics (Norton, 1981, 26). Norton's distinction between the formal and the theoretical foundations of British government on the one hand and the commonly accepted practices on the other encapsulates the debate between reformers and traditionalists. For example, some critics of reform and select committee scrutiny assert that because the Constitution provides for a sovereign and supreme Parliament, the House of Commons must give its approval to all executive-initiated legislation. Thus Parliament as an institution fulfills its constitutional role mainly through its power of assent.

Several MPs and academics, however, have questioned whether Parliament can indeed fulfill its constitutional obligation given the paucity of information and expertise available to individual members. With the few institutional mechanisms available for scrutiny, monitoring, or policy input, constitutional assumptions are undermined by the day-to-day reality of parliamentary government organized through political parties. When Gladstone addressed the House in the late nineteenth century about its role and the role of its members, he said, "You have been summoned here, not to legislate or to govern, but to be the constant critic of Government" (Ryle, 1977, 104). His dictum appears to have been accepted and practiced throughout much of the twentieth century as well.

During the period between the first two Reform Acts (1832–67), the relationship between the government and the House of Commons was one of almost mutual dependence. The House expected the government to exercise the executive authority, and the government looked to the House for support. The dynamics of this relationship prohibited the House from being taken for granted, as the outcome of votes was not a foregone conclusion and the House could, and did, replace one government with another. Although the executive continued to be chosen from Parliament, the relationship between the two changed significantly after 1867.

The Reform Act of 1867 stimulated a certain amount of national organization in order to increase voter registration and provide a list of possible candidates for constituencies lacking suitable local prospects. The national organization—at the time usually headed by the party's chief whip in the House of Commons—might encourage constituency organizations to name candidates wherever local party leaders had failed to do so or to attempt to arbitrate when the local party leaders were split. The Reform Act of 1867 also prompted the growth of constituency organizations in order to attract the new working-class voters. The first prominent example was the "Birmingham caucus," established by Joseph Chamberlain (Arnstein, 1976, 132). The individual Birmingham voter had the right to elect the caucus, or leadership, of his constituency party organization. But since most voters then, as now, did not bother to attend party meetings, this leadership remained in the hands of party workers and activists, who tended to choose party nominees. This procedure subsequently became standard in most constituencies.

The emergence of a large electoral role, the growth of party competition, and the development of large, centralized party organizations also changed the position of members within Parliament. Increased activity by the constituency party caucuses, together with the improvement in communications, served to tighten the relationship between an MP and his local organization (Butt, 1967, 90). Consequently, the parliamentary activity of an individual member was no longer only his own concern or that of a limited few; it was now also that of his constituents and party. Moreover, conflicts between constituent interests and party policy seemed rare or even irrelevant, for the electors no longer identified with members as individuals but increasingly with party, and it was on the strength of their party labels that members were elected (Norton, 1981, 16). And as mass parties assumed positions of dominance, the effect on Parliament and parliamentary life was profound. Norton notes that the organization of government and politics around party resulted in members of Parliament being dependent upon a party label for election to Westminster and deferring to party leaders once there. He adds: "The

House became a party-dominated institution, heavily dependent upon a Government for information and the generation of public policy. By the 20th century, the House was a marginal actor in the making of public policy. The relationship between the two was almost one of master (the Government) and the servant (the House)" (Norton, 1986a, 69).

Parliament's subservient position vis-à-vis the executive appears inconsistent with the formal, constitutional theory of a supreme and sovereign Parliament. But consistent with the demands and expectations imposed by party government, one would expect increased voting along party lines to occur in the House. Indeed, in 1836 the percentage of divisions where both parties cast party votes (90 percent voting on the same side) was only 23 percent. Voting cohesion diminished to 6 percent in 1860, when the fragmentation of parties was greatest. Following the Reform Act of 1867 and more centralized political parties, the percentage of party votes rose almost uninterruptedly to 76 percent in 1894. And by 1899, the number of divisions in which neither side of the House cast a party vote almost vanished to less than 3 percent of all recorded votes (Butt, 1967, 83). For one of the earliest "behavioral" works on voting in the House, see also Lawrence A. Lowell, *The Government in England* (New York: Macmillan, 1924).

Despite the restrictions imposed by party government on parliamentary assertion, nineteenth-century Britain's leading scholar and commentator on Parliament and the Constitution, Walter Bagehot, suggested other roles for Parliament. Writing in the year of the Second Reform Act, he identified a number of deliberative functions for the House of Commons. These extended well beyond "watching and checking ministers of the crown," a primary constitutional principle that tended to be neglected in subsequent decades. Bagehot conceived Parliament to have an "expressive" function: "All opinions extensively entertained, all sentiments widely diffused, should be stated publicly before the nation. We must take care to bring before [the] . . . legislature, the sentiments, the interests, the opinions, the prejudices, the wants of all classes of the nation" (quoted in Bagehot, 1974, 6:195).

Bagehot also perceived Parliament to have a "teaching" function, and to him this "teaching" or enlightenment necessarily implied change and reform. It did not mean that government's task was to maintain the status quo: "A great and open council of considerable men cannot be placed in the middle of society without altering that society. It ought to alter it for the better. It ought to teach that nation what it does not know" (Bagehot, 1974, 173). Perhaps not surprisingly, many of the members of Parliament I interviewed who complained of Parliament's subservient status placed a strong emphasis on Parliament's ability to educate the public about government policies. In fact, they felt that one of the most important functions of the post-1979 select committees was their teaching and educating role.

A third function of Parliament, according to Bagehot, was its "informing" role, which is to say the House of Commons was an arena of debate for issues not faced by either principal party: "Any notion, any creed, any feeling, any grievance which can get a decent number of English to stand up for it [is] . . . possible—an opinion within the intellectual sphere, an opinion to be reckoned with" (Bagehot, 1974, 174). Of course, Bagehot's sweeping generalities of the endless "valid" opinions—and opportunities to present them—seem unrealistic, but it is precisely this opportunity for debate that has been pointed to as confirming the constitutional relationship between the government and Parliament. It is also a function that opponents of reform through investigatory committees suggest is the most important one for the House, and committee service would only tend to deplete the attendance during such debates.

Bagehot also stresses the "elective" function of the House of Commons. His understanding of Parliament's elective role consists of two features. First, the House elects whom "it likes" for executive office and also exercises the power and privilege of dismissing those whom it dislikes. Second, the House is able to make such decisions because of the free will in judgment allowed to its members. He argues: "The house only goes where it thinks in the end the nation will follow; but it takes its chance of the nation following or not following it; it assumes the initiative, and acts upon its discretion or its caprice. . . . Because the House of Commons has the power of dismissal in addition to the power of election, its relations to the Premier are incessant" (Bagehot, 1974, 172).

While Bagehot stresses the formal constitutional powers of Parliament, executive-parliamentary relations changed considerably with the introduction and maintenance of party government. And although Bagehot's descriptive and constitutional analysis may have been fairly accurate at the time of the Reform Act, the influence of individual members and the House as a whole over government policy began to dwindle as party politics became increasingly important in the Westminster equation. Rather than being responsible to Parliament as the sovereign legislature, which the Constitution presumes, the prime minister was responsible to the party with the largest majority in the House. Indeed, party not only was the "tie that binds" but also served to restrict the Commons and its members.

The advent of mass suffrage and the growth of party deprived the House of Commons not only of its elective function, but also of another function ascribed to it, namely, the legislative function. One might expect a legislature to legislate and legislators to initiate legislation. But the degree to which a legislature's policy-initiating and - monitoring domain is free from other constraints (i.e., party dominance, executive popularity, and interest groups) can and does vary markedly. The executive, or government, assumes its authority not only through its majority of members in Parliament pledged to support its programs, but also because it can claim support from the electorate through the democratic, electoral process that sent representatives to Westminster. Because voters were presented with members of Parliament standing as party representatives and elected them on the basis of the candidates' party affiliation, a key voter-MP-government link was forged. Political parties developed party programs and manifestos that delineated the differences between parties as well as delivering to the electorate reasonable expectations and assurances of the likely policies the winning party would pursue in the next Parliament. In turn, government would enjoy the support of a majority in the House to facilitate its legislative program and to keep its electoral pledge with the voters. This relationship of mutual dependence through expectations and obligations allowed the government to claim a mandate not only for the pledges made during the election campaign but for subsequent policies pursued until the next election.

The notion of governing by a mandate became equally important in the executive's control of the parliamentary timetable. Redlich points out that, as the notion of the mandate developed, government-sponsored legislation, which was promised at the polls, began to be given precedence over the bills of private members. Moreover, private members had neither the facilities nor the information and expertise to prepare the complex bills that were becoming a feature of parliamentary life (Redlich, 1908). The result was a gradual domination of Parliament by the executive.

Executive ascendancy was also aided in the 1880s when ministers and backbenchers sought means to protect themselves from Irish obstruction in the House over the lingering issue of Home Rule. The reforms, introduced by Gladstone, "represented the watershed between the old and the new Government-managed Parliament" (Butt, 1967, 88). Closure, which has now become an institutionalized instrument for curtailing debate, was introduced, followed by the guillotine (in effect, a timetable motion). The traditional right of members to raise adjournment debates on what were considered matters of urgency was also severely restricted. The Speaker of the House was empowered to order a member to stop his speech if the Speaker deemed it irrelevant or repetitive, and the Speaker's power to "name" a member (usually resulting in temporary expulsion from the chamber) was strengthened (Norton, 1981a, 19; Redlich, 1908; Butt, 1967, 83–9; Mackenzie, 1950, 137–43). These procedural reforms may appear rather more evolutionary than revolutionary, especially in comparison to contemporary legislatures that have varied arrays of rules and procedures to process heavy legislative agendas. Nevertheless these and several other similar reforms that followed over the next twenty years did indeed mark "a watershed" for an institution that was to be manned by independent-thinking gentlemen who were in the House to debate "the great issues of the day." Such changes diminished the power of the individual MP and of minorities, while strengthening the government backed by its parliamentary majority. And although Gladstone introduced and justified such reforms in response to Irish obstruction, Redlich has observed that the action of the Irish members helped accelerate the reforms but were not the true cause of them: "The real motive power came from the alteration in the nature of British Government itself" (Norton, 1981a, 19).

The introduction of parliamentary reforms to dispense with the Irish problem served the government effectively in overcoming obstruction from other private members, including the Opposition frontbench. Moreover, these reforms were not repealed when the stated motive for their introduction (obstruction by Irish members) had been resolved. Governments ensured that the reforms remained in place and initiated further reforms to increase their powers and prerogatives in Parliament. The most important feature common to all these reforms was the restrictions placed on backbenchers and other private members to regulate the proceedings of their House and to debate freely issues important to them. Instead, control of the parliamentary timetable, the structure of chamber debates, and the introduction of legislation became the prerogative of the executive.

Paradoxically, the developments that made the Commons the dominant element of Parliament—the rise of a mass electorate, growth of national political parties, and the demands of the new electorate—also served to shift the locus of decision-making and policy formulation from the House to other bodies. Of the functions identified by Bagehot, the House lost its two most important: the elective function (choosing the government), which it lost to the electorate, and its function of legislation, which effectively passed to the cabinet. As Norton points out, party served as the conduit for this transfer: "Contact with the new electors could only be made through highly organized political parties and the support of the voters obtained through promising the passage of measures salient to their interests; such passage was possible only by the presence in the House of Commons of a party majority. The initiative for promising measures passed to the party leadership; election success resulted in the party leadership becoming Prime Minister and his lieutenants serving in the Cabinet. The Cabinet depended upon the support of a majority in the House; party ensured that the majority was usually forthcoming" (Norton, 1982a, 7).

Defining a Role for Parliament

What role, then, did or does Parliament play in the governing process? How can one reconcile party government through democratic elections with what the Conservative Lord Hailsham has termed "an elected dictatorship"? These questions form the central issues in understanding subsequent parliamentary reform and institutional change. Party government is an abstraction of European parliamentary democracy in the era of mass suffrage and can be seen as one historical answer to the problems of mass politics and class confrontation. Katz has argued that although most clearly based on academic interpretations of British practice, the party government model is an intellectual construct whose logic is far more coherent than is the actual operation of any real government (Katz, 1986, 42–43). He sees the party government model as representing the adaptation of the institutions of bourgeois parliamentary democracy (which were adaptations of the institution of royal government) to democracies with electorates numbering in the millions rather than the thousands. Katz suggests that this model retains legitimacy with democratic theory because government is made accountable to the general public by entrusting government to individuals organized into parties who owe their positions to electoral choice. But, although party government was to produce governments based on organizations accountable to the electorate, political parties in time "shifted from the channeling function (social demands and preferences brought to the consideration of policy-makers) to the steering function (their own ability to guide the socio-political process of allocation of resources)—their problem-solving capacity" (Pasquino, 1986, 139).

Parliament as an institution was the key in this shift by retaining its constitutional role as a sovereign and supreme body and by providing formal accountability to the electorate through elected representatives. And indeed accountability remained more formal than real. The responsibility of government to Parliament is a political relationship and as such it is not a matter of precise definition nor to be found in codified texts (Norton, 1982a, 98). Even if the power to defeat government were used more frequently, the fact would still remain that Parliament is not the government and does not govern. In a strictly procedural sense Parliament does formally decide many matters, but most votes are cast along party lines, and many issues are not discussed at all.

The issue of whether the House of Commons should properly be described as a "rubber stamp" is, to Rush, a different matter, "for whether Parliament is effective or not there is no mistaking its basic political function: to examine and question government policy and activity (or lack of it)" (Rush, 1986, 273). One cannot, however, so easily separate the issues of effectiveness and functions as Rush suggests. While one might support Rush's claim that examination and questioning of government policy and activity are a "basic political function", this role is also a constitutional one. As such, determining Parliament's ability to fulfill this constitutional obligation and responsibility to a very large extent assists in understanding its institutional effectiveness. Many current MPs interviewed stated that Parliament's role was indeed to examine and question the government's policy, but added that the institution had abandoned this role. They also envisioned the new select committee system as a means of asserting the House's constitutional responsibility. Furthermore, they added that party government carried the onus of responsibility for hampering the Commons from performing its scrutiny and monitoring functions.

Although Parliament effectively ceased to be involved in the making of public policy, it theoretically would execute its constitutional role through scrutiny and influence. But while governments were seeking even greater powers through procedural reforms in the House to expedite their expanding legislative programs more quickly, the Commons was not being allowed to develop correspondingly expert methods of scrutiny or information-gathering. The effects of streamlining procedures and of delegating more power to Whitehall, coupled with party discipline, resulted in drastically reduced opportunities for critical analysis by backbenchers (Downs, 1985, 55). Second, while scrutiny and influence are analytically separable terms, Norton argues that they may be conjoined as a single function of Parliament: "Scrutiny without any consequent sanction to effect influence is of little worth; and influence is best and most confidently attempted when derived from prior scrutiny" (Norton, 1985, 6).

Members of Parliament are aware of the House's constitutional authority and role in scrutinizing the government. And they tend to agree with Norton that their collective influence is best achieved through prior scrutiny. Select committees offer opportunities for Parliament both to influence and to scrutinize government activity. When I asked members in an open-ended question to describe the importance/power of Parliament, the response given most often was its role of scrutinizing the government. Moreover, when they were asked, "Do you think that the executive has become too powerful vis-à-vis Parliament?" more than 75 percent of the respondents replied yes. Of those who felt that there was indeed an imbalance between the two institutions, a follow-up question asked what they thought should be done to change the balance in this relationship. In response to this open-ended question, 85 percent believed that the expanded select committee system provided the means "to claw back power from the executive." Calls for parliamentary reform prior to the 1950s and 1960s almost invariably meant streamlining procedures within the House of Commons for the sake and benefit of the government. The legislature appeared to be perceived by the executive as the legitimator of cabinet policies. And indeed, Parliament's role became one of legitimizing what had been decided elsewhere.

Paradoxically, the very institutional trappings sought by party leaders to dominate the chamber, control the timetable, and ensure passage of most legislation through party discipline would also ensure reduced influence by those men when in Opposition. The positions adopted by party leaders on procedural reforms and the needs of the executive to govern efficiently differ markedly when out of power than when in government. For example, during his tenure as a cabinet minister and later as prime minister, David Lloyd George had little sympathy for parliamentary interference with the proposals of his ministry or government. His controversial "People's Budget" of 1909 was resisted by Conservatives in the House of Commons and took seventy sittings and 554 divisions before it was passed by a Liberal-Labour-Irish Nationalist coalition. Although stalling tactics could be used effectively by an organized Opposition, party government ensured victory. Nevertheless, in 1931, nine years after losing the premiership, Lloyd George testified before the House of Commons Select Committee on Procedure. The committee's remit was to gather evidence to consider what reforms, if any, might be needed for the House to address more efficiently the economic problems facing Britain. Lloyd George declared: "My . . . criticism would be that the control of the Executive by the House of Commons is confined to rather perfunctory dimensions, which does not excite any real interest, apart from an element of censure which is conducive to excitement, but does not achieve the real purpose of establishing control over the Executive. . . . The fact of the matter is that the House of Commons has no real effective and continuous control over the actions of the Executive" (Norton, 1981a, 201–2).

Several parliamentary scholars, including Marsh, Pasquino, and Norton, have argued that the increased involvement by government in the social and economic affairs of the nation has also served to decrease Parliament's role in the policy process. The growth of the Welfare State and the managed economy generated larger governmental departments and greatly increased expenditure accompanied by a mass of legislation difficult for Parliament to process because of its extent and, more significantly perhaps, because of its complexity. Access to information and expertise remained the province of the executive. Because debates in the chamber were the only significant means available for other MPs to challenge government policy, these debates were dominated by the government frontbench because of the expertise and specialist knowledge to which it alone realistically had access. Parliament failed to generate an institutional capacity to keep abreast of the increased legislation or to create avenues through which it could acquire expert advice on government-sponsored initiatives. But alternative forums for the purpose of gaining necessary specialist knowledge in order to create, initiate, or influence policies are incompatible with the theory and practice of party government. In short, these parliamentary tools would be unnecessary and redundant in an institutional environment whose members accept and promote the rules and norms of party government.

As government intervention in the economic and social life of the nation expanded, ministers became more dependent on diverse groups operating in these sectors. Policy increasingly was made by government in conjunction with outside groups, and the locus of policy making and influence moved even further from Parliament (Richardson and Jordan, 1979). Indeed, policy formulation was a process carried out between the elected (cabinet ministers), those who would execute the policy (civil servants and interest groups), and those who would be most immediately affected by the policy (interest groups). Tight party cohesion generally ensured passage of the legislation; members were assured of its acceptability, feasibility, and legitimacy because all relevant groups had been consulted and had given their assent. Marsh offers an interesting analysis of this process and Parliament's role in it by differentiating between the "private" and "public" dimensions of policy making in party government. In a two-party system of party government, a parliament is conceived as the setting for a "continuing election campaign." While the public face of politics is based on a contest for executive office between the parties, Marsh suggests that this struggle for office often distorts debate about the merit of issues (Marsh, 1986, 101). Indeed, lacking the expertise and specialized information available to the government frontbench, backbenchers and the Opposition often base their criticisms of government policy on moral or philosophical arguments. Furthermore, the government retains the advantage in defending technical and complex policies with, appropriately, technical arguments and justifications. On the other hand, the Opposition is largely left with scoring debating points in the chamber. Most of the MPs I interviewed argued that while debates and Question Time in the House are in theory opportunities to scrutinize and criticize the government and its policies, the chamber was "a farce," "a talking shop," "irrelevant," and "useless." In practice, given the lack of information to which they had access, members claimed the chamber was reduced to a forum for embarrassing a minister or scoring debating points.

The "benefit" of focusing public attention on general debate between adversarial parties is to leave policy making a "private" activity between ministers and departments. Cabinet ministers essentially deliver the agreed-upon policy to the House for ratification. Party government normally ensures passage. Marsh, too, points out that this process rests upon certain assumptions consistent with democratic values: "The 'private' character of policy-making and the concentration of the power of initiative in the hands of ministers presumes elections settle the 'political' dimension of policy-making. 'Private' policy-making presumes the parties are the exclusive agents for general interests and that they are capable of mobilizing sustained majority support" (Marsh, 1986, 101).

The current relationship between the executive and the House was one that was forged a century ago, and the Parliament that took shape in the late nineteenth century reflected the contemporary social and political environment. The House of Commons provided a forum for discussion and debate, but its members were not involved, nor did they wish to be involved, in detailed policy formulation. Parliament did not convene until 2:30 p.m. so that its members could pursue their professional and personal interests during the morning and attend to their "government service" sometime after lunch. For the most part in this laissez-faire, sociopolitical environment, MPs were content to defer to their party leaders. It is important to remember that the relationship that developed between the executive and the House was based upon mutual interests—ensuring support and passage of the majority party's election mandate. While the party in Opposition may have had little influence over government through Parliament, it did have an incentive in maintaining party government and a subservient role for the House of Commons. Given the alternating pattern of party control of the House (and by extension of the executive), reforms championed while in Opposition to change the institutional relationship would only hamper the party when next in power.

The rubber-stamping role often attributed to Parliament appears to be one the House has, until recently, accepted. The extent of backbench subservience can be understood in a like manner. Given that backbench MPs usually outnumber their frontbench counterparts by a ratio of three to one, why is it that a majority of MPs in the governing party willingly accept discipline from the minority who hold government positions? The most often offered response is party identification (Rose, 1981, 78). Party identity is claimed to be the tie that binds frontbench and backbench MPs to maintain a government in power. Moreover, members of the governing party share some collective goals, both ideological and instrumental. Although they may differ among themselves, they are united in wishing to secure their own and their party's victory at the next general election. Thus the goals of the individual MP are commensurate with the party's, although the former were often subordinate to and sacrificed for the latter. Until recently, any substantial division within a party on government legislation would force a government to resign and call for new elections, plunging all into political uncertainty.

John Mackintosh also views the members of a parliamentary party as like-minded individuals who form one politically cohesive and homogeneous whole. In addressing the issue of executive dominance over the legislature through party control, he ignores the possibility of any overt manifestations of intraparty dissent. He maintains:

To understand party loyalty, it must be appreciated that most MPs have spent years in their party before election to the House. They have joined it, worked for it and probably stood as candidates once or twice before election. They identify themselves with the party's general approach and any serious failures of high policy are personal calamities for them. They may want to change aspects of policy, they may at times disagree with members of the Cabinet including the Prime Minister, but despite this they still wish the party to be successful. Because of this, they will defend the party in public which means supporting the Prime Minister's action in the lobbies and in the constituencies. [Mackintosh, 1977, 62–63]

While it is agreed that Conservative or Labour MPs will share broad, fundamental views, simple identification with the "party's general approach" remains an inadequate explanation of party cohesion and parliamentary subservience. In identifying four possible factors accounting for party unity, Anthony King extends the version offered by Mackintosh:

1. The majority party wants to sustain a government in office; if too many MPs on the Government side rebel, that may be the end of the Government.

2. MPs fall into line because they hope to hold office or already do; the Executive remains the primary source of patronage.

3. There is an absence of positive, constituency-inspired incentives for breaking with the party.

4. There is the sense that the public will punish a divided party at the polls; most voters vote only for the party and MPs know it. [King, 1974, 81–83]

Although a combination of these four factors may provide strong explanatory variables for party unity, it seems unlikely that any single factor could produce the type of party cohesion that has traditionally characterized British politics. For example, the first factor does not explain unity on the Opposition side. Nor does it account for the whips' passion for mustering the full government majority. It also does not take into account that governments have indeed been defeated on major pieces of legislation without being followed by a resignation or parliamentary elections.

G. R. Strauss, a former Labour MP, supports some of King's assertions. Writing about the influence of Labour backbenchers upon a Labour government, Strauss maintains that the opinions of the backbench are rarely listened to. Nor do backbenchers wield any influence in setting the government's legislative agenda: "With Labour in Government, the influence of the backbencher on policy is small. Decisions are made in the secrecy of the Cabinet. Prior consultation with backbenchers is impossible and subsequent rejection politically impracticable. . . . The possibility of an early election makes it essential to avoid the image of an indecisive Government that can be diverted from its course by backbench pressures" (Strauss, 1972, 226–27).

The only time when Labour backbenchers are able to exert any influence appears to be in Opposition. These MPs are then subject to the frustrations of having achieved some influence in preparing party programs, manifestos, and orientations while their party is out of office but then being denied any role precisely at that moment when access to decisionmaking would be most important—when their party forms the government. Although some party members will be promoted to the frontbench, most will remain on the backbench to be joined by a few former frontbenchers who have been exiled, at least temporarily, to the backbench.

This lack of backbench influence is a manifestation of party government and a recognition of the principles of party government and party representation. As David Judge (1981) points out, this doctrine maintains that the MP is primarily a representative of his party, a delegate whose task it is to carry out the program offered to the electorate at the last election. Since candidates stand for Parliament on a party manifesto listing the policies to be pursued if the MP and party are victorious, the party is then committed to translate the manifesto into action. Individual MPs, pledged to these promises, are consequently obliged to support the party's program in the House.

Committees in a Party Government

The dominance of party government and the accompanying authority-hierarchical relationship between the executive and Parliament, and the government and backbenchers, also affects the voting behavior of MPs. In making the decision on how to vote and the stance to take on complicated bills in a complex world, the member's task was made easy by following the party cue. Judge suggests that conformity to the "party line" provides the backbencher with a relatively cost-free mode of decisionmaking, allowing him to reach a decision on any particular issue without necessarily having a detailed understanding of the subject involved (Judge, 1981, 11–12). But perhaps the more interesting point to be raised is the likely result of cross-pressuring cues. What might be the effects of an MP's receiving expert information from a bipartisan select committee when that committee's recommendations or evidence deviate substantially from the official "party line"? Unfortunately, this question has yet to be subject to academic scrutiny and thus no definitive answer can be given. Nevertheless, it would seem plausible to suggest that an alternative and equally respected or feared cue-giving structure could seriously erode both the necessity and the practicality of party dominance over Parliament. It could precipitate a critical reexamination of party government. Indeed, several members I interviewed stated that they had voted against their parties' positions on the floor of the House based on the recommendations of bipartisan select committee reports.

Challenges to party government are not a new phenomenon in British politics, nor are they limited to the postwar era. Backbench specialization through committee work, however, would further undermine the authority relationship inherent in party government. Specialization would result in further diffusion of authority, authority which up until very recently had been monopolized by party leaders. The norms of the House of Commons reflect the values of the most important and powerful actors in Parliament and so support the existing distribution of power and status quo. Thus Judge's research on backbench specialization in the House of Commons has led him to conclude:

In conforming with these norms, backbenchers have been led to accept as imperative the need for party loyalty . . . and, above all, the advisability of performing the generalist role within the House. Moreover, backbenchers have been socialized into the belief that conformity will positively assist their career prospects in the House. . . . And he adds: The perpetuation of generalist values in the House is in the basic interest of the executive, and as long as backbenchers remain convinced that their political careers should be oriented to the attainment of executive office, then they will continue to conform to those norms most likely to secure this goal. [Judge, 1981, 13–14; 22]

The second sense of persistence of party government relates to the continued adherence of those in power to its norms. Party government should persist in this sense so long as the structure of incentives that led individuals to adopt that strategy remains in place. Pasquino's research on party government leads him to conclude:

"Although party government involves costs for some people, once a system of party government is established, those who come to the top have a vested interest in its continuation, as well as in the continuation of their own parties. At the same time, many of the conditions of party government are subject to conscious manipulation. Thus barriers may be erected against those who attempt to pursue a nonparty strategy" (Pasquino, 1986, 63–64).

As long as executive office is the only available career goal and as long as party loyalty is the only avenue, or career ladder, to pursue, MPs are subject to the logical demand of pursuing these "choices" that ultimately serve to legitimate party government and the authority-hierarchical relationship. Should alternative career opportunities and structures be created in Parliament, party loyalty and party unity would diminish in importance as means of achieving career goals. I believe select committees can indeed be viewed as "alternative structures," allowing members to specialize and therefore removing them, to a degree, from the dictates of party leaders. At the same time, as several MPs have commented during debates and testimony, committee posts grant backbenchers more active and rewarding participation in the governing process than would be possible through years of service as mere loyal party men and women. Committee service can also guarantee meaningful parliamentary careers to those persons for whom the call to executive posts will never come. Furthermore, whereas backbenchers achieve a degree of freedom in policy formulation in Opposition but not when in power, the creation of departmental select committees would provide the structural prerequisites necessary to maintain a sense of continuity in backbench influence toward the executive, whether it be a Labour or a Conservative government.

Because party leaders are the granters of patronage, the power rests with them not only to reward MPs with parliamentary and executive posts, but also to remove noncooperative members from these positions. This situation becomes problematic for backbenchers who are assigned to committees by party whips. If these MPs are perceived as becoming too independent, the whips are able to remove them from the committees. In effect, then, Parliament can only scrutinize the executive if committee members understand, a priori, that they must respect party ties, placing them in a double-bind that effectively prohibits any real scrutiny. As Leader of the House in the mid-1960s, Richard Crossman understood this dilemma. His reforms were intended to provide legislators the opportunity to have careers as parliamentary specialists who would not be forever subject to the norm of party loyalty. But Crossman realized that the whips, acting within the rationale of party government, found such independence unacceptable: "They [whips] have to be able to impose discipline by giving people jobs and by taking them away and he simply can't understand why if members of the party behave awkwardly on a Select Committee he shouldn't remove them. Yet I want to see these Specialist Committees develop as a really effective control over the Executive. For this purpose they need to have a core of members who grow old and hoary in their service, not unlike the cadres of the American Congressional Committees" (Crossman, 1976, 327). Recognizing this problem, parliamentary reformers ensured that backbenchers serving on the select committees created in 1979 would not be subject to placement or removal by party whips.

The acceptance of the principles of party government, in both theory and practical-career terms poses an obvious dilemma for would-be reformers of the House. The reassertion of Parliament's power is dependent upon the fragmentation of the executive's power, but centralization of power in the hands of the government effectively means that it alone has the capacity to sanction the diffusion of power necessary for the rejuvenation of the legislature. Later discussion will address the peculiar circumstances that allowed the 1979 reforms to occur. The distinction between parliamentary government and party government should be made clear. The issue at hand is not merely the (re-)birth of a committee system within a parliamentary framework, but rather its rebirth within a legislative environment that is overshadowed by a traditionally strong party system. This dilemma posed several challenges for successive governments—Labour and Conservative. In the following chapters I examine governments' reform initiatives and subsequent responses to select committee experiments in the House of Commons.

3

Parliamentary Committees under Party Government

The development and dynamics of party government highlighted in the previous chapter had obvious ramifications for the creation and functions of parliamentary committees. In this chapter I examine more closely the use of parliamentary specialist committees prior to the 1966 Crossman Reforms. Given a system of party government supported by amateur and generalist members of Parliament, one would expect few calls for procedural reforms that would result in the creation of legislative committees. And for those committees that were created, one would surmise they were little involved with policy matters and primarily functioned as extensions of the executive in the House.

While these earlier committees may not have been completely subservient to the whims of the cabinet, it seems clear that the government would only support creating committees whose aims and purpose would be consistent with a government's overall interest in fiscal efficiency and management. Political constraints prevented committees from developing in the way traditional organizational theory and division of labor might suggest. Consequently, substantive procedural and institutional reform could not occur until a change in MPs' attitudes toward the role of Parliament and their place within it also shifted significantly.

Members were party men and women, and it was to party that they owed their primary loyalty. Moreover, as Norton illustrates, members characteristically stressed the centrality of the floor of the House, an emphasis that was consistent with prevailing notions of representation. Parliamentary committees were associated with specialization, but the principle underlying constituency representation was that of the generalist (Norton, 1986a, 10–18.)

Committees under Party Government

The committees created in the nineteenth century shared a common focus of ensuring efficiency and "value for money" for the government's policies. But these early committees were hampered in their efforts both by the lack of expertise and specialization of their members and by the growing interference of party politics in committee hearings and proceedings. Just as leaders of the majority party supported procedural reforms that would allow the government increased influence over proceedings in the chamber, so too was party pressure exerted on committees of the House. As legislative initiatives became more controversial, the executive's need for political control of committee proceedings led to greater emphasis on political considerations in determining their memberships (Walkland, 1979b, 245). Thus, these legislative committees lost many of their investigatory and deliberative characteristics and instead increasingly reflected the nature and spirit of the parent chamber. The committee chairmen, much like the Speaker of the House, adopted the role of impartial moderator between government and Opposition supporters who were placed on the committee by their respective party leaders. Moreover, leadership of the committees was granted to representatives of the government, including the ministers responsible for a particular bill. The experience and characteristics of these early legislative and financial parliamentary committees underscore the environment and expectations that would surround subsequent parliamentary committees.

Most observers of legislators and legislative politics point to legislatures' "power of the purse" to demonstrate their roots of power and influence. Indeed, the granting of supply to the government in return for consideration of grievance petitions was a centuries-old constitutional doctrine governing the relationship between king and nobles, Crown and Parliament, and later government and the House. But in practice, the granting of supply constitutes one of the formal rather than the real functions of the House. The introduction and continued importance of party government ensured that no government with an overall majority was likely to be denied supply.

Moreover, the Committee of Supply was in essence a committee of the whole House; the chamber suspended and reconstituted itself as the Committee of Supply. The ability of such an unwieldy body of several hundred members to subject the government's raising and spending of money to detailed and rigorous scrutiny proved virtually impossible for a number of reasons. First, and most obvious, the sheer number of potential participants made sustained scrutiny impractical. Second, the House of Commons and its members lacked the resources and information available to the government in appraising the merits of specific supply issues. And in fact, the Commons was dependent upon the government for information, a situation that began to change significantly only in the latter half of the twentieth century. Third, although the entire membership of the House was formally allowed to attend and debate during a Committee of Supply, few members attended and fewer still took an interest in financial matters (Norton, 1981a, 162–63). Indeed, members' attitude toward rigorous scrutiny of the government's supply figures was consistent both with the prevailing notions of representation and with the role members were to play within the confines of party government. Since members did not seek to become policy specialists and since members of the majority party would not mount attacks on their party's leadership on supply issues, it is not surprising that the Committee of Supply was characterized by rather general debate led by the Opposition frontbench. Norton has conclude that "with the steady growth of public expenditure, both in volume and complexity, and the increasing presence of legislation on parliamentary time, the Committee of Supply tended during the nineteenth century to become more and more an instrument for the criticism of administration rather than of finance as such" (Norton, 1981a, 163).

Supply days eventually were recognized as de facto Opposition Days; for approximately twenty parliamentary days the Opposition was allowed to set the agenda for debate. Although these days were set aside ostensibly for financial enquiry into the government's expenditure plans, they were utilized instead for sustained criticism of the government of the day by the Opposition—one of the only recourses available to the Opposition to define the parameters of debate and force the government to defend its policies, agenda, and record. As a consequence, however, the scrutiny of expenditure was negligible. And just as Irish obstructionism allowed the government increased control of the chamber, so too did this issue allow it extended protection from private members when the House went into the Committee of Supply. The ancient privilege of the House to raise its grievances before granting supply was finally eliminated.

This inability to undertake sustained and effective scrutiny of government expenditure had not gone on unnoticed by several members of the House. In 1902 a specially appointed select committee was created "to inquire whether any plan can be advantageously adopted for enabling the House, by select committee, or otherwise more efficiently to make an examination not involving criticisms of policy, into the details of National Expenditure" (Norton, 1981a, 163). Although the committee noted the advantages of select committees to gather expert information in an environment relatively free from the sharp party political divide characteristic of proceedings in the chamber, no action was taken as a result of this report.

This occurrence highlights two features of parliamentary life that tended to stifle an active and critical House. For one, despite some members' support for select committees to undertake the tasks handled so ineffectively by the whole House (Committee of Supply), they were nevertheless clear that any alternative should not be involved in any "criticisms of policy." Their attitude about the role of the House and its members on policy issues was consistent with their representative roles as they appear to have defined them, as well as congruent with and supportive of a parliamentary-executive relationship defined by party parameters. Second, the response of the executive not to pursue this report was also expected. There was little incentive for the executive to support a more efficient scrutiny of its expenditure plans by the Commons, despite assurances that policy matters would not fall within the proposed committee's remit. Any such committee would undermine the government's monopoly of information and expertise on expenditure matters, information that was presented to the House by the government and ostensibly at least formed the rationale for the members of the majority party to vote with the government on supply matters. Members enjoyed little, if any, access to alternative sources of detailed information that would contradict or undermine the government's position. Clearly it was in the government's interest to keep it that way.

Successive attempts by Parliament to monitor the government's expenditure plans were also ineffectual. In 1912 an attempt was made "to force Parliament to direct its attention to Supply, by the establishment of a select committee for that purpose" (Hanson, 1970, 44). But committee members soon realized they did not possess the specialist information nor access to informed specialist advisers that could match the resources available to the Treasury. Consequently, the committee functioned primarily as a useful tool for the government to examine ways in which policies could be executed more cost-effectively. Again the committee was not allowed, nor did it realistically expect, to question the merits of any policy. Indeed it focused on administrative efficiency "by choosing appropriate votes simply as a peg on which to hang its enquiries" (Hanson, 1970, 44; Chubb, 1952; Johnson, 1966; Reid, 1966).

As long as members of Parliament maintained this general lack of interest in the government's expenditure plans, or at the very least accepted that a select committee's role was not to consider the merits of government policies, any "checking of the executive" through committee was virtually nonexistent. In fact, such committee work aided the government; the Estimates Committee in practice was an additional instrument available to the executive to achieve administrative efficiency and lowered costs for the government. And because the merits and rationale for these policies were exempt from discussion, the government could look forward to money-saving rewards without political costs.

A select committee on National Expenditure, appointed in 1917, concluded that the form of the Public Accounts and the Estimates was inadequate for any realistic control over expenditure, whether it be departmental or parliamentary. But the committee's perception of what constituted "control" is substantially different from the connotation present-day parliamentary reformers would give this function. Members of the Expenditure Committee did not envision that control of expenditure included influence over or input into the policy/ expenditure process. This concern with value for money as opposed to the nature and merits of the policies themselves is in sharp contrast to the attitudes of committee members and other members of Parliament displayed after a comprehensive select committee system was introduced in 1979.

As the levels of government expenditure grew and Britain's economic vitality appeared to worsen in the late 1920s and early 1930s, so too did criticism of Parliament increase both from within and from outside the House. Butt has suggested that the most important reason for the new criticism of Parliament was the enlarged activity of the executive in the social and economic affairs of the nation. He wrote: "The flood of new government business with which members of Parliament were required to cope: the increased influence of the Cabinet and the bureaucracy: the sheer complexity of government activities—these were the new facts of political life which, after the First World War, raised the question whether Parliament was still adequate to exercise control over the executive and to guard the rights of the citizen" (Butt, 1967, 105).

Butt, however, wrote as an apologist for Parliament and seemed to overlook the question of whether the legislature had exercised any effective control over the executive during the previous thirty or forty years. Furthermore, he neglected to address whether Parliament and its members expressed any substantial desire to control the executive.

The prevailing norms of party government and the experience of those committees relating to supply and expenditure suggest little interest on the part of MPs. Although constitutionally empowered to maintain a more than adequate control over the executive, in practice the dynamics of party government, supported by the prevailing attitude of generalist and amateur parliamentarians, prevented any substantial exercise of the formal powers ascribed to the House. The result of procedural and parliamentary reform during this era underscores three identifiable characteristics defining the executive-parliamentary relationship: (1) the strengthening of the disciplinary and administrative powers of the Speaker; (2) the continuous extension of the rights of the government over the discretion of all parliamentary action in the House; and (3) the suppression of the private member, both as to his legislative initiative and as to the scope of action allowed him by the rules (Redlich, 1908, 206).

A more realistic appraisal should note the symbiotic nature of intentions and politics. Clearly, the tight political relationship of Parliament and the executive largely accounts for the relatively sketchy committee structure.

Procedure Committees' Examination of the Reform Question

The apparent subordination of the legislature to the needs of the executive had not escaped the attention of all members of Parliament. A Select Committee on Procedure was appointed in 1932 to examine what some viewed as a decline of the institution, and the committee recognized in its report that "one of the chief reasons for their appointment was the existence of a large body of criticism of Parliament, both by members and by representative citizens . . . " (HC 129, 1932, iii). Although the committee's remit was quite broad, it nevertheless refused to pronounce on any constitutional principles, which included commentary on executive-parliamentary relations. Rather, the Procedure Committee noted that such criticisms had existed since the Reform Act of 1832 and consequently various committees had considered the practice and procedure of the House since then and appropriate amendments had been introduced to the rules of Parliament. The committee concluded that the result of the rules changes was a reduction in the opportunities of the private member and conversely an increase in the powers of the executive so that the House might be able to process efficiently the ever increasing volume of official business that confronted it (Butt, 1967, 131).

The Select Committee on Procedure recognized the declining influence of the House over the executive, but at the same time it pointed to an adapting institution whose procedural reforms facilitated efficient and expeditious processing of government business. The report displayed little concern with the legislature's admittedly weakened position in the governing/policy process and instead rendered a favorable assessment of Parliament's efficiency in processing the government's agenda.

The committee's sole substantial recommendation was to enlarge the Estimates Committee; otherwise it maintained that the procedure of Parliament was "sufficiently flexible to meet all the demands made upon it," a conclusion described by Jennings at the time as ludicrous (Norton, 1981a, 202). In fact, when giving evidence to the Procedure Committee, the prime minister, Ramsay MacDonald, stressed that the role of Parliament was to expedite the business of government. And he supported the system of governing through the "usual channels," a euphemism for party elites' eschewing institutional constraints and formal rules. Having gone through the usual channels, party loyalty ensured relatively problem-free executive initiatives (HC 161, 1931, 5). When MacDonald was a member of the Opposition during the early years of Labour representation in Parliament, he argued before a select committee in 1914 for increased opportunities for private members to monitor and criticize government and supported a more active role for them in policy formation. Like many of his successors, MacDonald's enthusiasm for an expanded role for MPs and Parliament diminished with his transition to executive frontbench status.

Despite the disparate calls for constitutional changes emanating from within and outside of Parliament in the 1930s, the prevailing attitude toward reform remained essentially that contained in the 1932 Procedure Committee Report.

Shortly after the war, in 1946, a Select Committee on Procedure again considered the status and procedure of the House of Commons. The committee concluded that Parliament's reputation was as high as ever and that there was not, at the time, any compelling reason or support for changing the nature of the House. Of course, what remains most important in this committee's analysis of Parliament is the role committee members ascribed to Parliament and then used in evaluating it.

This favorable appraisal of the House's status rested on the a priori assumption that the legislature was of course not to legislate; rather, it should be able to process efficiently the government's business presented to it. This task, the committee concluded, was handled quite well by Parliament. But Parliament's formal and constitutional obligations of holding the executive accountable for its action received scant attention. The opportunities to challenge the government in the chamber on "the great issues of the day," coupled with the comparatively limited select committee work in reviewing cost efficiency appeared to satisfy the Procedure Committee's criteria for parliamentary accountability.

The committee's report suggested that the necessity and dynamics of party government had clearly displaced institutional prerogative and members' capacity to influence policy as a legitimate basis for evaluating parliamentary effectiveness. Moreover, while the Attlee government's reconstruction and welfare programs required unparalleled amounts of legislation and expenditure, a series of Procedure Committee reports recommended that standing committees should be used more extensively. The use of standing committees would allow the House to expedite even more quickly the government's legislative agenda; the government obviously welcomed the proposals. But as Downs also points out, the reforms were clearly one-sided, as the Attlee government was not prepared "to compensate for its increased use of standing committees with an enhanced role for select committees to help scrutinize the extra business that Parliament was technically obliged to oversee" (Downs, 1985, 55–56).

The distinction between standing committees and select committees is an important one. Standing committees, comprised of perhaps dozens of loyal party men and women, were useful for the executive in speedily processing legislative initiatives. Select committees, much smaller in membership, focused on information-gathering and fact-finding activities. As long as these latter committees also adopted the prevailing norms of party loyalty and discipline found on standing committees and in the House in general, government was realistically free from sustained scrutiny and effective criticism through parliamentary committees in toto.

Specialist Committees

While the use of committees by the House clearly has precedent, the contemporary departmentally related or subject-oriented select committees are essentially of recent origin. One of the first such committees was formed in the 1950s: the Select Committee on Nationalised

Industries. Following what was considered extensive nationalization by the postwar Labour government, Conservative backbenchers exerted pressure on their leaders to act more enthusiastically in the interest of private enterprise. These members did not wish to have these industries become inefficient organizations absorbing billions of pounds a year from the public purse in return for low productivity and competitiveness.

What these backbenchers wanted was a committee through which the state-run industries could be accountable to a minister in Parliament. Consequently, the government set up a select committee in 1953 to consider the relationship between the industries and the House. The specially appointed committee recommended that a Nationalised Industries Committee be created. It was not until two years later, however, that the government moved with extreme caution to appoint such a committee. The terms of reference for the new committee were so limited as to make any thorough examination of the state-owned industries impossible. When the Select Committee on Nationalised Industries met, Labour and Conservative members decided its terms of reference indeed were inadequate. Committee members received such strong support from the Conservative backbenchers that the government "capitulated" and agreed to expand the committee's terms of reference (Butt, 1967, 207).

Any discussion of select committees in the House of Commons usually includes an account of the Nationalised Industries Committee, but several significant features are often overlooked. For one, calls for reform emanated from the government backbench, not from party leaders seeking an extension of the executive's influence through the legislature. The existence of a Select Committee on Nationalised Industries was incongruent with the established pattern of utilizing Parliament for expediting and processing the government's agenda. This committee also received a much narrower but more politically sensitive remit than most previous committees. It was not to examine the forms of the estimates, accounts, or expenditures while searching for cost-efficiency; instead, it was to seek political accountability from a particular government sector and policy arena. Finally, it is also essential to note that backbenchers did not seek accountability to Parliament, ostensibly fulfilling a constitutional role. Rather, what was sought was accountability of an industry's activity to a minister in Parliament. The House was not about to request, nor would the government grant, a supervisory role for Nationalised Industries. Members of Parliament were clear in their calls for a committee through which state-owned industries could be held accountable to a member of the executive. They were not seeking a committee to which state-owned industries could be held accountable to Parliament. The government was nevertheless reluctant to create such a committee, but party leaders were secure enough in their power to nominate the committee's membership.

Four years after the Select Committee on Nationalised Industries was created, the Select Committee on Procedure of 1958–59 considered the question of employing specialized committees in the House. The terms of the committee's inquiry focused almost exclusively on a proposed Colonial Affairs Committee. Suggestions to review or debate the work of departments were not new, and the committee pointed out in its report that evidence was given on the subject before the Select Committee on Procedure of 1931–32—albeit twenty-seven years since evidence was last given to a Procedure Committee on the topic (HC 92-I, 1959, xxiv).

The committee's final report recommended that specialist committees not be employed by the House. In rejecting this particular method of parliamentary inquiry, committee members noted their concern with the constitutional difficulties specialist committees would present. The Procedure Committee concluded: "The main argument against this proposal, and one which convinces us, lies in the nature of the committee, which in our view would constitute a radical constitutional innovation." The report also stressed that such a committee would ultimately involve itself in controlling rather than criticizing the policy and actions of a particular department. The result, committee members claimed, would be to usurp a function which the House itself had never attempted to exercise. The report added: "Although the House has always maintained the right to criticise the executive and in the last resort to withdraw its confidence, it has always been careful not to arrogate to itself any of the executive power. The establishment of a colonial committee would not only involve this principle, but would also lead to the establishment of other similar committees" (HC 92-I, 1959, xxi).

The committee's interpretation of legislative-executive relations provides interesting insights. For one, it is not so readily apparent nor accurate to state that Parliament has universally chosen not to invade the executive's prerogative over the House. It would be more accurate to stress that Parliament has been reluctant to venture into what has come to be considered the government's purview, and has generally accepted its subservient role since the introduction of party politics into the parliamentary system. The political realities of party government that serve as mitigating factors in the relationship between government and Parliament should not be confused with the constitutional theory defining that relationship. Nevertheless, the Procedure Committee report tends to suggest that the organization of institutional relations through political parties has become embedded in constitutional principle. Upsetting this relationship would upset this now defined constitutional formula as well as the fundamental underpinnings of party government. No procedure committee would be prepared to recommend an alteration of this delicate balance.

Decline of Parliament?

The Procedure Committee's consideration of specialist committees for the House, amid continued debate in and out of Parliament regarding that institution's alleged decline in influence and impact on national politics and policies, reflected the criticisms levelled by academics and political commentators outside of the legislature. As early as 1949 Christopher Hollis's *Can Parliament Survive?* was published; in 1950 Lord Cecil of Chelwood called attention in a Lords debate to the growing power of the cabinet, and in 1952 Lord Campion in a similar vein noted the increasing subordination of the Commons to the executive. Analyses of parliamentary decline, and perceptions as to how that decline might be arrested or reversed, became a persistent theme in the late 1950s and continued throughout the 1960s. Bernard Crick's influential Fabian tract, *Reform of the Commons*, was published in 1959 and was followed five years later by his book *The Reform of Parliament*. An article by Professors Hanson and Wiseman, urging committee reform, also appeared in 1959, as did Michael Foot's *Parliament in Danger!* and Paul Enzig's *The Control of the Purse*.

Both Norton and Butt identify Britain's economic woes as the major catalyst to the "Decline of Parliament" debate. Norton suggests that postwar calls for parliamentary reform were offset by an evaluation of the social and economic reforms achieved by the Attlee government and the prosperity of the early and mid-1950s. These achievements, Norton argues, conferred greater legitimacy on the Westminster Model. The country appeared to be faring rather well, so there was little motivation to question the operation of the political system (Norton, 1982a, 100–101).

Butt, too, assesses the new reform era as a consequence of Britain's failure to solve its fundamental economic difficulties. But he does note that the critical examination of Parliament was part of a larger introspection of British politics and society, including a series of books published by Penguin, each of which asked what was wrong with one aspect or another of British life and institutions. Butt further contends that the prevailing "What's Wrong with Britain?" mood was undoubtedly heightened by the growing disillusion with the performance of the Conservative government under Macmillan in the early 1960s (Butt, 1967, 6).

Although Norton, Butt, and others suggest that previous criticisms of Parliament and concomitant calls for reform were associated with macroeconomic travails (particularly in 1929–31), remarkably less explanation is offered as to why reforms were accepted in the 1960s and not previously. While criticism and scrutiny of Parliament's role may be a necessary antecedent to provoke substantial reform, it appears that a shift in members' attitudes about Parliament's role and their role within it is equally necessary. As I pointed out above, earlier inquiries into Parliament's status by successive procedure committees yielded few results. This rejection of reform proposals reflected members' understanding and acceptance of a limited, subservient House vis-à-vis the government. What is starkly obvious in the 1960s, however, is an apparent frustration on the part of several MPs of both major parties with their own and Parliament's inability to have any significant influence on national policies.

Second, after the "Thirteen Wasted Years" in Opposition, the Labour leadership formally committed its party to an energetic and reform-oriented reign following the 1964 general election. That election not only brought Labour to power for the first time since 1951 but also marked a significant turnover in parliamentary membership.

Walkland suggests that although members' "initial surge of enthusiasm in the 1960's" had complex causes, the predominant one was the belated recognition by MPs of government's expanding role. The growth in influence of corporate agencies, particularly in the economic sphere, coupled with the increasing practice of policy making by government through a process of collaboration with producer groups, served to diminish the role of Parliament as the importance of primary legislation was reduced and the role of discretionary action by the civil service was enhanced (Walkland, 1985, v–vi). These developments were perhaps best epitomized by the creation of the National Economic Development Council in 1962.

Also important was a book by a group of Conservative MPs published by the Conservative Political Centre. Its fundamental message was that Parliament no longer had the capacity it had once possessed to oversee the executive. Their argument was predicated on the view that the government's involvement in an increasingly vast and complicated network of detailed and highly technical activity—particularly concerned with the economy—made it difficult for Parliament in its present form to scrutinize, control, or even understand these policies (*Parliament and Government*, 1963). William Rees-Mogg, a former Conservative candidate for Parliament, deputy editor of the *Sunday Times* and future editor of the *Times*, also wrote an indictment of Parliament: "The position of a member of Parliament in Opposition is now difficult enough, but the position of a backbench MP supporting a government in power has become almost absurd. . . . The ordinary Member of Parliament is by-passed on every side" (Rees-Mogg, 1964, 3).

Conservatives certainly were not alone in their criticisms of Parliament. Prior to the 1964 general election, a group of twelve Labour members of Parliament, ten from the House of Commons and two from the House of Lords, published a paper criticizing the inability of Parliament to perform its constitutional role ("Three Dozen Parliamentary Reforms," in *Socialist Commentary*, 1964). Like the Conservatives, they were critical of the executive's use of Parliament as simply a processor of government proposals.

Another article appearing that year in *Political Quarterly* summarized both the frustrations and the hopes of these Conservative and Labour reformers. In it, W. A. Robson wrote: "The status of Parliament has declined to a serious extent during the post-war era: and if this tendency is to be reversed the House of Commons must be prepared to assert its rights and authority more forcibly than it has done in recent decades. After all, the power of Parliament is intact; it is the will to exercise it which is lacking. No government, whatever its political complexion, is going to make the first move towards enhancing the status of Parliament: the initiative must come from the House of Commons" (Robson, 1964, 34). What was more evident in this article than in the works by parliamentarians, however, was an implicit recognition of the prior necessity of concerted action by a sufficient number of MPs to assert the institution's will.

Bernard Crick's *Reform of Parliament*, also published in 1964, was the principal academic work on the decline and reform of the House. It reflected the views of some Labour members and their academic supporters—including Professors Hanson and Wiseman and MPs John Mackintosh and Richard Crossman. Crick had no sympathy with the argument that Parliament had declined from some "Golden Age" in which it "governed," or for the idea that rule of 630 independent minds would either be possible or preferable to party government. Clearly Crick wanted Parliament to fulfill what Bagehot referred to as Parliament's educative/communicative role. He envisaged pre-legislation committees as the bridge between informal opinion, interest groups, and the executive. Above all, Professor Crick wanted to see members of Parliament, rather than external bodies or officials, involved in the task of scrutinizing government policy because he resisted the contemporary practice of depoliticizing political issues. That is to say, he opposed removing governmental problems from Parliament only to place them in the hands of Royal Commissions, Special Enquiries, and other extra-parliamentary bodies.

But the fundamental problem for realizing this plan of reform lay in the belief by Crick (along with other reform-minded MPs and academics) that parliamentary committees established to keep political issues in public debate through Parliament would not be a challenge to the government of the day. Parliament's communicative role emphasized by these early reforms, moreover, remained consistent with the prevailing frontbench interpretation of Parliament as processor—whether it be processor of legislation or processor of information. In both roles, parliamentary-executive relations would continue to be defined and guided by party politics that served to maintain executive privilege and prerogative in the House. Labour members generally agreed with Crick's observation that "Parliament should not and does not threaten the ability of the government to govern" (Crick, 1965, 79).

Most observers point to 1963–66 not only as the starting point of the parliamentary reform movement by academics but also as the beginning of a change in attitude among MPs concerning Parliament's role. Butt points out that while discontent is commonplace among new entrants to Parliament, the disillusion was particularly bitter among the new intakes of the 1964 and 1966 parliaments. A group of Labour MPs tabled a long and detailed motion setting out their proposals for reform of parliamentary procedure. The motion highlighted the frustration felt by several MPs with their inability to take an active role in the policy process. One of the members, Dr. Kerr, said: "We take the view that new members bring in new ideas and we have noticed the tendency that the longer people stay here in Parliament the more they regard the system as perfect and not needing improvement. . . . The present divorce of government policy-making institutions from the MPs is something we want to reverse" (quoted in Butt, 1967, 183).

In a House debate three years later, a leading Labour MP, Charles Pannell, queried the frustrations of members arriving to Parliament since 1964: "What is it that so discontents new members? What do they believe to be lacking? I believe that they ask from the House something which it cannot give them. They ask for participation in legislation and they want a voice in legislation before it has crystallized in a Governmental view. . . . If that is so all I can say with great regret the answer to that is further committees" (HCD, 1966/67, 745:622). I include this particular reference because it encapsulates and echoes the opinions of several anti-reform, status quo–oriented MPs during the early parliamentary reform movement in the 1960s. Pannell and others like him in the House clearly understood that different kinds of committees offered a practical means for members to take part in legislation and the policy process. They did not, however, believe that was an appropriate role for the House and its members.

There is also an explicit recognition in this speech of an institution bifurcated from its members. It is not the House as an abstract ideal that bestows powers and authority on its members. It is the members who give themselves, and consequently the House of Commons, authority to act. When reflecting upon this discontent and disillusion, Hanson identified the need for an attitudinal change among MPs. Although he questioned whether a body of amateurs, however public spirited and industrious, could have meaningful input into the policy process, he argued that parliamentary institutions are far more adaptable to new needs than is usually imagined: "We shall assume that an attempt at adaptation is worth making, and that something useful can come of changes in procedure, provided that they are *accompanied by corresponding changes in attitudes*" (Hanson, 1970, 42 [emphasis mine]).

These two features must be present for Commons to alter the dismal state perceived by parliamentary reformers and to make effective any mechanism for scrutiny Parliament might devise. Both institutional adaptation and attitudinal change are necessary prerequisites. Procedurally, committees could be created yet committee members retain their relatively amateur status vis-à-vis the executive if those committees were not given power to acquire and utilize expert and detailed information—regardless of how committed to a new role these members might be. Conversely, a committee bestowed with information-gathering and specializing capacities could fail to meet the goals of parliamentary reforms if the members still saw their role as a subservient one that should be confined to activity on the floor of the House.

The 1964–65 Procedure Committee Report

In 1965, once again, a Select Committee on Procedure examined Parliament's role "to carry out its functions as a check upon the executive more effectively, to bring that part of our operation more up to date" (HC 303, 1965, 26). Of course, checking the executive "more effectively" and bringing that "role up to date" can imply a variety of means, but the end result clearly points to increased scrutiny of government with potentially serious ramifications for party government. The chairman of the committee asked the assistant clerk to the House, D. W. S. Lidderdale, as an expert witness, if historically there had been greater use previously of select committees for conducting inquiries into matters of government administration. Lidderdale noted that while such committees were probably used for that purpose, they had rarely been used in the previous half-century. And he, too, pointed out Parliament's failure to keep up with government activity: "I would think that it is a failure, as it were, of the House to keep up with what has been happening outside, that the whole operation of Government has expanded and become more complicated and instead of the House taking more steps to scrutinize these various new fields it has allowed that to be done much more by departmental committees or things of that kind" (HC 303, 1965, 23).

The interpretation of the role select committees might play in increased scrutiny differed significantly between civil servants and academics. Unlike 1959, when the advice of reforming academics was shunned by the Procedure Committee, members of the Study of Parliament Group were asked to give extensive testimony in 1964–65. Members of the SPG, Professors Wiseman and Hanson in particular, supported the creation of select committees with the power to investigate government policy. Civil servants objected to any committees that would be enabled to monitor their departments' policies, and they also objected to the academics' assertion that civil servants should be expected to appear before a committee and answer questions about policies within their respective departments.

Unlike previous procedure committees, the 1964–65 committee's inquiry was based on the premise that the House had indeed declined in its ability to monitor the executive effectively. In particular, the committee recognized the need to improve the sources of information available to the House in carrying out its duty of examining government expenditure and administration. But in its report, the committee stressed it was "convinced that a main purpose of Parliamentary reform must be to increase the efficiency of the House of

Commons as a debating chamber" (HC 303, 1965, v). Committee members were convinced that Parliament's role in the governing process was the traditional one of providing an arena of debate for public scrutiny and criticism of the government. But to perform this task "efficiently" and "effectively," members must have access to expert and technical information. The committee concluded: "In order to achieve this latter purpose, Your Committee have come to the conclusion that more information should be made available to members of the way government departments carry out their responsibilities, so that, when taking part in major debates on controversial issues, they may be armed with the necessary background of knowledge. This requires that the House should possess a more efficient system of scrutiny of administration" (HC 303, 1965, v).

The more "efficient system of scrutiny" would take place on the floor of the House by members who would gather the necessary information through committee work. Consequently, the committee recommended the establishment of specialist committees as subcommittees of a new select committee developed from the Estimates Committee. The purpose of the new committee would be to examine how the departments of state carry out their responsibilities and to consider their estimates of expenditure and ensuing reports.

This inquiry and subsequent report were important for a number of reasons. First, the committee accepted a priori that MPs require better access to information. Given that Parliament was primarily an auxiliary to the executive to process its agenda, recognition of the necessity of specialist information suggests an ensuing alteration in parliamentary-executive relations. It was also apparent that individual MPs accepted increased scrutiny as part of their parliamentary duties. Second, the committee remained loyal to the perception of the House as a debating forum. Committee activity and inquiries were important in fulfilling Parliament's constitutional scrutiny function only inasmuch as it produced more adequately prepared speakers in debate. Third, criticism of policy was still not considered to be the focus of the proposed committees; that focus remained scrutiny of administration—consistent with what had become an essentially reactive role for Parliament in the policy process.

The debate that followed the appearance of this report was extraordinary, with representatives of all parties denouncing Parliament's alleged decline and placing the blame on successive governments for trampling the rights and duties of MPs and the House through party government.

Indeed, there was considerable discussion at the time whether or not structural changes in Parliament would be sufficient to arrest Parliament's declining influence and inability to scrutinize the executive properly. Many members recognized that a substantive alteration in the relationship between the executive and Parliament was realistically possible only when MPs themselves changed their perceptions of the House's role and acted upon them. In concluding the House debate on the Procedure Committee's report, Sydney Silverman, another Labour MP, effectively summarized the major theme of the bipartisan reformers: "Never at any time in our Parliamentary history has the average back-bench Parliamentarian had so little influence on any of the Parliamentary functions as he has now. We have little or no influence on policy. We have virtually no control over public expenditure. . . . We shall not make Parliament efficient, respected or worthwhile unless we succeed in attracting into our membership really energetic, progressive-minded young people anxious to make a career of the job" (HCD 1964/65, 718:1231–32).

As important and necessary as new MPs with correspondingly "new" attitudes may be for reform, Silverman overlooked the party's role in candidate selection. There is little incentive for the parties to recruit "energetic, progressive-minded" men and women to stand for Parliament, persons who want to be more active in the policy process and to assert Parliament's authority. Such members would be troublesome to party leaders and a challenge to the authority-hierarchical relationship between the backbench and the party leaders.

There were several opponents of the Procedure Committee's suggested reforms. Included among the opponents were members of the Opposition and government frontbenches, members who perceived and accepted their roles as amateur, part-time positions, and those who did not wish to remove scrutiny and the locus of power from the chamber. But even among this latter group were several MPs, including Michael Foot, who felt that Parliament's ability to hold government accountable was in serious decline. As I will demonstrate later in further detail, later debates on parliamentary reform were often divided between those supporting specialist committees and those who claimed that Parliament's role was and should be primarily to provide a debating forum. Moreover, it was Michael Foot who was Leader of the House when the Procedure Committee of 1977–78 issued its report calling for a comprehensive system of departmentally related select committees. Foot was hostile to that report and would not act upon it. His argument was essentially the same in 1965 as in

1978; he feared that more specialist committees would only serve to take important issues out of the chamber—out of the glare of public debate. Conversely, he wanted to strengthen Parliament's role through debates.

The Fourth Report of the Procedure Committee (1964–65) stressed that committees were to be used to give ordinary MPs more information, thereby making them more effective in debates. Moreover, what became an essential feature of subsequent committee proposals, the right to question ministers, was not even considered in the early 1960s. In fact, in comparison to subsequent proposals, these proposed reforms were exceedingly limited.

These early attempts at parliamentary reform were stifled by a number of obstacles. Chief among them was the persistent reluctance of successive governments to create committees in the House that would examine the executive's action and potentially threaten its prerogatives and hegemony in Parliament. The government of the day, it seems, would have little to fear from members of its own party under the norms of party government. But governments would be ill-advised and ill-served to establish institutional mechanisms through which Opposition members could publicize and criticize executive shortcomings. Equally important was the apparent reticence of many members of Parliament to undertake committee service for the purposes of monitoring executive policies. In order to foster an environment conducive to parliamentary reform, a perceptible shift in attitudes among MPs about their roles and the role of the House was necessary. This is precisely what appears to have occurred in the 1960s, a fact supported by my survey research of members in the 1980s.

The debates, the committee reports and testimony, and the academic critiques of Parliament highlighted in this chapter underscore a shifting understanding of the purpose of parliamentary reforms. While early appraisals acknowledged concerns with the then current parliamentary procedures, they were dismissed on the grounds that these procedures allowed the government to process its legislative agenda expediently. Subsequent reform discussion focused on Parliament's legitimate right to be empowered with specialist committees corresponding to executive policy areas, i.e., Nationalised Industries. A central issue in this debate was a potential committee's venture into "political issues." And although the Procedure Committee in 1959 rejected further specialist committees because of the "radical constitutional" problems they would engender, reformers remained committed to committees that would serve primarily to prepare members for debates in the chamber. The next step in this evolutionary cycle occurred with the return of a Labour government in 1964, coupled with a high membership turnover in the House. In the following chapter, I explore Labour's wavering commitment to specialist committees and the problems the government subsequently encountered from them.

4

Labour Commits to Reform

With only a slim majority following the 1964 general election, Harold Wilson called another election in 1966 in order to strengthen his party's parliamentary majority. In this election Labour increased its representation in the Commons from 317 seats to 363. Both the 1964 and the 1966 election brought in several new Labour MPs. A survey of new MPs was conducted by the *Times* shortly after the 1966 election. The ensuing article noted that the MPs canvassed expressed considerable discontent with their ability to influence important political matters and took "a dim view of the rusty machinery of Westminster." The article added: "The class of '66 are full of ideas and enthusiasm for reform. A Conservative says that the reformers have their remedy in their own hands if they will only use it. Until government backbenchers use their vote as a weapon against the executive, Ministers will ride roughshod over the rights of members, and the House of Commons will cease to have any real significance" (*London Times*, 6 June 1966). But the message contained in the *Times* article was still off mark. While it is true that reform would only be possible if members voted for it, the underlying argument (supported by many critics at the time) was that MPs lacked the courage to challenge party leaders. What were glaringly overlooked were institutional incentives and routinized norms that benefited incumbent MPs who were unlikely to support scrapping their familiar system. Second, as I pointed out in my last chapter, there were disputes among reform-minded House veterans for the proper route to follow—through debate or in committee. Furthermore, John Mackintosh, an academic supporter of parliamentary reform and a member of Parliament during the 1960s, pointed out that it was "starkly evident" that the House of Commons could not reform itself. Despite whatever cross-bench consensus could be reached in creating committees to increase parliamentary effectiveness, power nevertheless resided with the cabinet to create or dismantle committees and to decide who would be appointed or removed from committee posts. In these circumstances, he argued, "the only chance of reform is if some election throws up an executive willing to undertake such changes" (Mackintosh, 1969).

The Wilson cabinet in 1966 appeared supportive of parliamentary reform. Indeed, Wilson conveyed an impression to the public, MPs, the press, and academics of reform and modernization on a broad spectrum of social and economic issues. Labour was formally committed to developing new technologies, administrative methods, and innovative policies to address the social, economic, and political problems facing Britain. Supporters of parliamentary reform were heartened to hear from Wilson during the Queen's Speech Debate highlighting the government's priorities that his government intended "greater participation of Parliament in the process of government." He added: "The last two General Elections have proclaimed the determination of our people that not only the government of Britain but the structure of our society should be modernised. From this modernisation we cannot exclude Parliament" (HCD 66/67, 727:1086–87). For Wilson, modernization of Parliament included an extension of select committees.

Crossman's Commitment to Reform

The task of managing the government's reform agenda for the House was given to the new Leader of the House, Richard Crossman. In choosing Crossman, Wilson was able to appease backbenchers and channel calls for reform through the Executive. Crossman, while considered a critic of Parliament's secondary role, was as Leader of the House a member of the Labour government and the key person in guiding the government's agenda through the House. With Crossman in this key position, the government could provide an avenue for criticism and reform while setting the parameters of the reform discourse. Wilson may indeed have been genuinely interested in reforming Parliament, but he was not so politically naive as to allow the Conservative Opposition and frustrated backbenchers from his own party to take the lead in reforming the House so that it could scrutinize, monitor, and criticize his government more effectively.

Several years after the so-called "Crossman Reforms," many political commentators—including MPs—perceived Crossman as a great parliamentary reformer who tried assiduously to seek means though which Parliament could reassert its authority. Although the legacy of his name is synonymous with reform, Crossman's reform goals and those associated with him by latter-day reformers were quite different. To be sure, during his first speech as Leader of the House, Crossman charged that the authority of the House had been declining, was declining, and would continue to decline unless active steps were taken to stop it (HCD 1966/67, 738:470–612). Crossman remarked that the main cause of this decline was the fact that institutions developed under one set of conditions and designed to fulfill certain specific functions had been perpetuated under quite different conditions when old tasks had disappeared and new ones had been added. He added that an "effective reform must be an adaptation of obsolete procedures to modern conditions and to the functions we should fulfill in a modern highly industrialised community" (HCD 66/67, 738:481).

In stressing Parliament's declining capacity to fulfill its expected and constitutional role in a complex, industrial society, Crossman echoed the sentiments of virtually all would-be reformers—journalists, academics, and politicians. But most important, he argued that those who wished to restore the pristine powers of the House, to which current procedures were irrelevant, were in fact backward-looking. Rather than make the case that limited reforms could still ensure an effective and efficient parliamentary role, as previous Procedure Committees suggested, Crossman instead urged MPs to accept their present limited functions largely as they were and adapt their procedures to them. In short, the House was being asked to opt for what the government perceived as realistic reform and not the unrealistic expectation of conducting business as it was done a century previous.

Those members who were wary of reform and their place within a reformed House were thus reassured that a new, radical constitutional relationship such as the 1959 Procedure Committee Report feared would result would indeed not arise. For these MPs, Crossman offered "safe reform." And for those members who did wish to see substantive reforms and access to the policy process, Crossman conveyed a forward-looking scheme of substantially updating parliamentary procedure without upsetting the political balance between the Executive and the legislature. Crossman was quite clear: "It must be the Cabinet that runs the Executive and initiates and controls legislation, and it must be the party machines that manage most of our business, through the usual channels, as well as organising what was once a congeries of independent back benchers into two disciplined political armies. Since this is the structure of modern political power, the task of the reformer is to adapt our institutions and procedures to make them efficient" (HCD 66/67, 738:512).

Like many parliamentary reformers before him, Crossman linked parliamentary efficiency with government effectiveness. He accepted prima facie that the government must be able to govern and that Parliament's responsibility was to assist, not interfere, in that task. Subsequently, Crossman strove to achieve "ways in which, while leaving the Executive the necessary freedom of action, we can develop institutions detailed, continuous and effective in their control." For Crossman these twin aims did not appear irreconcilable "because a strong and healthy Executive is all the stronger and healthier if it is stimulated by responsible investigation and criticism" (HCD 66/67, 738:513). The operative word here is "responsible," and it would be left to the Executive to judge whether a committee was acting responsibly in its investigation and criticism of government policies. As I shall point out below, the Executive and the House witnessed some of their most serious confrontations when forced to judge if subsequent committee proceedings were in fact responsible. What emerged were two institutional perspectives and two divergent sets of criteria.

The common tie shared by the reformers in the 1960s was not only a normative concern with the "decline of Parliament" and an increasing inability of backbenchers to carve out a useful role in the House. They also shared an adherence to the Westminster Model and sought changes in parliamentary procedures that would restore the Commons to the position posited by the model. Theirs was the task of bringing Parliament up to date without distorting Executive-parliamentary relations.

These issues were particularly evident in the interminable debate over the committee structure of the House and the specialization of MPs, in which the reformers, especially Laski, Hanson, Crick, and Wiseman, attempted to design advisory agencies for the Commons "which would in no way transform the character of Parliamentary government but merely endorse existing tendencies" (Walkland, 1977). The early reformers displayed a respect for the rights of ministers and civil servants, offering committee secrecy and ministerial control of the committee's agenda and proceedings. Above all, the reformers strove not to upset the traditional relationship between ministers and the House. In so doing, there seemed to be little apparent awareness of the difficulty of reconciling the twin aims of strong single-party government on the one hand with comprehensive bipartisan investigatory powers for the House on the other. The difficulties one would encounter in reconciling these divergent goals were not merely issues for academic debate; they erupted on the floor of the House shortly after the Crossman Reforms were in place. MPs questioned the government's motives and charged the government with trampling on the rights and privileges of the House.

Committees Created: Proceedings and Assessment

The Fourth Report from the Select Committee on Procedure (1964–65) recommended specialist committees for the House as well as specialization of the Estimate Committee's subcommittees. Both recommendations were viewed negatively by Bowden during his tenure as Leader of the House, and it was not until the 1966 election and the replacement of Bowden by Crossman that the government took up the report's recommendations. The task of the Estimates Committee, through its subcommittees, was to examine in detail the Estimates for the current year and to investigate whether the policy implied in the Estimates might be carried out more economically. In the process it examined the management and spending problems of many departments. As the Fourth Report recapitulated, the task of the committee was "to examine such of the estimates presented to this House as may seem fit to the committee and report how, if at all, the policy implied in those estimates may be carried out more economically and, if the committee think fit, to consider the principal variations between the estimates and those relating to the previous financial year" (HC 303, 1965).

But the examination was carried out through subcommittees identified by a letter of the alphabet—A through G. Committee members may have acquired expertise in this particular type of inquiry, but they did not engage in or acquire specialization in a particular subject, field, or department. Hamilton pointed out in debate that while one or two subcommittees might conduct inquiries on military spending, for example, for two consecutive years, subcommittees were generally not defined by their area of specialization. Furthermore, an MP newly assigned to the Estimates Committee would not know to which subcommittee he or she was to be assigned, nor in fact the subject that his or her subcommittee would be investigating (HCD 65, 718:172–295). Thus if an MP had a particular policy interest, wished to channel his or her area of expertise into parliamentary activity, or was concerned with government plans in a certain area, then going to the Estimates Committee would not satisfy these goals. If one's interest was in Defense, one would have a one in six chance of being placed on a subcommittee investigating defense—if indeed defense was going to be one of the areas under scrutiny at all. One scrutinized for scrutiny's sake, without systematic policy direction or scope.

While Bowden was Leader, the government opposed specialization of the subcommittees on the ground that this would detract from the authority of the House of Commons, as the committee proceedings would empty the debating chamber. In truth, it was not the authority diminishing in the chamber that the government feared per se. Rather, it was the government's unbridled control of and authority in the chamber that it desired to sustain. If the government could confine the central locus of power and scrutiny of the House within the chamber, its policy positions would remain fairly secure, for there the government's power and influence remained supreme through party whips and party loyalty. Furthermore, the government implicitly acknowledged that the committee forum would be a particularly more effective means of scrutiny than the chamber. Members would empty the chamber for committee service only if the latter proved more effective in fulfilling Parliament's monitoring function. If Parliament's role is to scrutinize, criticize, and perhaps keep government accountable, the government's opposition to the Fourth Report was indefensible.

Crossman also established more specific subcommittees for the Estimates Committee in the 1966–67 Session. These included subcommittees for Social Affairs, Economic Affairs, Technological and Scientific Affairs, Defense and Overseas Affairs, and Building and Natural Resources. Admittedly, the breadth of a subcommittee subject was quite wide; but an MP could now seek a post on a particular subcommittee of interest. Moreover, a small group could also develop some expertise and specialization in a particular field. As a result of the creation of two (later three) specialist committees, however, the Estimates Committee was reduced in size from 43 to 36 members and the number of subcommittees from six to five. The Estimates Committee wished to avoid overlap with the specialized committees and as Wiseman points out was persuaded to return to "lettering" subcommittees as a means of introducing "a greater element of flexibility . . . which would ensure that no subject of particular interest or topical importance is overlooked and that every sub-committee has an equal chance of having such a subject allotted to them" (Wiseman, 1970). But although "flexibility" and subjects of "topical importance" were possible, specialization and expertise that could have accrued were now forgone. Again scrutiny fell to a few members (five) who attempted to monitor the Estimates of government departments—usually spending no more than one year on the subject—resulting in limited and rather ineffectual scrutiny.

The two specialist committees that were initially established were the Select Committee on Agriculture and the Select Committee on Science and Technology. During the debate on the Queen's Speech in April 1966, Wilson suggested the extended use of specialist committees: "Accordingly, the government will enter into discussions through the usual channels with the two Opposition parties on the suggestion of establishing one or two new Parliamentary Committees to concern themselves with administration in the sphere of certain Departments whose usual operations are not only of national concern but in many cases are of intensely human concern" (HCD 66, 727:1086). While the prime minister paid lip service to supporting an extension of House of Commons committees, his remarks indicated that such a system would be a matter for the respective frontbenches to consider, not the House. And, in fact, when Bowden was winding up the Queen's Speech debate a week later, he quite categorically denied a role for the House as a whole: "I do not think there is any point in sending the question to the Select Committee on Procedure. As soon as we [the government] have firm proposals we shall discuss them with the Opposition and discuss them with the House" (HCD 66, 727:1087).

An issue that had traditionally been the domain of the Select Committee on Procedure was usurped by the government. That this had not occurred previously is explained by the congruency of previous Procedure Committees and the governments of the day. Former committee proceedings on the subject, i.e., the 1959 Procedure Committee, addressed the reform issues consistent with the government's perception of the proper role of the House. Once attitudes among MPs began to alter on their and the House's role, it was no longer politically tenable for the government to permit a Procedure Committee to monopolize reform proceedings and recommendations.

To the Conservatives, Wilson's action appeared to substantiate their opinion that the prime minister was making a conciliatory gesture toward his own backbenchers. Conservative leaders also assumed their Labour counterparts would be cautious in introducing specialist committees and certainly would not allow scrutiny of departments responsible for major and/or contentious policy areas. In short, these would be politically marginal and "safe" committees. Butt (1967, 354) points out that in the exchanges between the frontbenches, Edward Heath, Leader of the Conservatives, let Wilson know that his party would be prepared to support a science and technological committee and also one for ad hoc specialized inquiries but that he was not anxious to go beyond this. The Opposition frontbench must assume the dual position of leading the attack and scrutiny of the government of the day and, as the Shadow Cabinet, be prepared to take the reins of power at the next general election. In this latter role, Opposition leaders must be wary of reform that would temporarily assist their role as critics of government but would also serve to hinder their powers and prerogatives when next they come to power.

As discussion continued under Crossman, the government itself became more cautious; the idea of specialist committees covering the Home Office, Social Security, or Defense were abandoned. Finally, on December 14, 1966, Crossman recommended implementing both the last report of the previous Parliament and the first report of the current Parliament as well as the main proposal in the earlier report on specialist committees. In doing so, he was able to give the impression that the government was accepting proposals from the House, but still retain the government's initiative in selecting those reports and specific recommendations as a prelude to reform. In advocating the two specialized committees—one on Agriculture, the other on Science and Technology, Crossman was charged by members of all parties with changing the recommendations and intent of the Procedure Committee to suit the government's needs and supporting it in the House under the guise of all-party Procedure Committee recommendations.

R. H. Turton, a Conservative former chairman of the Select Committee on Procedure, criticized Crossman on the floor of the House precisely because Crossman claimed he was implementing the Procedure Committee's recommendations on specialist committees. Turton stated: "He is doing the reverse; he is completely contradicting it. What we recommended on specialist committees, rightly or wrongly, was to take the Estimates Committee, broaden it out, extend its activities and make it a more wide ranging and powerful body. This is not being done and this is the weakness of the proposals for specialist committees" (HCD 66/67, 738:593).

Turton was correct; Crossman was contradicting the Procedure Report. But the government had no incentive to create a "more wide ranging and powerful body" to monitor, scrutinize, and criticize itself. Other MPs criticized the government for setting up an Agricultural Committee with a vague remit over a large department, and one on science and technology with a remit covering virtually any department. Few opportunities for specialization or for acquiring expertise would be possible from service on these committees. The government was on record as supporting parliamentary reform through committee extension but, more important, the subjects to be covered were uncontentious and politically nondivisive. The government whips were on for the final vote; there were 264 votes supporting the government's proposals and 177 against. Some members, notably David Steel, the future Liberal leader, voted against the proposal because they thought it would actually hinder further reform. Of those persons present to vote who would serve in a Thatcher cabinet, eight voted against this proposal, including Thatcher and her subsequent Leader of the House, John Biffen. Among those voting for the proposal were Michael Heseltine and John Nott, both of whom were dismissed by Thatcher following disputes about her leadership style.

What was also significant about this set of reforms and accompanying debate was the expectation of policy scrutiny. Crossman, speaking for the government, belittled those who thought it was still possible to make a sharp distinction between policy and administration and to form a select committee to deal only with the latter and be excluded from consideration of the former. He argued that "even a significant study of the work of the Committee on Nationalised Industries, for example, will reveal that this distinction is often very blurred, and that it is the blurring which enables the Committee to do its valuable work" (HCD 66/67, 738:485). Such a candid acknowledgment of the link between policy and administration as a legitimate area of focus in a committee's inquiry was a remarkable statement by any government. Perhaps Crossman felt self-assured in making this association, as the proposed committee's proceedings were thought to be politically neutral, and in its dozen or so years of existence the Nationalised Industries Committee had shown little indication of criticizing a party's policy nor questioning the Executive's prerogatives in this policy area.

Towards the end of the 1966–67 session, the Select Committee on Procedure issued its sixth report, which recommended a legislation-proposing role for specialized committees. The report noted that the Select Committee on Nationalised Industries had recently considered the form of the proposed corporation for the Post Office and offered appropriate recommendations. Expecting an expansion of specialist committees that would concern themselves with particular subjects or departments, the Procedure Committee interpreted the action of the Nationalised Industries Committee as a helpful precedent. As such, the committee noted that "it will become increasingly possible for such committees to consider ideas for legislation referred to them, or for them to propose legislation" (HC 539, viii). An endorsement from the Procedure Committee of a legislative role for specialist committees highlighted the apparent change in attitude toward the role these committees could potentially play in the House. It was certainly drastically different from the sort of observations made by the Procedure Committee in 1959.

The Science and Technology committee did not seek to criticize Labour or Conservative party policies, but it clearly defined its role in policy terms. During the debate on the committee's first report, Arthur Palmer, the Labour chairman, stated unequivocally, "It is definitely our business to attempt to help in the formulation of public policy, and this we have tried to do" (HCD 67/68, 765:952). He interpreted the committee's wide remit as an asset in enabling it to select its own subject of inquiry, hold inquiries into areas of broad public policy, and offer recommendations for future public policy. Neither he nor his committee members expressed support for the previous mode of committee inquiry, which examined past expenditures, previous policies, or former administrative practices.

Given that the committee assumed a policy-shaping role, the government's response was predictable. The government waited seven months before permitting a debate on the committee's first report, and it was a "take note" debate only—not a debate on the merits and recommendations of the report itself. When conducting its inquiry into nuclear energy, the Foreign Office refused to make the necessary arrangements for the committee's planned overseas investigations. The committee charged that the minister of transport was not at all cooperative and refused the committee's request for papers prepared in his department. Members also complained about the resentment and disdain from other government ministers, particularly in the Treasury (HCD 67/68, 765:951–1071; HC 381-XVII, 1967).

Backbench MPs from all political parties criticized the government's treatment of the committee, and the Labour frontbench was subject to a blistering attack for delaying a debate on the report and then scheduling it at 7:30 p.m., when the fewest members could likely attend. But Tony Benn, minister of transport, stated that the presence in the chamber of so many members who had devoted serious study and contributed thought and knowledge to a report subject to debate was unparalleled in parliamentary history (HCD 67/68, 765:967). Equally important for executive-parliamentary relations, the debate focused less on the nuclear power program and instead provided an opportunity for committee members to highlight the perceived arrogance and complete lack of cooperation they received from the government.

The Select Committee on Agriculture encountered considerably more difficulty in pursuing its inquiries than did Science and Technology. In particular, the Agriculture Committee had planned to travel to Brussels to speak with members of the EEC delegation. The Foreign Office contacted the clerk of the committee to inquire what precisely this House of Commons committee intended to do in Brussels, who the members would speak with, and in general learn all the details of the committee's inquiry. The clerk was then directed by the Foreign Office not to mention the conversation but to keep the ministry informed. Furthermore, the chairman of the committee was forced to petition Parliament for permission to leave the country. The other committee members had been waiting at the airport for several hours when permission was finally granted at 6:30 a.m. (Wiseman, 1970, 206–9). The government asserted in its defense that the objection was not to members of the committee visiting the Commission in their capacity as members of Parliament but as members of a House of Commons committee.

As with the Science and Technology Committee, there was a period of several months between the publication of the Agriculture Committee's report and the debate on the report. And, as with the debate on the Science and Technology report, this latter debate was characterized by criticisms and outrage at the government's treatment of a House of Commons committee. The government was also criticized for holding the debate on a day in which the committee's chairman informed the government he would be physically unable to attend. John Mackintosh, a member of the committee and of the government's party, criticized his frontbench for the many problems and obstacles created by the government in the committee's work. He, too, noted the refusal of departments to comply with requests from the committee for information: "All these arrangements were turned down and we got a reply, a Departmental Observation which said: '. . . . but Government departments cannot accept a general obligation to produce all papers for which a Parliamentary Committee asks, particularly'—and I emphasize these words—'those relating to internal administration.' It is precisely the internal administration of a Department which we were set up to investigate" (HCD 67/68, 764:135).

Despite Crossman's assurance that policy and administration were intertwined and provided legitimate, insightful areas of scrutiny, the Agriculture Committee was persistently hampered in fulfilling its remit. But this committee posed a qualitatively different dilemma for government. Other committees of inquiry—Nationalised Industries, Science and Technology, for example—would examine the administration of programs in which various departments might have a role. They did not seek to inquire nor to challenge the administrative practices of a specific department of state. While Agriculture appeared to be the least politically contentious of the departments, the committee's actions nevertheless threatened the heretofore unquestioned inviolability of ministerial–civil servant relations and confidentiality. This perceived intrusion was one that neither ministers nor civil servants had any desire to facilitate or allow. Consequently, two sets of perceptions emerged. On the one hand, the government could claim that the committee's requests would undermine the traditional principle of minister–civil servant relations and ministerial responsibility. On the other hand, the committee could claim a right to investigate administrative practices because its authority was granted by a resolution of Parliament, extending from support and recommendation of the Executive. Moreover, parliament's constitutional role is to hold the Executive accountable, a role that the committee assumed it was fulfilling on behalf of the Commons.

Soon after the Agriculture Committee began encountering difficulties with the government, Crossman announced details about the committee, explaining that the original intention of the government (only now revealed) was that a departmental committee should spend one session on a department, then move on. The committee reported on 3 July 1968 that it would soon complete its current inquiry and asked to be reconstituted. There was no response from the government, however, and on 6 November the chairman was told the terms of a motion appointing the committee and ordering it to report by 31 December. The rest of the committee first saw the motion on the Order Paper the next day, 7 November. A government whip quickly moved it the same evening, but the late night vigilance of Labour and Conservative committee members blocked an order that would have required the committee to report in an impossibly short time. After the motion had been blocked for several days and an amendment had been put down by members of the committee, the government withdrew its motion and made a concession extending the life of the committee to 28 February. The length of this extension was determined by the government without consultation with any committee member.

Crossman was aware of the difficulties these committees were creating for the government, and he sought to avoid establishing new ones. He persistently argued that one could not go much further in setting up specialist committees because of the lack of members to serve on them. Nevertheless, the government put forward a motion to extend the membership of the Select Committee on Agriculture from fourteen to twenty-five members when the committee became troublesome. Not all of the additional eleven members were people who wanted to be on the select committee or interested in agriculture. But they were safe party men, obedient to their respective frontbenches, and consequently could be depended upon to reign in the committee's activities.

On the 12 February 1969, a Special Report was issued by the Agriculture Committee outlining its history. The report was a peculiar one because it contained nothing about agricultural policies; rather, it was wholly a sharp attack on and condemnation of the government. One must bear in mind that the chairman and a majority of the committee were members of the governing party. Without shrillness or hyperbole, the report carefully documented the government's duplicity, breach of faith, dishonesty, and heavy-handed tactics. Parliamentarians expect governments to employ the various means available to them to maintain their strength and priorities. And, in fact, the government's response to the committee's activities could not be considered surprising. What was surprising, however, was for a House of Commons committee to produce a unanimous report in which the government's lugubrious tactics and actions were detailed for the public record. What had been traditionally considered as "parliamentary politics" and business through the "usual channels" was now presented in terms of the government's "indefensible" actions which involved the "repute of Parliamentary government."

The report claimed the packing of the committee was unjustified, that granting a remit of one session rather than one parliament violated the government's original commitments, that limiting the number of specialist committees because of staffing considerations was "indefensible," and that the government had locked out MPs in the policy-making process in deference to ministers and producers' organizations—essentially only those groups that agreed with the relevant department's policy position. And finally: "We *deplore* the decision to disband the Committee of Agriculture at a time when it was becoming familiar with its task, developing its expertise and had identified so many questions which urgently call for further investigation" (HC 138, 1969 [emphasis mine]). If indeed the committee was evolving in the manner suggested by this statement, one can appreciate the government's rationale for impeding the committee's pace and, failing that, abolishing it, as the government indeed did.

In the final analysis, party bonds and party whips were strong enough to ensure that the government's motion to disband a House of Commons committee, a move "deplored" by the committee members, was successful. The committee's report recognized but lamented the power of the government to control specialist committees. Motions to set them up, to nominate, add, or drop members, and motions relating to their powers and terms of reference were all brought forward by the government. As Shell pointed out, these powers indicated clearly the subordinate position in which the Commons found itself in relation to the government (Shell, 1970). And during a debate on the government's "winding up" the Agriculture Committee, Alexander Lyon, a Labour MP, spoke out against his party leadership: "The essence of the issue before the House is this. Should the House be the final controller of its own select committee procedure, or should the matter be decided by the Front Bench?" (HCD 68/69, 773:829).

During the 1960s the answer to this question was still very clear. But what was also striking from the debate, reports, and press conferences was an embryonic change in the perceived duty of MPs in the policy process. In addition to detailing the obstinacy encountered from the government in obstructing a committee's inquiry, members also criticized the contemporary policy process in which MPs were consistently excluded from the consultation of ministers, civil servants, and interest groups. Noting the difficulties some of the new committees had encountered from ministers and civil servants, as well as its own experience over the past twenty-one years, the Select Committee on Nationalised Industries decided to conduct an inquiry into ministerial control. The committee observed that any committee appointed by ministers to undertake a fundamental review of the role of ministers themselves and to comment on how they had performed this role would understandably be dubious (HC 371-I, 1968).

The report was highly critical of the policy process that offered MPs only a reactive role; it challenged the notion of ministerial control and responsibility for assorted departments, boards, and commissions, and it suggested more active involvement for Parliament as a whole in both formulating and evaluating national policies. The government took eleven months to reply to the committee's report. The form of the reply was rather peculiar in that it was not a formal listing of specific recommendations followed by a terse reply—as had been the case with previous government replies to committee reports (Cmnd 4027, 1970). The government instead accepted minor points such as "that spending departments should take the initiative in bringing together the industries for discussions of common problems" (para. 13). It waffled on others: "The Committee proposed that the Air Transport Licensing Board should be abolished. The government will bear this recommendation in mind during its consideration of the report of the Committee of Enquiry into Civil Air Transport" (para. 25). On others, it simply rejected recommendations: "The Government have given very careful consideration to the closely argued case in the Select Committee's Report for a Ministry of Nationalised Industries. They have, however, concluded that the disadvantages of a major change in the machinery of government on these lines would substantially outweigh the advantages" (para. 32). A close reading of the command paper reveals an outright rejection of any and all committee recommendations that venture into the internal administration and policy domain of a minister's department as well as policy recommendations directing the cabinet to act in specific ways.

Crossman's earlier praise of the Nationalised Industries Committee's inquiries that blended administrative and policy concerns was now nowhere to be heard. Most important, this sort of committee activity was acceptable, and indeed perhaps welcomed, only when the committee's investigations focused on individual industries. It was blatantly unacceptable when the committee inquired directly and specifically into ministers' administrative and policy options vis-à-vis these industries.

The government's reply extended beyond a formal command paper. Prior to publishing the response, the Commons experienced an extraordinary debate over whether to reestablish this committee at all. During more than twenty years of existence, neither Labour nor Conservative governments had questioned the committee's existence. But its recent report on ministerial control and a proposed inquiry into the Bank of England placed the select committee in jeopardy. The committee's activities had transgressed what the government clearly saw as its exclusive domain, and the committee was prepared to continue this type of inquiry.

In a compromise between committee and government, the committee was reappointed with terms of reference allowing it to investigate the Post Office, the Independent Television Authority, and Cable and Wireless, Ltd. The committee was critical of its inability to conduct effective inquiries into these subjects previously; the government conceded the committee's right to hold these inquiries as long as the Bank of England was exempted.

The government defended its stance on the Bank of England issue ecause of a potential breach of confidentiality in the bank's proceedings. This debate also drew senior Labour members in opposing the position taken by their party leaders. Ian Mikardo, who had served in Attlee's government, was the current chairman of the committee. He reiterated that past inquiries were carried out with complete discretion when investigating confidential transactions of nationalized industries. Mikardo argued: "So the question is not whether an investigation into the Bank of England should be carried out within limits. That goes without saying. The question is—who decides the limits? I do not believe that it can be seriously held that a Committee of this House is not capable of deciding its own limits" (HCD 68/69, 777:1195–96).

J. T. Price, a former government whip, echoed the speeches of many present in the chamber on the government's treatment of the committee: "I think it is wrong for a senior Committee of this House to be placed in the invidious position of being at the receiving end of decisions about which we know so little. . . . I want to persuade the Government to put away childish things and to grow up and be a little more mature about these matters. . . . This is a key matter for us. We are in the dark about our financial institutions" (HCD 69, 777:1207–8).

To be sure, it was not the case that MPs were not "in the dark" before and now suddenly found themselves to be so. Rather, many members of Parliament no longer felt this situation was justifiable or acceptable. This particular issue was not one in which knowledge of or access to a policy area had declined in recent years; instead the fundamental issue in this case was an assertion of a committee's right to inquire into areas it thought the House should be more knowledgeable of and potentially should involve itself in to a much greater degree. To that end, Mikardo, in an extraordinary move, issued an amendment on the floor of the House to the Leader's motion on limiting the committee's investigation. Mikardo moved "to establish the principle that Select and Specialist Committees of the House are independent bodies responsible only to the House, and are not creatures of Ministers who can limit their activities" (HCD 69, 777:1191). In the ensuing vote, the government (Labour) whips were put on, but Mikardo received unanimous support from the Labour and Conservative committee members. Thirty-nine other Labour MPs voted against their party leaders and supported Mikardo's amendment. At issue was a fundamental constitutional principle and institutional prerogatives. Although some Conservatives also supported the amendment, they by and large abstained. In the end, the government won, but only by 40 votes—the same as the number of Labour MPs who could not vote for the government's position and subsequently abstained.

The End of Crossman's Reforms

The experience of these three specialist committees in the 1960s underlines four important features. First, the committees moved their inquiries beyond a narrowly defined focus on administration of government policies. Second, the topics they wished to consider were far more searching than the government apparently intended when the committees were created. Third, there was a widespread acceptance among committee members and by several other members of Parliament that the committees' activities reflected precisely the sort of work the House and its members should be performing. The observations and recommendations of the 1959 Select Committee on Procedure seemed strangely archaic. And finally, the acrimonious procedure debates on the floor of the House and the special reports issued by the respective committees displayed frustration among MPs from all political parties with the Executive's domination over the House and its proceedings.

Those new institutional arrangements also fostered a change in the political relationship between Parliament and the Executive, a change that neither side found easy to accommodate. One Labour MP who served in Wilson's cabinet was critical of Crossman's duplicity and the government's retreat in its commitment to specialist committees. But she also noted the growing support in Parliament for these committees: "Richard Crossman was a liar, a cheat, and a bully. He was insufferable. Cabinet meetings at which he presided were like academic seminars. He really wanted to see some reform, but he did not anticipate the kind of problems and powers that these committees would have. Agriculture is an excellent example; the government was happy to close it down because they produced a great report on CAP which embarrassed the government. Harold Wilson also wanted to get rid of them as did the rest of the cabinet, but the political realities were pointed out to him, so they were allowed to stay" (Interview, 2 July 1987). As the Crossman diaries also helped to reveal, ministers and their officials were not sympathetic to the establishment of bodies designed to keep their work under critical review.

In 1969, the last year of the Labour government, MPs reassessed the performance of the specialist committees. During a debate on the

Consolidated Fund Bill, which coincided with the Procedure Committee's evaluation of specialist committees, MPs defended the committee's activities and suggested other committees as well. At the heart of their defense of previous committees and support for new ones was again a fundamental concern with the technical aspects of contemporary government policies.

Julian Ridsdale, a former Conservative defence minister, called for the creation of a Defence Committee. Anticipating the reluctance from a government to create such a committee, he stressed that much of this committee's proceedings would be in secret and would be devoted to questions of the military's "adequate strength" and "preparedness." He argued that "having been a defence Minister for over two years, I do not believe that Parliament can be nearly well enough informed to look into all the items it should examine except through the median of a Select Committee." And in support of better-informed debates, he added: "I do not believe we can adequately discuss the nuclear role of Polaris submarines and their effectiveness, the American nuclear shield, or the part nuclear warfare will play in the future at Question Time or in debates on the floor of the House. . . . [W]e must have far more debates in depth than we have been having especially in the technical and nuclear world of defence in which we now live, and because of the cost of modern weapons and their technicality" (HCD 68/69, 778:1453–56).

Ridsdale's concerns were echoed by many others. One Labour member noted that he had become a "convert" to specialist committees after attending an all-party defence seminar in which there had been more agreement between the parties than had ever been possible during defence debates in the chamber. Another Labour MP rose to note that debates had suffered because of the shape of the chamber, which is not particularly well arranged for "logical and cool debate of technological subjects." The proper forum, he suggested, was the Science and Technological Committee, which of course had been abolished. He, too, reiterated that Parliament was "in danger of failing to cope with the challenge of modern technology in defence." Patrick Wall, vice-chairman of the Conservative parliamentary committee on defence, summarized the frustrations of many MPs with the existing arrangements: "We all realize that Parliament today is held in pretty low esteem by the nation. . . . The real reason for this state of affairs is that, when we have major debates in the House, everyone knows that a decision has been taken already and nothing anyone says will alter it. . . . And most Members on the Government side and all on the Opposition side have no function at all, except to talk in an attempt to direct policy" (HCD 69, 778:1453–56). Indeed, reformers objected both to their reactive roles in the policy process and to their inability to discuss complex, technical policy issues with the government frontbench in a forum conducive primarily to politicized exchange and scoring debating points.

Reformers argued that the superiority and virtual monopoly of information possessed by the Executive and its ability to withhold this information from Parliament meant that members could neither accurately foresee what issues were coming up for discussion nor make known their own opinions and preferences prior to decisions being taken by the government. As Nevil Johnson (1970) points out, a strength ening of select committees was intended to help remedy this situation. Johnson, however, is critical of the value of information as the justification for major extensions of select committee scrutiny. With hindsight as his guide, he notes that few attempts were made "to work out how additional flows of information might be related to parliamentary functions or powers, still less to specific stages of governmental activity." He suggests a vagueness and naïveté among parliamentary reformers (including academics like Crick) for valuing information as an end in itself that could not be channeled into the formative stages of policy development (Hanson and Crick, 1970, 226–27).

But Johnson's criticisms of these committees neglect two related and important aspects. While the chamber remained the primary avenue available for monitoring and criticizing government policy, select committee service provided its members and other MPs with the detailed information to be used in debates, which of course they had lacked previously. Moreover, opponents of select committees who feared this work "upstairs" would detract from the chamber's importance were soon to find that committee members desired more time in the chamber to debate committee reports and to utilize the information gleaned from their committee service in debates. Second, the fact that information was not utilized systematically by the government or to alter substantially the dynamics of the policy process can hardly be blamed on backbenchers. It was the government who curtailed the life of some committees to avoid the development of expertise among their members, restricted terms of reference, packed committee memberships, reconstituted committees late in the session, refused to supply papers, hindered efforts to conduct inquiries abroad, provided inadequate staffing, and delayed debates on committee reports. In short, the government created formidable obstacles for these committees in collecting, processing, and utilizing information.

Nevertheless, the committees produced some quite influential reports; even Johnson gives due credit to the Science and Technology Committee. Its first report covered the nuclear reactor program and its second, defence research. In addition, following a request from the government it inquired into coastal pollution (as a consequence of the Torrey Canyon disaster). Johnson concludes that the committee was able to make valuable contributions because "it has not shied away from important topics and has shown a preference for weightiness and substance before political glamour" (229–30). The major difference between these inquiries and those of other committees is not that other specialist committees pursued politically glamorous topics at the expense of substantive and important topics. Rather, because these inquiries were deemed important and substantive, they were also politically controversial for ministers and their departments. The Science and Technology Committee operated in a substantively different political milieu; it was not associated with corresponding ministers and officials to monitor nor with departmental policies to criticize and scrutinize.

The committee also succeeded in establishing the principle of a select committee meeting regularly in public, of ministers and officials giving testimony to a committee when called, and, after a considerable confrontation between the Executive and Parliament, the freedom of a committee to travel and hear evidence from whomever it wishes. However, it remained unclear what direction select committees would take in the near future. Government still obviously had a great deal of leverage in influencing their creation, proceedings, and abolition.

When Crossman first proposed establishing committees, he explained that he hoped to set up two more of these departmental committees each year until all domestic policy was subject to scrutiny. Certainly the whole tenor of Crossman's speech reflected this idea, and there are no Hansard references to the word "experimental" meaning termination after one or two sessions. Three years after the announcement of the Crossman Reforms during a debate on the lessons learned from the committees' activities, John Silkin wound up the debate for the government with an entirely different message: "The time has come for the Government to take stock of this whole experiment, for experiment it was, of Select Committees. . . . But the House must consider not only the experiment as a whole, but the experiment individually. . . . This is a matter which must be carefully thought out and given some study, and I assure the hon. Gentlemen that this is what the Government intend to do" (HCD 68/69, 778:1471). In his speech, Silkin made it clear that the government certainly had a role in the evaluation of prior committees as well as in proposing new changes for the House.

Four months after this debate, the Select Committee on Procedure issued its report on the use of select committees in the House of Commons. While giving evidence to the committee, F. A. Bishop, who served nine consecutive years in the cabinet or as the prime minister's private secretary, noted that Parliament's response to policy decisions of the executive was controlled by the way in which the Executive presents its decisions and its actions. The result, he argued, has meant that Parliament has concentrated on scrutinizing decisions that are short-term rather than long-term and on their financial implications. For him, the fundamental question was "what should Parliament's job be in our modern industrial society?" (HC 410, 1969, xxxiv).

Bishop's concerns and questions formed the basis for the committee's ensuing report. The committee concluded that the existing system of select committees for scrutinizing policy and its execution were inadequate. First, the range and terms of reference of the Estimates Committee were not wide, and it noted that the recommendations of the Procedure Committee's Fourth Report (1964–65) had never been implemented. And second, the report referred to the manner in which specialist committees had developed, resulting in a number of problems with the Executive. Subsequently, the committee recommended a restructuring of the House's committee system. The committee's goal was to "seek the provision of information for the House on the present day system of planning public expenditure and to propose means by which the House can scrutinize government decisions on plans and priorities and can check on their execution by Departments of State" (HC 410, 1969, lxi).

The Procedure Committee also noted that the extent of the Commons' control of public expenditure depended upon the relationship between the House and the Executive. These recommendations shied away from the problematic issues of direct policy involvement and instead returned to focus on expenditure and policy execution. But the intended role of the proposed system was nevertheless clouded by the report's rather vague conclusion: "Although there are limits to the degree to which Governments can be expected to disclose their plans and future thinking, yet over the years the power of the Executive has tended to increase, and this tendency has left its mark on the working of Parliament. Your Committee believe that the main outline of the proposed changes in procedure should be embarked upon without delay if the House is to develop its proper influence in these fields" (HC 410, 1969, lxxii). But what is the House's "proper influence"? The respective frontbenches would have a different set of criteria than many on the backbench. In the end, the committee recommended changing the Estimates Committee to an Expenditure Committee and operating through a general subcommittee and eight functional subcommittees. The order of reference of the committee would be "to consider public expenditure, and to examine the form of the papers relating to public expenditure presented to this House" (HC 410, 1969, lxxiii).

The Heath Years

The Labour government was replaced in 1970 by Ted Heath's Conservatives. As in the past, the incoming government pledged support for a Procedure Committee's recommendations but nevertheless made substantial arrangements before submitting them for parliamentary approval. The Conservatives also followed the trend of the Labour government in abolishing departmental select committees and restricting specialist committees to a few subject areas. And as Walkland pointed out, those specialist committees were limited in their creation by the government's assessments of the role they could play in assisting official objectives (Walkland, 1979a). This well-established pattern of utilizing parliamentary procedure and the chamber as adjunct and aid to government priorities was thus continued. Moreover, one cannot discern a noticeable difference in the attitude of the two parties toward parliamentary committees; both acted consistently in asserting and defending the prerogatives of the Executive.

The Heath government, with William Whitelaw as Leader of the House, proposed a new Expenditure Committee, which the Conservative frontbench saw as neatly fitting into a packet of administrative reforms based on the reports of the Plowden and Fulton committees as well as the Procedure Committee of the previous year. Conservative support was based on the premise that the Expenditure Committee could be useful in realizing more efficient economic planning and management. But unlike Labour's early views on the desirability of bringing Parliament closer to the policy arena, the Conservatives maintained their view that committees could be valuable in seeking economies, monitoring profligate Whitehall spending, and pursuing efficiencies and rationalizations in spending programs. To this end, the Expenditure Committee would function in a manner consistent with the government's aims. Similar aims were instrumental in convincing an initially skeptical Prime Minister Thatcher to support the 1979 reforms as a means to control a civil service hostile to her view of the role of government and her political philosophy.

The government, however, was not prepared to surrender its primary responsibilities in these endeavors to parliamentary committees. Committees could be an auxiliary in the government's attempts to find economic efficiencies, but it clearly remained with the latter to set the pace and breadth of this agenda. As such, the proposed Expenditure Committee would consist of only forty-nine members (only six more than the Estimates Committee), an insufficient number to staff the Procedure Committee's proposed eight subcommittees. The result was to limit to six the number of subcommittees that could be appointed and to restrict both the range of subjects that could be covered and the number of members eligible to serve on a subcommittee looking at a particular matter (Cmnd. 4507, 1970; HC 588-I, 1978).

In addition to changes the government imposed on the Procedure Committee's recommendations, there seemed to be a fallacy in the committee report itself. In moving beyond its formal remit, the Expenditure Committee mirrored the experience of previous specialist committees. Members of the Procedure Committee believed that members of the Expenditure subcommittees would accept dictation from the chairman of the full committee, meeting together with the chairmen of the subcommittees, as to how the subcommittees would proceed. But subcommittee members decided that the House needed them to scrutinize matters generally and not from the narrow and exclusive viewpoint of expenditure and so determined for themselves the scope and focus of their respective inquiries, producing reports that were not vastly dissimilar from the reports the Estimates Committee had produced before them.

D. A. M. Pring, senior clerk in the House, noted in later testimony that although "an academic blueprint" can be produced for how committees ought to work, committee members in the end decided how they would actually work. He further acknowledged that a subcommittee usually felt obliged to find some expenditure link before it would adopt a subject for study but, once it found one, felt able to embark upon the study without limiting itself to questions of expenditure. And in fact, in the Procedure Committee's report calling for the creation of a new and comprehensive system of select committees, the Procedure Committee blamed the "unsystematic character" of the then current committee system "because the House has at no point taken a clear decision about the form of specialization to be adopted." The House had taken no decision because it was left to committees themselves to determine how they were to operate, and they consequently interpreted their orders of reference with "considerable latitude" (HC 588-I, 1978).

Whatever criteria may be employed, the Expenditure Committee did not fulfill the expectations of many parliamentary reformers. Walkland charged that the committee reports were not unlike the low-key, Royal Commission-type reports issued by the previous Estimates Committee. And he concluded that the Expenditure Committee's activities had "probably not resulted in one penny of public money being allocated differently" (Walkland, 1979a, 195). Perhaps they were not intended to secure these economies, but then one must ask what was their role? Ann Robinson also concluded that the Expenditure Committee had neither "much concrete impact upon Government decisions about public spending" nor more than "a limited amount of influence on the policy making process" (Norton, 1981a, 144).

On the other hand, some MPs did credit the Expenditure Committee with a degree of indirect influence. William Rodgers, chairman of the committee, suggested that the "taking of evidence itself, which, of course, is taken in public, widely reported, has influenced government policy in a very substantial way" (Granada Television, 1973, 142). For Rodgers, it was far more important to inform Parliament and its members about government policies and priorities than to strive for consistent policy influence. There were, moreover, some committee reports that appear to have had a marked effect on government industrial policy. For example, in 1975 the Expenditure Committee criticized the conditions of government assistance to British Leyland, and the matter received widespread publicity. When the government gave substantial financial assistance to Chrysler UK in December 1976, the terms of the agreement (which was also the subject of an investigation by the Expenditure Committee) were very much tougher and followed most of the committee's recommendations for cases of this kind, although no formal acceptance of the recommendations had been acknowledged by the government.

Labour Returns to Power

Most of the critical Expenditure Reports covering macroeconomic and industrial policies were issued during Labour's return to power. Conservatives, in comparison, were treated much more lightly by the committee. Midway through Labour's tenure in office, the Expenditure Committee was clearly regarded by most parliamentary reformers as a stop-gap reform. Although the committee system appeared more systematic than in the 1960s, it nevertheless lacked, in the words of one leading Tory backbencher, the "necessary constitution" to undertake a vigorous scrutiny role (Downs, 1985, 57; Du Cann, 1976).

A year after the October 1974 General Election, Labour again committed itself in the Queen's Speech to a major review of the practice and procedure of Parliament. Shortly thereafter there was a day-long debate on procedure. Most of the members taking part were backbenchers, many of whom later went on to be active members of the present select committees. Some of these MPs, such as Paul Channon and Giles Radice, were strong supporters of extended select committees and went on to become members of their respective frontbenches in the early 1980s.

Edward Short, as Leader of the House, opened the debate for the government. He was particularly concerned with Commons committees being transformed into committees resembling the American congressional system. The result, he claimed, would "certainly represent a shift of power from the Executive to Parliament" (HCD 75/76, 741:969–70). Acknowledging the resurgent popularity of parliamentary reform, Short clearly articulated the relationship—as he saw it—between the Executive and the legislature. As the government spokesman, he left no doubt as to the dynamics of that relationship; parliamentary reform must ultimately result in strengthening the government. He stated that "clearly the Government must govern. . . . They must also be able to secure from Parliament any necessary extension of their executive powers and to implement their election pledges, by legislation or otherwise. Whatever changes we introduce should reinforce and not undermine effective government" (HCD 75/76, 741:965). He did not deny a role for Parliament, but the tasks he outlined for it in this arrangement would constitute mere reactions to the Executive. He mentioned that Parliament should scrutinize the exercise of executive power, monitor its activities, and debate the great issues of the day. But he avoided any reference to or suggestion of previous government statements calling for Parliament to be more active in the policy process. Moreover, the scrutinizing, monitoring, and debating duties did not imply that Parliament had a role in setting the legislative agenda, nor in fact that government need be responsive to recommendations and proposals as a result of the fulfillment of these tasks. Above all, government must be able to govern.

Short also proved very adroit in recalling the basis for reformers' arguments in the past and anticipating the same logic in the current debate. Previously, advocates of select committees had argued that the government had necessarily extended its influence and activities into the social and economic spheres of the nation. That successive governments had accepted and even encouraged these new duties was not questioned. Parliamentary reformers did however contend that parliamentary structures and functions had failed to develop that could fulfill the accountability expected by the public and required by the constitution. Consequently, select committees were envisaged as the means to correct this imbalance. It was clear from the government's tone that it did not intend to strengthen Parliament vis-à-vis the Executive. What the Labour frontbench did hope to achieve was a strengthening of parliamentary committees to assist the Executive with its expanded role and responsibilities. Thus the government was able to wrap itself in the cloak of parliamentary reform while simultaneously guarding its prerogatives and rights. For the first time the government acknowledged parliamentarians' concerns about the Executive's burgeoning role in the nation as a whole. But rather than dismiss this argument and the concomitant reform proposals, government emphasized their agreement and called on Parliament to assist the government in governing. The ensuing debate focused less on Parliament's constitutional responsibility to achieve executive accountability and more on defining Parliament's legitimacy in "this modern society" and exploring all available means to govern a "complex industrial nation." In this endeavor, select committees might be useful to government and satisfy reformers seeking a role for Parliament.

Not all reformers were so easily swayed. Several Conservatives wished to "restore to Parliament its power and its will to exercise an effective influence on future policies and to control public expenditure" (HCD 75/76, 741:993). In particular, Conservatives argued for legislation to be much more carefully prepared and scrutinized. This would, of course, provide an opportunity for the Opposition party— in this case the Conservatives—to influence the proposed legislation of the majority party, i.e., Labour. Thus, the Conservative party could use institutional structures to influence the policies put forth by the Labour party. Given the fractious tendencies of the Parliamentary Labour Party, the Conservatives' influence could be more substantive than if Labour were a relatively homogeneous, united party. As I will point out in later chapters, these same reflections were important for the 1979 Select Committees.

The Labour government received its most striking criticism from members of its own party during this debate. Calls were repeatedly made for committees that would possess a pre-legislation function. But these Labour members also recognized the need for a change in how backbenchers perceived their role and the role of the House. In an especially long speech, William Hamilton acknowledged that the changes he and his colleagues advocated would not be possible because there existed no sustained assertion of parliamentary will. He charged that too many members try to curry favor from party leaders, both for frontbench posts and for honorary titles: "We are bedeviled by the party system of Government. Let us take the example of the Whips. The House would be healthier if they were declared redundant. . . . We have a Procedure Committee and all the machinery that is needed to reform the procedures of the House; only the will of the House is lacking" (HCD 75/76, 741:1002–3).

The second major point made during the debate was the opportunities presented to backbenchers through select committee service. Several members of Parliament have often claimed that being a back-. bencher is particularly frustrating when one's party is in power. Not surprisingly then, Labour backbenchers sustained the debate on the issue of backbench participation in Parliament in its latter stages. Members pointed to the contributions backbenchers were able to make in the parliamentary process that would not have been possible without the presence of select committees. They also noted that backbenchers were generally responsible and constructive in their inquiries, and service provided them with access to the detailed information increasingly necessary for debates in the chamber. In short, past select committees could be judged successful because they had provided a role for the backbench—a matter the subsequent Procedure Committee would examine closely.

Although Crossman has often been credited as the initial force behind committee reforms in the House, subsequent proceedings suggest less than enthusiastic support from him and his party's leaders. The Conservative leadership under Heath proved equally reluctant to accept committee activities that challenged Executive policies and prerogatives. But the experience of the specialist select committees in the 1960s and later the Estimates and Expenditure committees highlights important parliamentary developments. First, members appeared willing and able to pursue inquiries independent of the government's priorities and concerns. When the government reacted to the committees' activities by placing formidable obstacles in the way of their proceedings (to the point of abolishing a committee),

committee members publicly challenged government ascendancy in the chamber and received cross-party support from other sympathetic members. Second, the government was politically unable to return to the pre-1964 status quo; the abolition or termination of specialist select committees necessitated a replacement. While the Labour leadership may indeed have viewed these committees as an "experiment", its success or failure nevertheless now required yet another committee mechanism in the House.

Both Labour and Conservative governments moved adroitly in creating similar successive committee systems (Estimates and Expenditures) that placated reformers' wishes for subjecting additional policy areas to committee investigation. But just as governments in the past have used Parliament—through the chamber—to process their agendas, the Estimates and Expenditure committees were also seen as useful instruments for the government to seek budgetary efficiencies and economies. Furthermore, those committees had large and vague remits and were hampered by shifting policy priorities and inquiries. Few opportunities for specialization and in-depth investigations existed, which of course made them acceptable to the Executive but ineffectual monitors of parliamentary reformers.

While reformers often stressed the importance of committee service in enhancing informed debate on the floor of the House, they now began to suggest that informed debate was only a by-product of committee work. Parliamentary committees should be able to investigate, monitor, and scrutinize government departments independently of any subsequent action in chamber. And governments should be responsible for their policies to Parliament—through select committees. Following a Procedure Committee report that recommended extended staff and resources for MPs in light of the increased demands on members, the committee once again announced an inquiry into the use of select committees. This report, the current committee system, and the attitudes of the committees' members are examined in the remaining chapters.

5

The 1979 Select Committee Reforms

The Select Committee on Procedure inquiry of 1977–78 was one of the most time-consuming and thorough investigations any Procedure Committee had undertaken. There were several factors that contributed to the committee's decision to investigate parliamentary reform and select committees once again. Chief among them was an acknowledgment of the unsatisfactory state of the current committee structure. The difficulties encountered by the proceedings of the Expenditure Committee and specialist committees had become highly politicized and publicized issues. In its subsequent report, the Select Committee on Procedure noted that the experience of these investigative committees was an important catalyst in determining the committee's final recommendations.

This chapter highlights the context of the political and parliamentary variables that influenced the committee's proceedings and decisions. More specifically, I will emphasize the way in which the expectations and understanding of parliamentary government expressed in this report exposed a significant departure from previous reports and indeed parliamentary practice.

Strained Relations between Specialist Committees and Government

Shortly after the Procedure Committee began its investigation in December 1977, there was an adjournment debate in the House on the recent exposure of the loss of more than £200 million through the speculative operations of the crown agents (HCD 77/78, 574:1024–94). Importantly, the debate focused not primarily on the loss itself but rather on the inability of current parliamentary arrangements either to detect the missing millions or to monitor the crown agents. Members of Parliament were indignant that the government was aware of the speculation losses but had failed to inform Parliament. Once again the House acted, or actually held a debate, only after the revelation was made by the Press.

Members from all political parties called repeatedly for a system of select committees that would presumably prevent the occurrence of this sort of scandal. The debate also provided a forum to draw the attention of Procedure Committee members to this apparent breakdown in scrutiny and urged committee members to view this situation as a glaring example of the deficiencies in the present committee arrangements. Reformers did not seek more committees per se; they sought more effective committees.

The Select Committee on Overseas Development had indeed begun an investigation of the crown agents but had abandoned its inquiry for two reasons. First, the dissolution of Parliament for the February 1974 general election also meant that the select committee would be dissolved until it could be formally reconstituted in May. Second, one of the committee members, Mrs. Judith Hart, became minister of state for Overseas Development. The select committee chose not to proceed further with the crown agents inquiry in deference to Mrs. Hart's promise to take action. After the second election in 1974, the minister finally established a committee of inquiry, presided over by a judge, and, in the words of the Overseas Development chairman, "there did not seem to be a need for the committee to mount a further inquiry at the same time" (HCD 77/78, 574:1069–70). The committee's decision to eschew parliamentary scrutiny in deference to a trusted minister and an extra-parliamentary investigating body was criticized by the press and by MPs during the December 1977 debate. Parliamentary arrangements had failed initially to uncover the scandal, and when the issue was exposed, the committee responsible abdicated its responsibilities to a government-appointed tribunal.

Ironically, that this debate occurred at all was due to Mrs. Hart's refusal to commit the government to appointment of a tribunal under the Tribunals of Inquiry [Evidence] Act of 1921. Consequently, John Mendelson, a member of the minister's party, placed a motion to discuss on the floor of the House the loss of the £200 million. He argued: "The country is fed up with promises of further considerations. If we want a certain type of action we as a Parliament had better say so. . . . That is the decisive reason why I cannot accept my right hon. Friend's [Hart's] assurances on this matter" (HCD 77/78, 574:1091–94). In the subsequent vote, Mendelson's motion was approved 158 to 126 over the objections of the government frontbench.

At the same time the attention of the House was being drawn to the crown agents affair, the Select Committee on Nationalised Industries issued a series of reports detailing the difficulties encountered in its recent inquiry (HC 26-I, 1977; HC 127-I, 1977; HC 238, 1978). In the first two reports of the session, the committee repeatedly drew attention to the difficulty it had encountered in obtaining reliable information from both the British Steel Corporation (BSC) and the government departments. The committee's reports questioned the motives of the government and the BSC in adopting such an uncooperative relationship, and concluded that the BSC had either "turned a blind eye" to the economic realities facing it or had "deliberately avoided revealing the true situation to the sub-committee . . . and also failed to make the true situation clear to the Department of Industry" (HC 238, 1978, vii; HC 127-I, 1977).

These reports were intended not only to highlight the corporation's management affairs but also to question the "proper relationship of Government Departments, nationalised industries and Parliament" (HC 238, 1978, xv). Indeed, the committee claimed in its conclusion to the Fifth Report that there was no need to summarize the particular findings of the report as its protracted relationship with the Executive was so starkly evident. The lessons learned from the BSC inquiry were, however, largely irrelevant to the corporation itself. Instead, the committee focused on the broader issue of select committee tasks and powers: "This inquiry has proved beyond doubt that a strong Select Committee system is essential if the House is to carry out its proper task of examining the workings of Government Departments and public corporations. It is also essential, whatever structure is decided for Select Committees, that committees be prepared to use their full powers to send for such persons, papers and records as the thorough pursuit of their inquiries demands" (HC 238, 1978, xiv).

Withholding of information from parliamentary select committees was a fundamental issue that divided reformers and anti-reformers and, in the main, frontbench and backbench. Unfortunately, Parliament adjourned for the Christmas recess shortly after the publication of the Nationalised Industries Committee's Second Report. When it reconvened in January, however, a two-day debate was requested to consider a department's or agency's ability to withhold information sought by a committee of the House. This issue also dominated Prime Minister's Question Time, in which Michael Foot, Leader of the House and an opponent of select committees, was standing in for Prime Minister Callaghan. As Leader of the Opposition, Margaret Thatcher led the attack and defended the rights of a select committee to obtain the information it requested: "Is not the Select Committee charged with the duty of making an objective assessment and reporting to the House? How can it do that if vital figures and facts are denied to it? This is a publicly owned industry. Ought not the Select Committee to be in possession of the facts?" (HCD 78, 941:1855)

Thatcher's persistent questioning of the government for its apparent support of denying full information to a select committee is important for two reasons. First, it suggested Conservative party support for strengthened parliamentary select committees. And second, it marked the first time that an Opposition Leader had championed the prerogatives of a select committee over the objections of the government frontbench. In the past, both frontbenches had recognized their shared interests as competing Executives in maintaining hegemonic authority both in the chamber and in committee. Consequently, the Opposition frontbench would not challenge seriously and caustically the government's treatment of a select committee. But Thatcher apparently chose to dispense with long-standing convention.

In defense of his government's departmental refusal of information to the select committee, Michael Foot did not deny that documents were withheld. Rather, he claimed the department's actions were not "out of the ordinary" and that in this respect both the BSC and the government had "abided exactly by the normal conventions in this matter" (HCD 78, 941:1855). But the premise of the committee's inquiry and complaints asserted that the government could not ignore House of Commons committees. The conventions that Foot defended were precisely those arrangements that hampered Parliament in fulfilling its constitutional role of accountability.

These time-honored conventions, perpetuated by respective frontbenches, were under attack for undermining the House's constitutional position in parliamentary democracy. It was not a case of the House arrogating powers and responsibilities to itself. Reformers understood they were performing the duties to which they were obligated by the constitution, despite the ruminations of the government and the informal but accepted conventions of the past. But conventions can only be successful when the parties entering into them mutually choose to maintain them. The government's reliance upon and support of conventions increasingly questioned by one of the principal actors necessitated an alternative defensive strategy by the government. A fellow Labour MP, critical of the department's actions, questioned Foot on the government's stance on this affair. Again Foot maintained that automatic compliance with select committee requests for information "would be a serious departure from the way in which select committees have previously operated" (HCD 78, 941:1855–59). By and large, committees in the past had operated in a manner similar to Foot's scenario. But the major point of the committee's reports and this debate was the legitimacy of these conventions. Foot would not concede any change that would undermine the Executive's superior role and prerogatives. Conservative MPs supported Sir Keith Joseph's motion to approve the committee's reports and implement the recommendations. One of the major recommendations was to hold a debate during government time prior to the announcement of the government's policy decisions so that the unanimous recommendations of the select committee could be taken into account by ministers. The result would be a routinized and formal pre-legislative role for the House.

Since the government was unwilling to allow time for this debate, the Opposition granted at least one of the two days the committee requested. The government's amendment required only that the House "take note" of the reports. The issue of the Executive's relationship with parliamentary select committees was no longer a procedural question but rather a political issue, with the respective party leaderships taking opposing positions. This issue provided the Conservatives with an opportunity to embarrass the government, which was one of the expected tasks of an Opposition in a debating forum. Dr. Russell Kerr, one of the Labour committee members who had moved a week before that the House "take note" of the reports, thought the Conservatives' tactics were a "brilliant parliamentary manoeuvre." He added: "Put simply, it is that the majority on the Select Committee, namely the eight Labour Members, will be so embarrassed by the terms of the Motion before us which, on one reading, means that we would have to vote against approving our own reports . . . and will be forced either to vote with the Opposition tonight or abstain" (HCD 78, 941:1058–59). What had become a party political issue divided the House largely on party lines. The Labour government won support for its amendment 302 to 254.

The Parties' Stance on Reform

Unlike past debates on select committee powers and reforms, there now appeared a fairly clear difference of opinion between the Labour and Conservative frontbenches. To many, the Conservative party seemed the party of reform while the record of the 1960s and mid-1970s demonstrated Labour's relatively poor commitment to select committees—despite its association with the "Crossman Reforms."

Because a government has a vested interest in maintaining Parliament's relative subservience, one might expect Labour leaders to regard parliamentary reforms and reformers with more than slight trepidation and disdain. And whereas the Conservative party was relatively homogeneous and deferential to the party leadership, Labour's leadership was confronted with clear factions within the party. Plagued by serious internal dissent, the Labour leadership was apprehensive about establishing new channels through which disgruntled and frustrated backbenchers could criticize party chieftains. There is an important difference between dealing with the internal discord of a political party (notably Labour) whose quarrels may at times find themselves in the press and a daily manifestation of this dissent played out between Parliament and the Executive.

Ian Marsh has suggested that the left wing of the Labour party has not emphasized parliamentary reform because its "ideological roots in Marxism predisposes the left towards measures which build from class as the key political grouping" (Marsh, 1986, 17). But Marsh has conceded that the Left has been supportive of parliamentary reform as a corrective to excessive bureaucratic power and as a step toward its goal of more direct, party-based participation.

In contrast, my survey research indicates that the left wing of the Parliamentary Labour party is no less supportive of parliamentary reform and select committee assertiveness than other Labour MPs. While just over a third of the members interviewed placed themselves in the left wing of their party, only 8 percent of all Labour MPs did not express a desire for further committee reforms and extension of powers. Moreover, all Labour MPs who served on a select committee since 1979—regardless of ideological leaning—found select committee service important and rewarding. And of the more than 80 percent who believed that the Executive had become too strong vis-à-vis Parliament, 90 percent stated that continued use and development of the departmentally related select committees was the best way to change the current imbalance of power.

The only Labour MPs who consistently expressed dissatisfaction with select committees were indeed on the extreme left wing of the party, but they had not served on a committee and only constituted 10 percent of Labour MPs interviewed. While other Labour MPs mentioned the important work of the committees in monitoring the

Executive, particularly the Thatcher government, whose policies were anathema to Labour, members of the Extreme Left opposed any reforms that supplemented or supported the parliamentary "establishment." One member of the Extreme Left stated that Parliament's purpose was the "perpetuation of bourgeois democracy," and he disliked select committee proceedings because of the blurred party distinctions they provoked: "They are there to achieve consensus, and I am not into consensus. The obligation of Labour MPs should be to the Labour and Trade Union movement only. You are drawn into discussions with them [non-Labour MPs] and have to go on trips with them outside the House and when your defenses are down the next thing you know you are socializing with them" (Interview, 15 March 1987).

By virtue of forming the government, Labour was forced to take a clear stand on the role of select committees and their powers. On the other hand, there was no need for the Conservative party to define its position clearly. Select committee reports and the deteriorating relations between the committees and the Executive provided the Opposition frontbench with precisely the type of evidence and arguments employed during Question Time each day on the floor of the House. Nevertheless, there was genuine support for extension of committee powers among many Conservative backbench MPs and a few on the frontbench.

The experience of Conservative and Labour governments with parliamentary select committees also differed vastly. Labour had witnessed serious difficulties in their relationship with specialist committees in the 1960s and mid- and late 1970s. But the Conservatives as government were limited in their experience to the 1970–74 period under Ted Heath. Their tenure in office conveniently coincided with the creation and operation of the relatively ineffectual Expenditure Committee. As I pointed out in the preceding chapter, this committee—through its subcommittees—posed few challenges or problems for the Conservative government. The committee's inquiries focused primarily on questions of administration and cost-effectiveness. It tended to examine the bureaucracy's role in administering government policies rather than the merit of the policies themselves. The Expenditure Committee's activities were thus consistent with the Conservatives' traditional interest in parliamentary reform—to seek economies in the administration of national policies that entailed few political risks. Tory support for a Commons role in this endeavor had been a continuing theme among Conservatives that can be traced to Hill and Whichelow's *What's Wrong with Britain?*

Members' Concern with Scrutiny

During its long inquiry, the Select Committee on Procedure gathered evidence from both opponents and supporters of further and extensive committee reforms. In its final report, the committee conclusively sided with the reformers. More than a decade of select committee activity had produced a substantial number of MPs who had been involved in committee service. And with declining turnover rates in the House, a substantial number of MPs with successive election victories and growing seniority in the Commons favored continued parliamentary scrutiny through select committees. Moreover, as the preceding chapters have suggested, senior figures from both political parties who had served on their respective frontbenches were also committee members and during debates and in committee reports had supported the rights and powers of select committees.

The premise of the Procedure Committee's ensuing recommendations reflected an endorsement of two persistent and related themes shared by parliamentary reformers who testified before the committee. First, reformers noted that government spending and programs continued to grow rapidly but the House had failed to achieve any effective or constitutional role of scrutiny through previous reforms. Second, reformers asserted that the British public held Parliament in particularly low esteem precisely because of its inability to influence the Executive and hold it accountable. This latter view was also expressed in an *Economist* editorial that criticized the "undignified, inefficient, undemocratic and, above all, unparliamentary government that is Britain's lot today" (5 Nov. 1977, 11–16).

During his testimony to the Procedure Committee, Edward du Cann, chairman of the Public Accounts Committee (PAC), detailed Parliament's inability to monitor the Executive. He suggested that the House of Commons had "very much fallen behind other legislatures and the United States in particular" in performing its monitoring role (HC 588-II, 1978, 135–36). Du Cann and Procedure Committee members also would not accept the argument made by Enoch Powell that select committees were not needed because ministers were constitutionally answerable to the House—a ritual performed daily on the floor of the House. While du Cann accepted Powell's understanding that a minister is answerable to the House, he would not concede that effective accountability necessarily ensued: "In my view Ministers are not questioned by this House, not interrogated by this House, not examined by this House, in the detailed way in which they should about the development of policy and its results. . . . I am saying Parliament is inefficient; Parliament is not surveying expenditure; Parliament is not examining Ministers; Parliament is not questioning their policies in adequate depth. It is not giving adequate financial surveillance and I want to establish the machinery if it is possible which would enable that duty to be discharged" (HC 588-II, 1978, 143).

Select Committees Created

When the Procedure Committee finally issued its report in 1978, the lead article in the *Times* announced that the report "may prove to be a historic document in British parliamentary history." But it also acknowledged "all the forces of inertia and tradition are ranged against any substantial parliamentary reform" because "it would shift the balance of parliamentary activity" (4 Aug. 1978, 13). Admittedly, the tenor of the article suggested exaggerated optimism, but it was correct in recognizing the institutional norms and interests inhibiting comprehensive reform. Moreover, the assessment by the *Times* did reflect reformers' optimism for a report recommending substantial reform in parliamentary procedure and practice.

Walkland's assessment of the politics of parliamentary reform, written when the Procedure Committee had just begun its inquiry, rested on a simple proposition. This proposition, recognized by Redlich at the turn of the century, claimed that the primary detriment to House of Commons procedures—especially those that govern its relationship with the Executive—is its political structure. In the previous chapters I discussed and analyzed this political relationship between the Executive and the House through committee reform in the Commons. Reform proposals submitted by the government consistently sustained the government's prerogatives and ascendancy in the House. Walkland's pessimistic appraisal of procedural reform noted the political relationship between government and the House: "[This relationship] has been taken for granted by procedure committees of the House, and the changes which have ensued have in no way been directed at the basic pre-suppositions of this political structure" (Walkland, 1977, 191).

As long as Procedure Committees accepted a priori this relationship, subsequent reforms were indeed marginal. Continued maintenance of the authority/hierarchical relationship by successive governments continued to impede committee effectiveness, despite institutional and procedural reforms.

When the Procedure Committee was appointed in 1976, the government vigorously stressed that the committee should not seek fundamental changes in the relationship between the executive and the legislature (Downs, 1985, 58). But the Procedure Committee rejected the government's warning and indeed challenged the "basic presuppositions of this political structure." The committee recognized that any reform would prove ineffectual if governments consistently remained assured of their legislation being passed, granting backbenchers a "worthwhile" but essentially marginal role on a committee with few real powers. The committee also sought to alter the point at which select committees were consulted or informed of policy decisions. Rather than serving as reactive mechanisms to policies that had already been decided upon by the Executive, the Procedure Committee recommended that select committees "investigate the actions of government at 'every' stage in the development of policy" (Downs, 1985, 158). This emphasis reflects a dramatic shift not only from an administrative to policy orientation, but also from the views expressed in previous testimony concerning the role of select committees. Supporters of this interpretation claimed it was inappropriate, a break with tradition, and ill conceived to conduct inquiries in a policy field in which the government had not yet formed a firm policy position.

Some scholars and parliamentarians have suggested that previous Commons reforms resulted from the initiative of governments (Norton, 1985, 42; HCD 76, 902:991–92). Such unilateral action, they contend, resulted in the politicization of reform proposals that would as a matter of course be opposed by the Opposition party. Second, because the "onus for creating new committees rested with government" and it felt confident in abolishing them, select committees were thus in a sense the creature of government.

This analysis assumes that the government's introduction of reform proposals based on Procedure Committee reports amounts to unilateral initiative from the government. Granted, successive governments chose which committee reports and specific recommendations contained therein to recommend to the House. Nevertheless, as these were "House of Commons matters," Procedure Committees undertook the necessary prerequisite inquiries and were responsible for addressing reform issues and consequently placing them on the government's agenda. An alternative and more plausible explanation should instead focus on the traditionally parallel attitudes of legislative-Executive relationships and MPs' roles shared by members of the Procedure Committees and the government.

The preceding chapters highlighted earlier Procedure Committees' reluctance to question the accepted political relationship. Instead, when Procedure Committees did claim that there was indeed a proper and legitimate role for parliamentary select committees, they universally sought a scrutiny-constitutional role for them, but without restricting the government's ability to govern. It is not simply that governments initiated and monopolized procedural reform; rather, Procedural Committees offered recommendations generally consistent with the Executive's interests. Relations between the Executive and the legislature became strained in the 1960s and 1970s when members of some of the specialist committees transgressed the Procedure Committee's intentions of legislative scrutiny through the existing political structure.

As long as successive Procedure Committees and specialist committees accommodated the Executive's political ascendancy in the House and worked within the parameters defined by that framework, governments accepted parliamentary committees that did not invade its policy domain. Indeed, that national policy was the exclusive purview of government was one of the key propositions governing Executive-legislative relationships. When select committee members interpreted their remit to include policy scrutiny and, moreover, thought policy input and activism were proper roles for themselves and their committees, government refused to cooperate and concede this role to them. In 1966, Crossman's support for procedural reform focused primarily on attempts to make the House more efficient. After a decade of experience with specialist committees, backbenchers wanted both efficiency and effectiveness. The 1977–78 Procedure Committee acknowledged these twin aims and asserted that the House should be involved at every stage of policy development and administration. Parliament must be involved and seen to be involved in influencing national policies. The report issued by the committee departed significantly from previous assumptions and conventions governing the House's relationship with the Executive.

The initial section of the report addressed the relationship between the executive and the legislature, a relationship the committee argued constituted the crucial feature of parliamentary government and one about which there was widespread concern in the country. But the committee did not agree with those who argued that these concerns could be addressed simply by processing the government's agenda more expeditiously through the House and then finding a "worthwhile role" for the backbencher. Instead, the committee concluded: "The essence of the problem . . . is that the balance of advantage between Parliament and Government in the day to day working of the Constitution is now weighted in favour of the Government to a degree which causes widespread anxiety and is inimical to the proper working of our parliamentary democracy" (HC 588-I, 1978, viii).

In addressing procedural reform, the committee dissented from previously held notions and government expectations of Parliament-as-processor. The committee acknowledged that in the past most changes in procedure were designed to permit the House "to deal with the greatly increased volume of public legislation" (HC 588-I, 1978, xii). But the constitutional requirements of scrutiny, monitoring, and accountability by the House had lapsed seriously. The committee's concern did not lie in designing institutional means and mechanisms through which the House could more expeditiously and efficiently "deal with" the workload presented to it by the government. Rather, the committee desired to create the means necessary for the House to perform consistently its constitutional and historic role vis-à-vis the government. To this end, the report stated: "We have approached our task . . . with the aim of enabling the House as a whole to exercise effective control and stewardship over Ministers and the expanding bureaucracy of the modern state for which they are answerable, and to make the decisions of Parliament and Government more responsive to the wishes of the electorate" (HC 588-I, 1978, viii).

The committee's report also noted that the development of more effective means of scrutinizing the expenditure, administration, and policy of government departments as well as more adequate procedures for calling ministers and civil servants to account for their actions has been a recurring theme of parliamentary reform proposals throughout this century. But the committee system that had developed in response to the need to relieve the pressure of business on the floor of the House or to demands for the House to perform new functions involving detailed investigations unsuited to a large assembly was "unplanned and unstructured" and "decidedly patchy" (HC 588-I, 1978, ix-li). Because the committee premised its recommendations on the belief that the House must fulfill its legislative obligations, piecemeal and sketchy scrutiny could no longer be the norm in the present-day Commons. The report charged: "The House should no longer rest content with an incomplete and unsystematic scrutiny of the activities of the Executive merely as a result of historical accident or sporadic pressures, and it is equally desirable for the different branches of the public service to be subject to an even and regular incidence of select committee investigation" (HC 588-I, 1978, lii). In defense of its strong position, the committee claimed it was quite clear that there was a widespread desire in and out of the House for a new select committee structure to achieve these aims.

During the inquiry, the Procedure Committee reexamined the benefits and drawbacks of previous and existing specialist committees. The committee concluded that "one of the main responsibilities" of any new committee system "should be to continue and develop the work of the Expenditure Committee and its sub-committees in examining the expenditure and administration of the civil and public service" (HC 588-I, 1978, liii). But they acknowledged the weaknesses of this committee and, rather than make alterations to it, decided that an entire new system was appropriate.

Perhaps most important, they recommended a committee system empowered with a much broader remit than had previously existed. As to the continuing problem of whether select committees should examine questions of administration only, the committee left little doubt: "We recommend . . . a system of new, independent, select committees, each charged with the examination of all aspects of expenditure, administration and policy in a field of administration within the responsibilities of a single government department or 2 or more related departments" (HC 588-I, 1978, lv).

Above all, the Procedure Committee wished to avoid limiting the nature and scope of any future select committee inquiry, including questions of government policy. Indeed, the committee believed that many excellent reports of previous select committees had gained much of their impact and importance precisely because they involved "subjects of major political importance." And finally, the committee expressed a strong desire that committees' familiarity with their respective departments would eventually enable them to respond quickly to current problems and new policy proposals.

In developing this role, the committee envisioned select committees becoming "the eyes and ears" of the House, "drawing the attention of Members to matters which require further political consideration." This function would then provide MPs with better information sources in "scrutinizing and criticising the activities and proposals of the Executive" (HC 588-I, 1978, lxiii). The Select Committee on Procedure sought to move the House and its committees from Royal Commission-type inquiries, the publications of which usually came long after the initial subject had been removed from the political agenda. As indicated in some of the passages quoted above, as well as other parts of the report, select committees were to be timely, relevant, and influential in policy proposals. They were not to be an avenue to offer essentially post hoc, reactive reprobations of administrative practices. These were clear and significant departures from previous expectations of the role the House and its select committees should play in the parliamentary process.

It would be very difficult, if not impossible, to divorce parliamentary reform from the twin problem of legislative subservience, and clearly the Select Committee on Procedure understood this. The issue was not simply to create a system through which the executive might be monitored, but rather to establish the means of parliamentary scrutiny that would also work to achieve a more influential role for Parliament. Simple monitoring of the executive would be insufficient for parliamentary assertion; the ability to influence the government was crucial.

Although the recommendations from the Select Committee on Procedure called for twelve departmentally related select committees, the final total was raised to fourteen to allow for monitoring of the Scottish and Welsh offices as well. Given the desire to establish some means of monitoring the Executive and its departments, these recommendations are not particularly surprising; in fact, they are rather predictable. Other committee recommendations, however, seemed more than "of an evolutionary kind," and some members clearly thought them to be revolutionary.

This Procedure Committee also differed from its predecessors in recognizing that its aim of providing the House with more effective means of scrutiny could be achieved only if the government's ability to control the new committee system was closely delimited. In order to pursue the duties required, the new departmental committees were to be granted a greater degree of independence. Therefore, the Procedure Committee sought to insulate committee members from Executive hegemony and the dominant value system "through the development of a normative 'sub-culture' and an alternative career structure within the House" (Judge, 1981, 92; HC 588-I, 1978, lxxviii–lxxix).

One recommendation in this report that appears innocuous enough at first sight was that chairpersons of select committees should receive extra payment for their additional parliamentary duties. Some incentive was to be built in to entice backbenchers to take on the extra duties of chairing a select committee. Implicitly, since payment was to be offered, it would be expected that these chairpersons would be hard-working individuals, prodding and pushing their respective committees into significant parliamentary structures.

Taken in isolation, the payment of committee chairs would be insufficient to ensure favorable backbench responses to the idea of committee service. To further remove backbenchers from the pressure of party leaders, the new select committee members would be chosen by a newly created bipartisan Select Committee on Selection. This committee alone would be empowered to place, replace, and remove select committee members, and threats of removal and committee-packing, which had marred previous select committee proceedings, would be impossible to make. Prior to this new system, select committee members were nominated by the House on a motion, usually after 10:00 PM, tabled by the deputy government chief whip after consultation with the other political parties and with interested members. The only opportunity open to members "who are aggrieved by the proposals" was to block the motion until the government changed its mind or provided time for debate. Such action, the report noted, "is naturally unpopular since it can involve open discussions in the House of the rival claims of Members for nomination to committees" (HC 588-I, 1978, lxxv). But it was also unpopular with reformers in the House because of the government's direct influence on committee membership.

The decision rule has had a significant effect on events and has helped to ensure that the new committees will be free of any obligation to follow party policies. Indeed, the selecting group, the Committee of Selection, refused to pick anyone who had any official standing in the political parties: ministers, shadow ministers, whips, and private parliamentary secretaries (PPS)—that is, anyone associated with the frontbench party hierarchy.

The principle that these MPs should not be members of investigatory select committees was upheld when the Committee of Selection removed a PPS from the Energy Committee and an Opposition spokesman from the Committee on Welsh Affairs. In the latter case, the removal was resisted by the MP concerned, Alan Williams, who had been elected chairman of the select committee. Following debate, however, the House upheld the decision of the Committee of Selection by a vote of 127 to 0 (*Parliamentary Affairs*, Summer 1980). Despite conflicting evidence given during testimony on finding sufficient numbers of MPs to undertake committee service, the Procedure Committee did not believe that the new proposals would impose significantly greater demands on members. The proposed system would entail only fifteen more members than the current system: Expenditure, forty-nine members; Nationalised Industries, fifteen; Overseas Development, nine; Race Relations, ten; Science and Technology, fourteen; and PAC, eight. All of them were to be replaced with the exception of PAC.

All new committees would also be appointed under permanent standing orders, and their memberships set for the duration of each parliament. Both measures were designed to give a sense of continuity to the committees' work and to avoid the ad hoc nature of previous select committees. Furthermore, permanent standing orders would make it impossible for a government dissatisfied with the reports of a particular committee simply to pass a resolution to have the committee "wound up," as had been done with the previous Select Committee on Agriculture.

There was also to be an extension of the convention whereby members of the Opposition parties could chair certain committees while still maintaining a majority of government party members. On the one hand, Opposition leaders would be hard pressed to denounce these committees as tools of the government when fellow party members were chairing them. And on the other hand, members of the government might find it difficult to ignore recommendations that apparently had the support of backbenchers from both sides of the House. Opposition chairmanships could be a means to whittle away at the adversarial nature of parliamentary politics, placing a premium on consensus, and questioning the utility of party government. This, at least, was a reservation expressed by opponents of backbench assertiveness and parliamentary reform, as well as by members of the Extreme Left in the Labour party.

Throughout the report, the Procedure Committee addressed the desirability of professional, full-time MPs in the House in contradistinction to the traditional notion of the MP as a part-time amateur. Committee members concluded that "the work of a Member of Parliament should be a full-time job, particularly if the proposals in this Report for increasing parliamentary scrutiny of the Executive are accepted." They further argued that any parliamentary arrangements designed to enable MPs to pursue outside employment conflicted with the committee's notion of a "modern and effective parliamentary system" (HC 588-I, 1978, cxvii).

In order to encourage and reward those MPs who sought a full-time post in Parliament and a "possible career alternative" for those undertaking committee service, the report contained numerous recommendations for extended staff and research support. The committee's remit did not include an inquiry into staff services for members, but the committee noted that committee reform and members' staff were clearly linked. Members could not pursue the duties expected by the Procedure Committee nor could committees "secure greater surveillance of the Executive" without additional staffing and resources: "Any broad inquiry into the procedure and practice of the House must take account of one over-riding factor: the ability of Members, and of the institution as a whole, to undertake the total volume of work required to fulfill the traditional functions of the House, the new demands and expectations of constituent and interest groups, and any new functions designed to improve the efficiency of the House as a representative assembly. . . . [W]hat is required is an acceptance by the House—and by the country at large—of the urgent need to provide Members with adequate assistance in performing the increased work required by the House" (HC 588-I, 1978, xi).

Contrary to the advice of the Clerk of the House and several other witnesses, the committee recommended full-time, expert staffs for the new select committees. The committee acknowledged the benefits of appointing temporary advisers with expertise in the relevant area of a given inquiry. But committee members were concerned with creating a corporate identity for each committee whose members and staff could develop long-term relationships with the corresponding departments, ministers, and officials. Temporary advisers were better suited to Royal Commission-type inquiries, but in order to sustain the influence and dialogue necessary for the committees "to examine the purposes and results of expenditure programs and to analyse the objectives and strategies behind the policies of departments," full-time, expert staffs were required (HC 588-I, 1978, lxxx). The report clearly suggested that although temporary advisers may have been adequate for the traditional post hoc inquiries into expenditure and administration, full-time staffs and advisers were required for the persistent monitoring and influence of departmental policies.

Reformers in the House of Commons argued that since government departments had established their own philosophies over a period of time and since new measures took considerable time to negotiate, these processes should be opened up in order for the public and members of the House to make their views clear while principles were still being settled. Select committees were not intended to be tied to producing particular reports but were to collect information and let the House and public know what disputes existed and what agreements were being reached within ministries and between ministers, civil servants, and interest groups.

The superiority of information possessed by the Executive, coupled with its ability and indeed practice of withholding this information meant that members could neither accurately foresee what issues were being considered nor effectively articulate their own opinions and preferences before decisions were reached. A strengthening of select committees was intended to help remedy this situation. They were also designed to be able to address various subject areas more effectively than would be possible for the House of Commons as a whole. The ability to gather and process information without the spectre of party control looming overhead is a prerequisite for effective legislative scrutiny. Many of the reformers assumed that a comprehensive, bipartisan committee system was a necessary ingredient for parliamentary assertion.

One of the most important, and controversial, recommendations made by the Select Committee on Procedure concerned the information to which the new select committees would have access. The committee's justification for reexamining the power of select committees to secure necessary information was based in part on the conflict between the Nationalised Industries Committee and British Steel. The circumstances of the case demonstrated to the committee the limited powers and the practical and procedural problems that could hinder a committee's inquiry. In Section 7 of the report, the committee recommended that select committees should be empowered by the House to demand the presence of all persons, papers, and records a committee deemed necessary to carry on its inquiry.

Historically, powers had been granted to select committees merely to send for persons, papers, and records. And it was noted that ministers in the past had created and then hidden behind conventions that prevented them from producing the information the committee required. The authors of the First Report acknowledged this problem and wished to break with those conventions "with a view to ensuring that such powers conform with the present requirements of investigative select committees and can, if necessary, be enforced" (HC 588-I, 1978, lxxxviii). The problem was never identified with a particular political party, but seemed rather to be a government-Executive tendency that committee members thought needed to be rectified.

A related problem that select committees encountered concerned the source of their powers. The Clerk of the House submitted a memorandum to the Procedure Committee explaining that a select committee could not have delegated to it powers the House itself does not possess. Moreover, limitations had been imposed requiring the House to issue an Address to the Queen to obtain papers from a department headed by a secretary of state. It had been accepted since the middle of the last century, however, that a select committee with power to send for papers and records had no power to send for papers which, if required by the House itself, would be sought by Address. Since most government departments were now headed by a secretary of state, the power of select committees to order the production of necessary papers was in practice limited to a few departments. In the mid-1800s, four or five of the fourteen or fifteen Cabinet posts were secretaries of state. When the Procedure Committee undertook its inquiries, the number of secretaries of state in the Cabinet had risen to fifteen out of twenty-four. Of the departments to be monitored by the proposed committee system, only two, Treasury and Agriculture, were not headed by secretaries of state. The Procedure Committee found no justification for either the proliferation of secretaries of state or the limitations imposed on committees to obtain information from them.

Second, select committees' power to require the attendance of persons did not extend to members of either House; those members who did respond to a committee's request to appear before it did so voluntarily. But their status as volunteers also cast doubt on their obligation to answer all or any of the questions put to them. Furthermore, there was a long-standing convention that committees requiring evidence from a government department usually left it to the department to nominate its witnesses.

The Procedure Committee also reexamined the conventions guiding the relationship between the civil service and select committees. The committee sought, and eventually secured, a Civil Service Memorandum explaining what evidence and guidance was to be given by the Civil Service Department (CSD) to other government departments concerning the treatment of requests from select committees for papers and records and for the attendance of departmental witnesses. The committee found the contents of the document to be largely unobjectionable. But members were "distressed" with the extension of the conventions guiding ministerial–civil servant secrecy to the internal dynamics of a department. Civil servants were advised in the memo not to disclose information about " 'the level at which decisions were taken,' or about 'the methods by which a subject is being reviewed. . . . ' They should 'refuse access to documents relating to inter-departmental exchanges on policy issues,' and in response to requests for documents relating to the internal administration of a Department, it would 'usually be more appropriate to offer specially prepared papers describing the organisation of the Department or particular parts of it, rather than existing documents such as departmental directories or organisation charts' " (HC 588-I, 1978, xci–ii).

The Procedure Committee concluded that such conventions would deny committees essential information in attempting to scrutinize governmental departments. It recommended that "select committees should regard any refusals to provide information of this kind . . . as a matter of serious concern which should be brought to the attention of the House" (HC 588-I, 1978, xcii–ii). Because of these and several other conventions that hampered committees in their quest for information, the Procedure Committee recommended that the House confer upon committees the power to order the attendance of ministers and the production of papers and records by all ministers, including secretaries of state.

Frontbench Response

Michael Foot, Leader of the House in the late 1970s, was one of those most opposed to any parliamentary reform that would enhance the power and role of backbenchers. Only reluctantly did he direct the Select Committee on Procedure in 1977 to conduct its inquiry on committee reform. As a member of the Procedure Committee, he persistently defended the "chamber first" side when reviewing the role of the House and its relationship with the Executive. Only one other member of the committee joined Foot's objections to the final report and recommendations. And as Leader of the House he successfully blocked for months any debate on the report and its recommendations.

Given Foot's reluctance to shift focus from the debating chamber, and the status of his party and his position within it, his opposition was not surprising. Foot opposed the establishment of a select committee system on the grounds that such a system would be a potentially powerful channel through which latent backbench power could be exerted. In his testimony to the Select Committee on Procedure, he stressed that the role of the backbencher could be strengthened by making more time available for general debate. His testimony indicated that through debate MPs could "look," "listen," and "examine"

matters, but avoided the fundamental problem of members' participating, influencing, and becoming involved in the governing process. Foot may have wanted to see members of Parliament participate
more fully, but in his view their actual influence should nonetheless
remain ineffectual, reactive, and negligible in any forum other than
debate in the chamber.

Foot's notion of Parliament as a forum of debate was supported
by his view of the adversarial relationship in an Executive-dominated
parliamentary system. His interpretation coincided with those of
former Leaders of the House and Procedure Committee members
that suggested that parliamentary reform should serve to facilitate
the Executive's responsibilities and burdens: "Modern industrial societies are so complex that you are bound to have all the time an Executive that has to take powerful action to deal with economic
problems, and Parliament must adapt itself to try and ensure that is
possible. . . . It is a credit to the House of Commons not a debit that
we have adapted as much as we have done. You cannot solve it by
saying the Executive should not be so rapacious. All modern Executives are rapacious, for very good reasons" (HC 588-II, 1978, 76).

Moreover, like the members of Labour's Extreme Left whom I interviewed, Foot opposed select committees because of their consensus nature. Their work was in sharp contrast to the adversarial,
partisan nature of the parent chamber. Foot stated in testimony: "I
am suspicious of select committees, partly because they work on a
non-partisan basis, and the basis of the House of Commons in my
opinion is a party argument, and the basis of our democratic politics
in this country is based on that in my judgment" (HC 588-II, 1978,
68). But it was precisely this organization of legislative life around
party politics that increasing numbers of MPs found objectionable.
The continued norm of adversarial politics ritually performed on the
floor of the House by the respective party leaderships reinforced the
role of the backbencher as "lobby fodder." Policy positions were defined by opposing frontbenches, and it was the expected duty of the
backbenches to support their respective frontbenches for what had
become party policy. Furthermore, it left the individual MP with few
structural channels through which to participate actively in the parliamentary process and emasculated the institution's opportunities to
perform its constitutional obligation of accountability.

Richard Crossman's diaries reveal that during the early years of
select committee experimentation, a majority of the Wilson government were fundamentally opposed to appearing before specialist

committees dealing with policy issues. James Callaghan called such a proposal an outrage (Crossman, 1976, 308). Ironically, the Select Committee on Procedure issued its most assertive recommendations for further parliamentary scrutiny during Callaghan's premiership. Had Callaghan been reelected, it is most unlikely that the recommendations would have been implemented. Foot and Callaghan were not alone in their opposition to increased parliamentary scrutiny and assertion. Ministers who had supported parliamentary reform through specialization and committee work before attaining executive office had become opponents of the extension of parliamentary power once they entered the confines of the Cabinet.

When the Procedure Committee's recommendations were debated at Downing Street before the Labour government fell, only five members of the Cabinet spoke in favor of the reforms: Tony Benn, Shirley Williams, David Owen, William Rodgers, and Joel Barnett (Hennessey, 1980d, 14). That these particular persons should find themselves on the same side during a Cabinet debate seems unusual. They may not have found parliamentary assertion in and of itself especially appealing, but rather hoped to see departmental select committees function as checks on the excesses of opposing Labour factions.

If previous governments had opposed the restrictions and constraints select committees might impose upon them, the necessary question to address is why the Thatcher government was so quick to embrace an extension of reforms designed to challenge executive hegemony and authority. What seems clear is the existence of a peculiar set of circumstances and predilections that allowed the Conservatives to support the Procedure Committee's recommendations.

For one, the timing of the publication of the First Report toward the end of a parliament meant that promises made by the Opposition frontbench could less easily be forgotten in the eventuality of a return to office. While Labour was reluctant even to address the recommendations of the Procedure Committee and was correctly perceived as opposing the new reforms, the Conservatives, partly as a function of the adversarial relationship, supported the reform package.

Second, the personal commitment of Norman St. John-Stevas was an important factor. As Shadow Leader of the House, he recognized that the old instruments of Question Time and the adjournment debate had become inadequate as a mean of parliamentary control of the Executive. Claiming that the most important function of Parliament is to check the Executive, which includes scrutinizing policies and holding ministers and civil servants to account for them, he supported the reform proposals. He too asserted that the balance of power and influence had steadily shifted from Westminster to Whitehall. And whereas the Executive had become more professional and the powers and resources of Whitehall had increased immeasurably, the legislature remained "dismally amateur" and MPs' available resources static and unchanged (St. John-Stevas, 1982, 21).

Upon the fall of the Labour government, St. John-Stevas secured the insertion into the Conservative General Election Manifesto that a Tory government would give the House "an early opportunity" to come to a decision on the proposals put forward by the Procedure Committee. The 1979 manifesto proclaimed the Conservative party's concern for the erosion of the role of Parliament: "The traditional role of the legislature has suffered badly from the growth of government over the last quarter century. . . . [W]e will see that parliament and no other body stands at the centre of the nation's life and decisions. . . . We will seek to make it effective in its job of controlling the executive" (Marsh, 1986, 7).

As Leader of the House, St. John-Stevas displayed a dedication to procedural reform that was significant in maintaining the momentum for change in the first session of the 1979 parliament. He also convinced a reluctant Cabinet and prime minister to support the reforms, arguing that the duties of select committees would in fact be commensurate with the government's objective of monitoring the Whitehall bureaucracy. The ideological predilection of key Cabinet members, including the prime minister, for "rolling back the state" was consistent with St. John-Stevas's argument. Thatcher's vision of less state activity also meant greater restraint of bureaucratic discretion in policy formulation and implementation through closer ministerial control of Whitehall departments. In this respect, an extension of the parliamentary select committee system could be rationalized as an invaluable ministerial aid in monitoring individual Whitehall departments.

Clearly this was not the intention of parliamentary reformers, nor the effect of actual committee experience. One Conservative MP commented early in 1980 that had St. John-Stevas not acted so swiftly, the inertia and fear of backbench power that had afflicted many previous Labour ministers would probably have defeated him as well. Within only a few months after establishment of the select committees, there were five or fewer ministers who still supported the new committee system. He added, "It is a good thing Norman moved as quickly as he did in setting up the select committees. He would not get it through now. The P.M. is violently opposed" (Hennessey, 1980d, 14).

The third important factor was the considerable and growing backbench pressure to accept the First Report's recommendations. The strength of all-party consensus on the need for structural reform in the 1979 parliament was possibly greater than at any time in the preceding thirty years. The influx of new members with more "professional" attitudes toward their parliamentary duties, coupled with the experience of minority government and its wider scope for independent and dissenting action for most of the post-1970 period, contributed to the widespread sense of dissatisfaction with the conventional backbench supportive role in the House. Although not sufficient conditions, all were necessary conditions for the passage of the 1979 select committee reforms.

This Procedure Committee report did indeed mark a significant departure from previous inquiries and recommendations. Committee members charged that Parliament's status was indeed subservient to the Executive, and consequently needed to be rectified. While other Procedure Committees also acknowledged Parliament's weakened position, they also concurred that this was appropriate. Parliament as processor and legitimator of government policies—coupled with the ability to raise and occasionally debate the great issues of the day—appeared to be enshrined in Constitutional practice, particularly in a system of party government.

The 1977–78 Procedure Committee, however, based its inquiry and recommendations on an alternative assumption. Rather than accepting government hegemony and party ascendancy as givens and then attempting to design committees to evaluate only the administration of policies, attention instead focused on strengthening Parliament as an institution in its relationship with the Executive. The Procedure Committee premised its investigation on the notion that Parliament should assert its institutional authority and play a more active role. To this end, the committee sought to establish independent committees capable of monitoring and potentially influencing government policies and to insulate committees from party politics and possible recriminations.

Although the necessary institutional structures—select committees—may have been established, the other necessary ingredient in fulfilling the committee's aims was a sufficient number of backbenchers whose attitudes about Parliament's role and their roles within it would coincide with those expressed by the committee in its report. Select committees without the "appropriate" men and women to serve on them would only perpetuate and reflect the dilemma of the parent chamber—institutions with significant powers in theory but little interest, will, or ability to assert them. In the following chapter, I begin to explore and compare more systematically the attitudes of these committee and noncommittee members toward parliamentary service.

6

Defining the Role of a Member of Parliament

The preceding chapter highlighted the political realities of parliamentary reform: executive reluctance to strengthen legislative investigatory bodies, committee members' frustrations with imposed limitations in conducting inquiries, Procedure Committee assumptions about the proper role and powers of select committees in a parliamentary system, and changing orientations of MPs toward their roles as legislators. The Procedure Committee's report of 1978 was all the more pathbreaking because of what it expected of members of Parliament. For the proposed committee system to be successful, effective, or relevant, members' attitudes about their jobs, about Parliament, and about committee service necessarily had to differ from the assumptions predicated in previous Procedure Committee reports.

The committee's belief that the requisite attitudinal changes had indeed occurred, that MPs were in some ways different from those of, say, twenty years before, was supported by various behavioral evidence. Committee members were aware of the unprecedented backbench dissent and rebellion in the 1960s and 1970s. They noted the increased calls for more staff and better resources, particularly by, but not limited to, recent entrants. They monitored the attempts of the then current committees to pursue broader, policy-related inquiries. And they took evidence from clerks, academics, and MPs who charged that while Parliament had apparently abdicated its constitutional role of accountability in recent years, members were seeking to "claw back" this power they had lost.

The Procedure Committee's report raised high expectations for the proposed departmentally related select committees. The new committees were to monitor, scrutinize, and influence government policies and their administration. They were to be the "eyes and ears" of the House in its relation with government departments. Furthermore, the select committees were expected to be able to respond quickly to current problems as well as maintain long-term oversight of expenditure programs of their respective departments. The result, Procedure Committee members hoped, would entail greater participation and influence in the parliamentary process by backbenchers, increased accountability of the Executive to the legislature, better information access to members of Parliament, and of course a reassertion of the House's role in policy formation and evaluation. To achieve these desired aims, the onus of responsibility would fall to the members of the new committees. Although the necessary institutional structures were created, they would remain relatively ineffectual without a corresponding interest, dedication, and will among their members. For the new system to be successful, the backbenchers seeking places on the committees would need to possess attitudes commensurate with those expected and anticipated in the Procedure Committee's report.

Awareness of the attitudes of legislators toward their roles in the legislature and their motivations and goals in the assembly assist one in deciphering how and why these members may react to or interpret various political phenomena. In this case, for example, knowing an MP's attitude about his or her role in the House, the emphasis placed on specialization, policy making, scrutinizing the Executive, and party loyalty provides a useful profile of the "type" of MP he or she best fits. Does one seem content with the generalist, party-loyal, chamber-oriented role characteristic of prior generations of backbenchers? Or does one attempt to specialize in a given policy area, place less emphasis on loyalty to party leaders, and more generally pursue an active career in Parliament? Answering these questions becomes crucial in understanding whether members are really willing and able to meet the current expectations and to perform differently than the previous procedure committees thought possible. New institutionalized mechanisms may be created, but if the men and women serving on them do not share commonly held attitudes about using these processes, then the experiment is sure to fail. The combination of new institutions, such as select committees, and members with corresponding attitudes to make the committees function as intended creates a much more feasible environment for success.

The Procedure Committee staked its proposals for a new committee system as well as the accomplishments it was to achieve on the belief that the House of Commons was characterized much more by active professionals than by gentlemen amateurs. In fact, during the debates on the "Crossman Reforms" in 1966, opponents of select committees saw in this experiment "the thin end of a wedge which, if driven home, they were afraid might exclude the part-time MP from the House altogether" (HCD 66/67, 738:492). To such an allegation Crossman replied that the composition of the House had changed since the war and that the Commons needed to adapt its procedures to the needs of newer members, particularly for those who sought to be full-time legislators. Twelve years later the 1978 Procedure Committee claimed that an MP-as-part-time profession was indeed inconsistent with current parliamentary practice and obligations. Full-time, professional MPs were expected to ensure the responsibility of monitoring, influencing, and criticizing government policies and administration through select committee service.

MPs' Career Backgrounds and Parliamentary Career Interests

The change in the type of men and women coming to Parliament since the war that was noted by Crossman reflected a larger socio-economic trend in Great Britain. Like other western, industrialized societies, the postwar years marked a period of economic expansion, shifts in the labor force and industrial infrastructure, and an increased role for the national government in the management of the nation's social and economic standing (Halsey, 1986). From 1961 to 1981, manual workers had declined from 60 percent of the workforce to less than 48 percent. And conversely in the same time period the white-collar, nonmanual workforce in Britain had increases sharply from just over a third of all workers to well over half (Halsey, 1986, 163–64). And despite an increase in the number of persons in employment, total employment in the manufacturing sector continued to decline, to less than 5.5 million workers by 1986. (See Figure 6.A.)

While backbenchers had become increasingly restless in the House during the 1960s and 1970s with their leaders' policy decisions, successive Labour and Conservative governments had tried to bring business and labour to the bargaining table through a number of neo-corporatist arrangements. Instead of enshrining the consensus policies of the 1950s and the vision of a classless Britain with promises of near-full employment and a generously funded Welfare State, Great Britain witnessed increasingly sharp social cleavages and divides. Gallup found that the "class struggle" had not been laid to rest with the emergence of Butskellism. Nor was it only brought to the fore with Margaret Thatcher's version of conviction politics in the 1980s. Rather, the 1960s and 1970s marked an era in which a majority of the British public believed a class struggle did indeed exist in their country (Abercrombie and Warde, 1988, 165). As Figure 6.B indicates, less than half of Britons polled in 1964 felt that a class struggle existed in Great Britain, but by 1984 nearly three-fourths felt this way. And, while in 1964 almost 40 percent thought there was no longer any class struggle, only 20 percent held this view twenty years later.

While the New Jerusalem envisaged by Beveridge and the planners in Whitehall in the 1940s sought to protect the least well off in society, welfare provisions were targeted at the very young and the elderly. But by 1971, almost half of the poorest quintile in Britain were of working age, and by 1982 the proportion had risen to three-fourths. In short, the bottom 20 percent on the economic ladder in Britain were not the elderly but rather those of working age. And, in fact, the largest single group identified by family status were single men and women of working age. (See Figure 6.C.)

The publication *Social Trends* presents a picture of Britain in the 1970s and 1980s in which most of the population is better housed, better educated, and living longer than any other previous generation. This increased standard of living comes at a high price, particularly when the nation suffers from entrenched regional economic decline and the North–South divide has certainly become more exacerbated than perhaps at any time since the Industrial Revolution. Policy makers were then faced with this dilemma: the state has accepted the responsibility of active, interventionist policies in Britain's social and economic affairs. But the costs to government to maintain this Social Contract, as Harold Wilson called it, had outpaced the Treasury's capacity to pay for it. Moreover, as Cain et al. (1987) so poignantly demonstrated, voters were no longer willing to accept the passive, party-loyal actions of their local MPs when those decisions seemed to affect negatively their own personal condition or the economic conditions of the constituency as a whole. Despite the long-held assumptions about party loyalty, party voting, and supportive backbenchers in the Westminster Model, the British electorate had come to expect their members of Parliament to put the constituency's interest above the party's (Cain et al., 1987, 116). The economic pie appeared to be shrinking, but there were more demands on its pieces. Members needed to cultivate constituencies for the "Personal Vote"; party ties had loosened. Electors expected and rewarded good constituency men and women. Voters could not and would not be satisfied with traditional, part-time, amateur backbenchers who deferred all policy issues to party elites.

In order for members of Parliament to pursue their legislative tasks on a full-time basis, however, most MPs have had to abandon,

FIGURE 6.A. EMPLOYMENT IN MANUFACTURING, 1966-1986

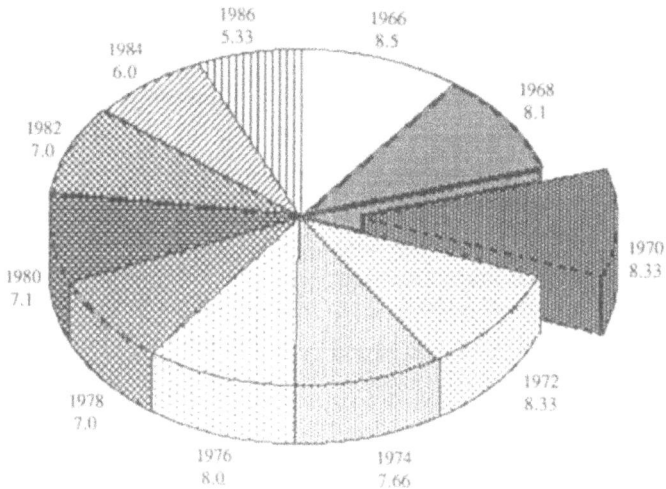

FIGURE 6.B. PERCEPTIONS OF "CLASS STRUGGLE"

Question: There used to be a lot of talk in politics about the "class struggle." Do you think there is "class struggle?"

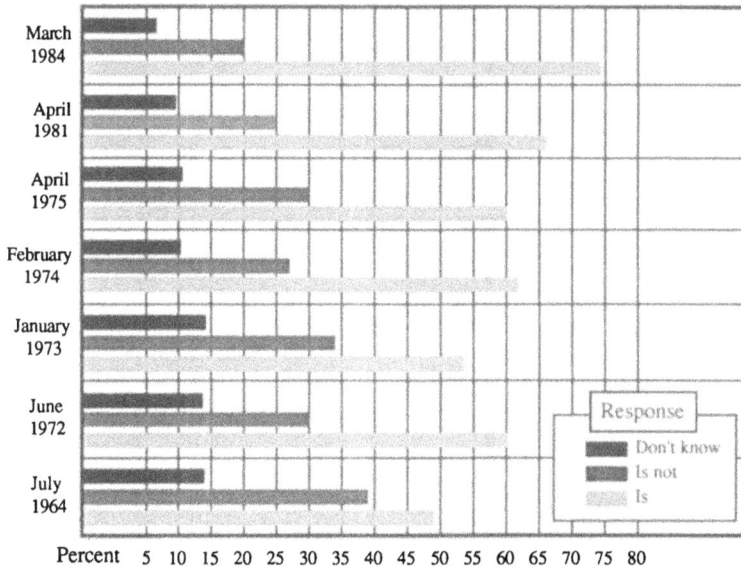

Source: Gallup Poll, reproduced from N. Abercrombie and A. Warde, Contemporary British Society (Cambridge: Polity Press, 1988), 165.

FIGURE 6.C. COMPOSITION OF THE LOWEST INCOME QUINTILE BY
FAMILY TYPE

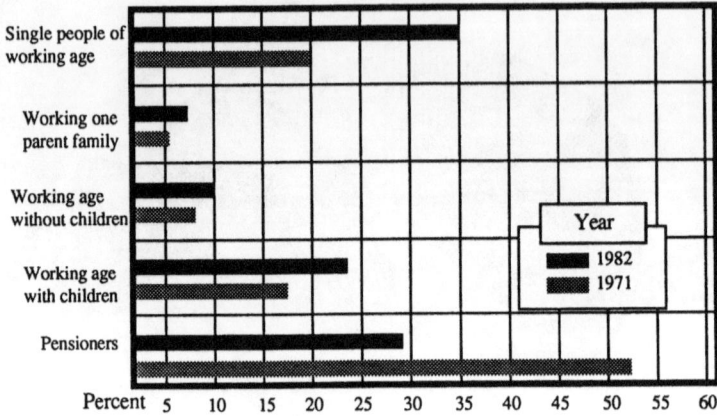

Source: Gallup Poll, reproduced from N. Abercrombie and A. Warde, <u>Contemporary British Society</u> (Cambridge:
Polity Press, 1988), 144.

FIGURE 6.D. OCCUPATIONS BEFORE ENTERING PARLIAMENT FOR
ALL MPS INTERVIEWED

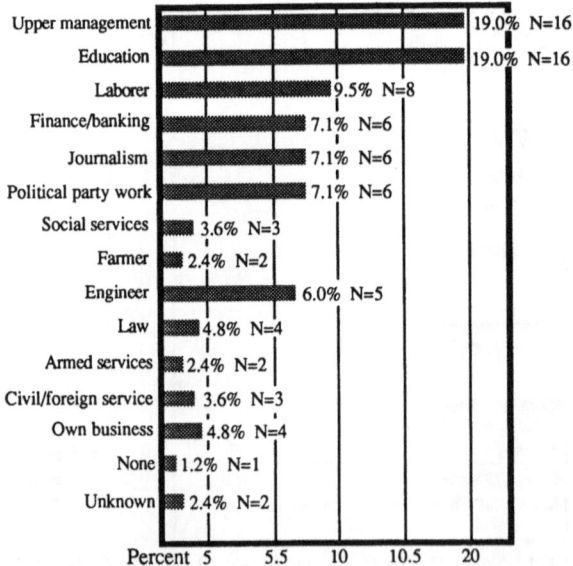

Sources: Personal Interviews; <u>Dod's Parliamentary Campaign</u> (London: Hansard Society, 1985); <u>Times Guide to the
House of Commons</u> (London: Times Publishing, 1984).

at least temporarily, careers in other fields. Only 7 percent of the MPs interviewed had pursued careers affiliated with their respective political parties, and less than 3.6 percent worked in the Civil Service or Foreign Service. Consequently, approximately only one in ten MPs had had careers that could be considered to have any political or government dimensions. If the job of an MP was to be considered a profession, then an overwhelming majority were outsiders. Further, there is little opportunity for training in any analogous institution, as there would be in Canada, the United States, or Australia, for example, through service in state or provincial legislatures. For most, election to Parliament meant entering a new field and a new institutional setting. Figure 6.D shows the variety of occupational categories of MPs surveyed for this study.

This figure also demonstrates more systematically the shifting occupational backgrounds of MPs suggested by Crossman in 1966. It is clear that white-collar workers predominate. Farmers account for a mere 2.4 percent of the MPs, as do former officers in the armed services. Both groups were traditionally regarded as exemplifying the amateur, loyal, part-time backbencher, especially in the Conservative party. Figure 6.D suggests that these occupations have been eclipsed by others. Almost 40 percent of the MPs listed their occupations in the areas of education or upper-management positions for large companies. The other major white-collar jobs include finance and banking, journalism, and engineering. By and large, from 1958 through the most recent parliamentary cohort of 1987, Conservative MPs largely come from professional and business backgrounds, with the ratio of professionals declining slightly and businesspeople increasing during that period. For Labour, there has been a marked decline of MPs-as-workers and an increase in members from the professions (Halsey, 1986, 316).

Knowing that an MP is a banker rather than a barrister may offer little information about that member's attitude toward his or her role in Parliament. Nevertheless, the experiences gained in these occupations are useful in understanding many legislators' perceptions of their current positions. Members of Parliament who entered politics after a career in a well paid white-collar occupation repeatedly mentioned the frustration they encountered in their newly acquired profession. MPs, regardless of age or party, complained of the lack of staff and supportive resources to enable them to pursue the active roles they had envisioned for themselves when they entered Parliament. But they were even more vocal when discussing their frustration in "getting things done" in Parliament because of the limited structural opportunities that would conceivably allow them to process their own interests and agendas. One Conservative MP elected in 1979 put it this way: "I find this place very frustrating, especially compared to the business world I was in and my experience in local government. There, in both instances, we got things done. This is my biggest criticism of this place; it is so difficult to get anything done" (Interview, 2 May 1987). And although he had been a PPS for the past five years, he had decided to abandon this first rung on the frontbench ladder in favor of a position on either the Select Committee on Trade and Industry or the Select Committee on Transport because these areas were important to his constituency interests. Feeling that his frontbench prospects after serving five years as a PPS were limited, he decided to pursue select committee service precisely in order to pursue his interests, represent his constituency's interests, and generally "get things done." For him and others who were selected to serve, the frontbench no longer monopolized political access to the policy process. And, as will be pointed out below, for those who desired the frontbench route, an alternative—and perhaps more appropriate—avenue to follow other than the traditional backbench subservience lay in committee service.

Another MP, elected in 1983, was representative of those who complained of the workload in the House and the lack of accompanying resources to handle it: "The capacity of MPs to cope with the workload and the hours, and be expected to master the detail, is what no one else in any other profession would seriously be asked to do. I was an executive in industry for quite some time, and I would never be expected to do the sorts of tasks and master them without the backup in resources and staff" (Interview, 23 Feb. 1987). This comparative lack of professionalism and professionalization in the House had led him to adopt a more cavalier attitude toward his role and tenure as a legislator. Without substantial changes in his ability to pursue his role actively and at the level he expected of himself, he indicated that he would step down from national politics within the next five years. Interestingly, he went on the Select Committee on Energy because energy was a particularly important issue in his constituency and also because he could maintain relations and foster new contacts in the energy industry. Select committee service was important for both constituency and personal reasons, as he had worked in the energy industry prior to entering Parliament. And at age thirty-six, he intended to return to this field if his parliamentary career did not yield the results he demanded. Like many of his parliamentary colleagues, he expected to take an active role in the House. He chose to eschew the amateur-gentleman legislative role.

But to be active and professional, more resources were necessary. Granting these resources, however, would not necessarily be in the Executive's best interest.

The perceptions and attitudes of these two MPs are of course not universally held. But they do represent the attitudes of many former white-collar professionals interviewed. And as the House becomes more and more characterized by young, educated professionals, one can expect to see a similar rise in frustration among this legislative cohort unless they receive promotions to responsible frontbench positions or find meaningful alternative roles on the backbench.

Ronald Butt acknowledged in 1967 that the newest MPs were "invariably disappointed by what they find to be their positions and status once they arrive at Westminster" (Butt, 1967, 181). This disappointment, he added, was particularly acute for those men and women who entered politics "to get things done." Butt's analysis suggested, however, that the disappointment felt by new entrants was a perennial problem—or at least one that followed each general election. As they were socialized into the norms of the House, they accepted their relatively ineffectual and passive role, and further, he implied, these MPs' disappointment would soon dissipate. Although Butt noted the presence of disappointment, he failed to appreciate its pervasiveness among new MPs in the early and mid-1960s. And he also appears to have overlooked the increasing number of MPs who entered politics to pursue active careers in Parliament. The preceding chapters highlighted the fact that much of the impetus for parliamentary reform emanated from the new entrants of the 1960s. Barker and Rush's 1970 study confirmed this impression; they also found some association between the background of MPs and the extent to which they favored parliamentary reform (Barker and Rush, 1970). And in 1981 Geoffrey Smith, parliamentary correspondent for the *Times*, observed: "The young, aspiring MP has not largely sacrificed any other career . . . in order to be lobby fodder for his party in the Commons and a glorified welfare officer for his constituents at home. He wants to determine policies, to influence events. He finds, however, that his opportunities for doing either are severely circumscribed on the backbenches and that his prospects of being called to the frontbench are limited by the laws of arithmetic. . . . This explains why there is mounting frustration among MPs and why it is the younger ones who are in general the most ardent supporters of parliamentary reform" (Ornstein, 1981, 38–39).

The prevalence of particular employment backgrounds among MPs is highlighted in a comparison of committee members from 1968 to 1987. Three successive panels of committee members are profiled

FIGURE 6.E. OCCUPATIONS BEFORE ENTERING PARLIAMENT FOR MEMBERS OF 1968-1969 ESTIMATES COMMITTEE

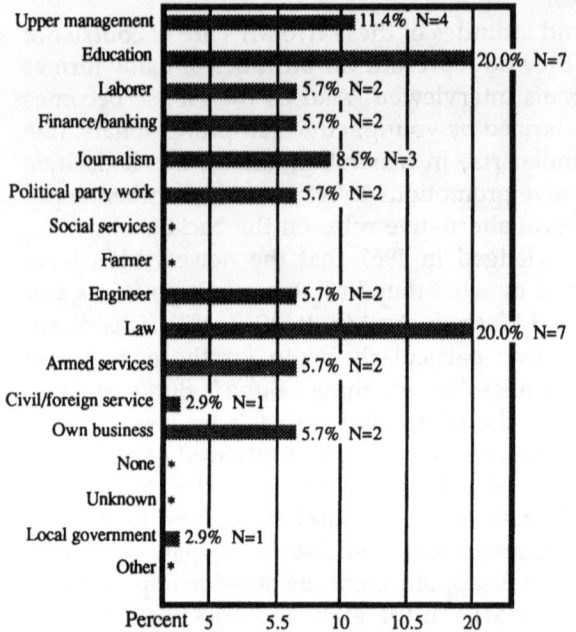

Sources: Personal Interviews;
Dod's Parliamentary Campaign
(London: Hansard Society, 1970);
Times Guide to the House of
Commons (London: Times
Publishing, 1984).

*No MPs fit this category.

Occupation	Percent
Upper management	11.4% N=4
Education	20.0% N=7
Laborer	5.7% N=2
Finance/banking	5.7% N=2
Journalism	8.5% N=3
Political party work	5.7% N=2
Social services	*
Farmer	*
Engineer	5.7% N=2
Law	20.0% N=7
Armed services	5.7% N=2
Civil/foreign service	2.9% N=1
Own business	5.7% N=2
None	*
Unknown	*
Local government	2.9% N=1
Other	*

Percent   5   5.5   10   10.5   20

here. Because the departmental select committees were created in 1979, there are no directly parallel units of analysis prior to this time. But in functional terms there were some corresponding committees in the 1960s and 1970s—the Estimates and Expenditure committees. (There were some other similar committees—Nationlised Industries, Agriculture, Science and Technology, and Overseas Development— that are comparable to current select committees, but the number of members on these past and current committees is so low that no meaningful interpretation could be made from the data.) Figures 6.E, 6.F, and 6.G demonstrate the similarity between the committee members' backgrounds from the last Estimates Committee in 1968/69, the last Expenditure Committee in 1977/78, and the sample of select committee members interviewed in 1986/87 for this project.

By and large, one does not find any glaring discrepancies in occupational backgrounds. Members serving on the Estimates and Expenditure committees, however, were generally seen as aberrations in Parliament and were singled out as the "parliamentary work-horses," unlike their more reticent and genteel fellow backbenchers. During debates and testimony to successive procedure committees, these members displayed continued frustration with their inability to

FIGURE 6.F. OCCUPATIONS BEFORE ENTERING PARLIAMENT FOR
MEMBERS OF 1977-1978 EXPENDITURE COMMITTEE

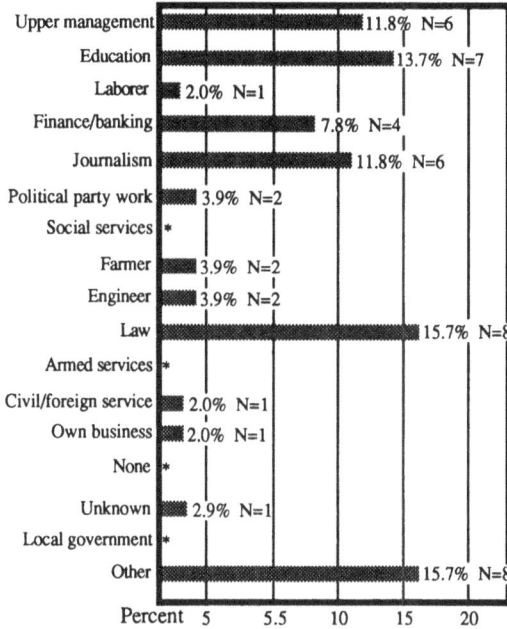

Occupation	Percent
Upper management	11.8% N=6
Education	13.7% N=7
Laborer	2.0% N=1
Finance/banking	7.8% N=4
Journalism	11.8% N=6
Political party work	3.9% N=2
Social services	*
Farmer	3.9% N=2
Engineer	3.9% N=2
Law	15.7% N=8
Armed services	*
Civil/foreign service	2.0% N=1
Own business	2.0% N=1
None	*
Unknown	2.9% N=1
Local government	*
Other	15.7% N=8

Percent 5   5.5   10   15   20

Sources: Personal Interviews;
Dod's Parliamentary Campaign
(London: Hansard Society, 1979);
Times Guide to the House of
Commons (London: Times
Publishing, 1984).

*No MPs fit this category.

FIGURE 6.G. OCCUPATIONS BEFORE ENTERING PARLIAMENT FOR
COMMITTEE MEMBERS INTERVIEWED, 1986-1987

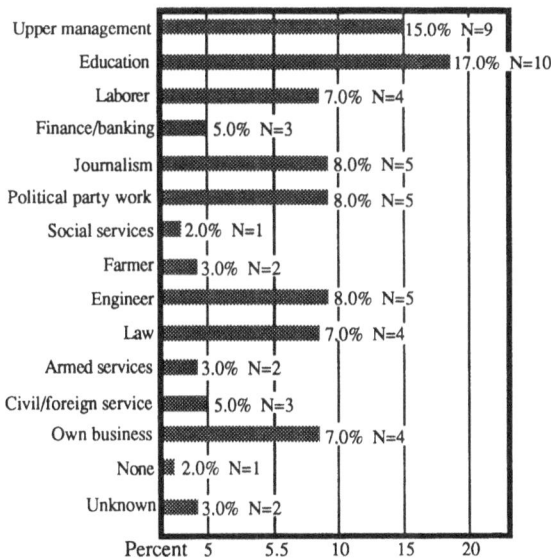

Occupation	Percent
Upper management	15.0% N=9
Education	17.0% N=10
Laborer	7.0% N=4
Finance/banking	5.0% N=3
Journalism	8.0% N=5
Political party work	8.0% N=5
Social services	2.0% N=1
Farmer	3.0% N=2
Engineer	8.0% N=5
Law	7.0% N=4
Armed services	3.0% N=2
Civil/foreign service	5.0% N=3
Own business	7.0% N=4
None	2.0% N=1
Unknown	3.0% N=2

Percent 5   5.5   10   15   20

Sources: Personal Interviews;
Dod's Parliamentary Campaign
(London: Hansard Society, 1985);
Times Guide to the House of
Commons (London: Times
Publishing, 1984).

pursue meaningful inquiries and to investigate policy decisions, and were generally disappointed with the apparent disdain shown them by party leaders. Frustrated and disappointed with their marginalized role in the policy process, these earlier committees faced high turnover rates and extremely low attendance rates. By the late 1970s, these committee members were less and less an aberration and more representative of the House as a whole. The old parliamentary committees would have to give way to meet the desires increasingly obvious in the House. Parliament supported a minority government, and many in the House recognized that the time had come to modernize Parliament's capacity for oversight to meet the needs and challenges of an increasingly restless and rebelling backbench.

This emphasis on carving out a role that includes an active, policy-influencing dimension also appears in the interview data I collected. Given a tacit recognition of pervasive frustration among recent entrants to the House, surely a parliamentary career must bring with it some rewards, some appeal to those who choose to seek re-election. To address this issue, members of Parliament were asked in an open-ended question, "As an MP, what do you find most appealing about being in politics?" Table 6.1 gives a breakdown of the six response categories offered by MPs. Overall, approximately 60 percent stated that politics was appealing to them because of the involvement it offered in shaping national policies. Many, however, were quick to point out that although there were opportunities to involve oneself in national policy matters, this did not necessarily mean there were sufficient avenues for them in the House to be as active and involved as they would like. An MP could try to introduce a Private Member's Bill, for example, but the likelihood for passage is very slim. One could move for an emergency debate on a self-selected issue, but a favorable decision from the Speaker is by no means assured. The chances of being called upon in debate are few, and the likelihood of significantly altering or shaping policy in the chamber is even more remote. Frontbench MPs were also more likely than their backbench counterparts to stress a more directly involved and active component in policy making. One Labour spokesman said, "I like being able to make some impact on public policy and actually being involved in this process at the national level to some degree." And another spokesman added, "For me, the most appealing part is the opportunity to get action on the areas one regards as important" (Interview, 4 Feb. 1987).

Frontbenchers should, and do, have greater capacity to "make an impact" or "get action," but for their backbench counterparts these opportunities are far more limited. For these MPs, then, there exist

TABLE 6.1. APPEAL OF BEING IN POLITICS FOR MPS

Question: As a member of Parliament, what do you find most appealing about being in politics?

Response	All Members of Parliament		Conservative		Labour		Non-Select Committee		Select Committee	
	%	(N-84)	%	(N-41)	%	(N-38)	%	(N-24)	%	(N-60)
Access to policy/ decision making	60	50	73	30	50	19	62	15	75	40
Seat of power	35	29	22	9	47	18	25	6	38	23
Serve constituents	21	18	24	10	13	5	29	7	18	11
Pursue ideology	11	9	2	1	16	6	8	2	12	7
Good club	5	4	10	4	0	0	16	4	0	0
Honor/privilege	4	3	2	1	5	2	0	0	5	3

too few formal, structural opportunities to participate actively in the formulation of national policies. This situation is especially apparent for members of the Opposition party. Given the Conservatives' continued parliamentary majority during the past thirteen years, coupled with Mrs. Thatcher's distaste for consensus politics, the Parliamentary Labour party as a whole, and especially individual Labour MPs, have been unable to define or influence substantially the policy agenda since 1979. While MPs may find solace in shaping Labour's policy positions, implementation and action are only possible after some future Labour general election victory.

One would expect, then, to find a marked difference between Conservative and Labour MPs in viewing "involvement" as an appealing part of being in national politics. Labour has found little opportunity to shape public policy since 1979 and, as a result, little access to the policy arena, a factor influencing their perception of its appeal. For many Labour MPs, the appeal of politics may at least temporarily be less important than other opportunities the job presents. Indeed, the data confirm this. While almost three-fourths of Conservative MPs stressed the appeal of "involvement," only 50 percent of Labour MPs did so. For Opposition MPs, there was virtually as much appeal for them in "being where the power is and decision made" as with actual involvement. Conversely, and as expected, less than half as many government as Labour MPs found this to be appealing to them. One of the longest serving MPs and a member of Labour's National Executive Committee explained it this way: "True, we are currently in opposition, but one still feels one is sitting in the center of being spun. You get a chance to know what is going on, a chance of being in the know. I do get a chance to know what is being discussed in government in Britain more than virtually anyone else" (Interview, 25 Feb. 1987). And as an SDP member remarked: "You may not always be in a position to substantially alter events, but you do get a ringside seat to what is going on" (Interview, 3 Feb. 1987).

Whether one finds it appealing to be involved in decision-making or be present at the seat of power where decisions are made, the evidence suggests a commonly held concern among MPs with national policies and policy making. And while being formally locked out of the policy-making process over the course of several years, half of Labour MPs still stressed the appeal of making decisions at the national level. This, too, may reflect some appreciation for articulating Labour's position to be implemented in a future Labour government. As subsequent data analysis will indicate, this emphasis on the policy dimension of the legislator's role persists when members are asked further questions concerning their role in the House.

The notion of MPs as amateurs, generalists, or part-timers once corresponded closely with the belief that they were in the House because it was "the best club in Europe" and service was an honor and privilege bestowed upon them (Granada Television, 1973). But these parliamentary attributes have largely ceased to be significant enticements for men and women to enter Parliament. Nor do these factors appear to have significant appeal to current members. Less than 5 percent of the MPs interviewed found whatever "club atmosphere" may exist appealing. Nonetheless, all of those who did mention this factor as an appealing part of national politics were Conservative members. An even smaller number (3.6 percent) mentioned the honor and privilege of serving as appealing to them. One Conservative MP answered the question this way: "Well, basically for me I find it an honor to be here and a privilege to serve in the Mother of Parliaments. The fact, because of dates of birth and the rest of it, I've never really been in anything [other] than public service all my life. I was in the diplomatic service and after fifteen years of that it was obvious I really hadn't the capacity for commercial life. Parliament seemed the obvious career then" (Interview, 20 Jan. 1987).

About 11 percent of the members interviewed stated they found being in politics appealing because it offered them the opportunity to articulate and champion a particular political philosophy or ideology. With the exception of a few Liberal/SDP MPs, these were self-styled ideologues who represented the Extreme Left in the Labour party and the Extreme Right in the Conservative party. But they had divergent, preconceived opinions concerning the utility of select committees as a means of pursuing their ideologically based goals. The Labour MPs, who indicated they came to Parliament to "champion the class struggle," were not interested in committee work because of what they perceived as the "sloppy consensus" that took place there. Conservative MPs did choose to serve on select committees where they attempted to pursue single-issue causes, e.g., removing Britain from the EEC. When they realized that select committees were an inappropriate avenue to achieve these aims and an improper forum for class-based or adversarial politics, they resigned from their respective committees.

The Liberals, on the other hand, found select committee service a useful means to pursue what they identified as moderate, middle-of-the-road policies, which they felt by and large reflected Liberal party policies. One senior Liberal MP said of the appeal of politics: "[It is] the ability to get a platform for Liberalism as I understand it and represent not just the views of my constituency—which are very important—but also as far as possible the views of Liberals throughout the country. I also correspond regularly with Liberals throughout Great Britain who have no Liberal MP." And, as a long-serving member of one of the most prestigious select committees before becoming a party spokesman, he added, "I think many of the committee's findings have helped to move public opinion toward the Liberal and Social Democratic way of thinking" (Interview, 3 Feb. 1987).

Describing the Job of an MP: The Participant's View

Discovering what MPs find appealing about being in politics sheds light on their motivations and rationale for entering Parliament. It also highlights what an MP may do in the House to seek and receive job satisfaction. But this does not provide sufficient information to determine how an MP defines his or her job in the House. Clearly, many members find being at the seat of power and decision making quite appealing, but it is difficult to imagine that they see this as necessarily part of their jobs as members of Parliament. And members may undertake a series of mundane tasks that hold little appeal whatsoever. Consequently, a follow-up question asked them to describe how they perceive their jobs as MPs, asking them, "What do you do here?" This question allowed MPs to define more precisely the duties and tasks they perform. Again, this was an open-ended question and the responses were subsequently coded into seven categories encapsulating all the offered responses. These are presented in Table 6.2.

TABLE 6.2. MPS' DESCRIPTIONS OF THEIR JOBS

Question: How do you describe your job as a member of Parliament? What do you do here?

Response	All Members of Parliament		Conservative		Labour		Non-Select Committee		Select Committee	
	%	(N-84)	%	(N-41)	%	(N-38)	%	(N-24)	%	(N-60)
Constituency work	67	56	68	28	66	25	58	14	70	42
Make policy	31	26	34	14	29	11	25	6	33	20
Demanding/ hard work	27	23	32	13	26	10	21	5	30	18
Petition grievances	17	14	15	6	13	5	4	1	22	13
Debates	14	12	12	5	18	7	25	6	10	6
Support party	12	10	7	3	13	5	0	0	17	10
Campaign for interests	10	8	0	0	13	5	8	2	10	6

Although only one in five MPs found constituency work appealing, two-thirds mentioned it as part of their job tasks. This was by far the most frequent response and was emphasized equally among Labour and Conservative MPs. As a sub-sample of all MPs, however, those members who had not served on select committees were generally less inclined to mention constituency work as part of their jobs. But this was mentioned in an equally high proportion (more than 2 to 1) to other job components.

The job of an MP has also meant a greater allocation of legislative time to constituency work than was the case even twenty years ago; but that does not mean the MP uniformly enjoys it at the same rate. This newly placed focus has been explored by several legislative scholars (Cain, Ferejohn, and Fiorina, 1979a, 1987). Alf Dubs, Opposition spokesman on Race Relations and Immigration, spoke of his job as an MP in the following way: "I would say I spend most of my time, much to my surprise compared to what I thought before I got here, on individual constituent problems—far more than I thought I would. What is not clear to everybody is that the inner-city areas like my constituency [Battersea] have enormous weighty constituency problems compared to other areas. From watching the secretary go through the post bag, I find that inner city post bags are up to three times more than other ones. [Why?] Well, because there are a number of inner-city problems—unemployment, social security, housing difficulties. So I spend far more of my time on that than I do on policy or other types of things" (Interview, 24 March 1987). Despite the attention Dubs paid to constituent problems, he lost his seat, which Labour had held since 1896, in the 1987 general election—a result perhaps of an influx of Conservative voters in this recently gentrified area of London.

Of course, one of the explanations for increased attention to constituent affairs and the gap that exists between it and the appeal one receives from it is the increased expectation among constituents that MPs will actively pursue this task. James Marsh points out that the change in attitude to, and scope of, constituency casework came in the 1960s "with the growth of community politics, which meant that local issues and problems were exploited by local parties, at that time usually the Liberal Party" (Marsh, 1985, 69). Some Conservative MPs who begrudgingly accepted this "glorified welfare officer" role also blamed the Liberals for their party's emphasis on "pavement politics."

When describing their jobs as MPs, long-serving members from both parties were quick to point out the changes they have seen in constituent expectations and members' responses. Said one Conservative MP: "It is incredible how in the twenty-three years I have been in Parliament the workload has increased, especially from constituents" (Interview, 5 Feb. 1987). But a few retiring Labour MPs disliked employing staffs to conduct constituency affairs. One senior retiring Labour MP stated: "This place has become too professional and the attitudes of the Members have changed a lot since I came in 1964. I am against all these research assistants and such, you lose contact with your local constituents and what is really going on in the world. With this professionalization, you find you don't get the attendance on the floor the way you used to" (Interview, 13 May 1987). These attitudes, however, were expressed only by members who had been elected to Parliament in 1964 or before. Overwhelmingly, MPs said they were in the House "to protect constituents if they get mucked around by government or departments" or "to take up the individual problems of my constituents. That is the bread and butter role—local politics." Another Labour MP who had been in Parliament for three decades and had served in Labour's frontbench continuously since 1969 effectively summarized the attitudes expressed by most MPs: "You are there to influence events, but as a backbencher, you make a small contribution to those policies; you mostly do constituency interests. Select committees are important here as they afford you the opportunity to do something else" (Interview, 30 June 1987).

Nevertheless, nearly a third of the MPs did describe their jobs in terms of influencing, shaping, or making policy. While 33 percent of those MPs who had chosen select committee service described their jobs this way, only one in four non-select committee MPs did so. Further questioning revealed that select committees provided the avenue for policy involvement for many backbenchers while their non-select committee backbench colleagues lacked the structural opportunities to take part in the policy process. The Procedure Committee had hoped that committee service would indeed provide a useful means for increased backbench participation in policy areas. The initial impression suggests that select committees have indeed facilitated members' ability to fulfill this part of their job responsibility.

The "job description" for MPs posited by the Westminster Model suggests a role orientation suited to and largely limited to activities in the chamber. Here the frontbenchers hold the monopoly of power and the party leaders determine the scope and nature of debate. The debate over the "chamber first" and "committee men" role gained prominence in the 1960s as members increasingly pressed for more active participation and influence through committee service. And those who worked on the early select committees pressed party leaders to allow more time for debating committee reports in the chamber.

Long-serving MPs such as Enoch Powell and Michael Foot have persistently argued that the job of an MP is to argue the "great issues of the day" through the thrust and parry of debate on the floor of the House. This is the best way, they contend, to hold government accountable where it must defend its programs and policies under the glare of public scrutiny. On the other hand, supporters of select committees maintain that MPs' ability to hold government accountable through scrutiny and criticism in the chamber is little more than a charade, given the lack of access to the detailed information necessary to perform this role at a realistically competent level.

John Selwyn Gummer, a Conservative MP, articulated the views of reformers on enhancing the chamber's role through committee work. He complained that the chamber was not "effective enough" because members concentrated upon the "ping pong of party political differences which are bound to arise if you haven't got an intelligent argument to put forward." He added: "What we are asking is for the kind of investigatory Select Committees which would make it possible for those of us who are debating and who wish to debate . . . but the fact is that we believe that we want to make the chamber more effective. . . . And what we are proposing is that we want the information about that which is being legislated about in the House of Commons, that information which is not available at the moment. . . . If we had such Select Committees I believe that the

FIGURE 6.H. ROLES MPS MOST WISH TO PLAY IN PARLIAMENT

Question: Which of the following roles do you most wish to play in the House?

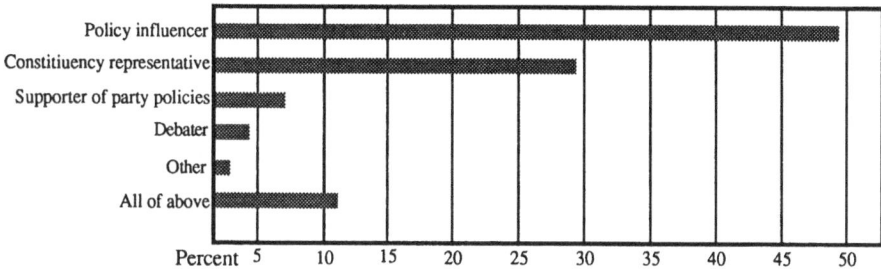

chamber would be a better place to be in, it would be a hotter and more difficult place for Ministers, it would be a more exacting place for back-benchers, but it would mean that the public for the first time for a long while would feel that its interests were properly represented" (Granada Television, 1973, 169–71).

Despite the chamber-oriented role ascribed to members of Parliament by the Westminster Model, few MPs emphasized this side of their own work when describing their jobs. Only 14 percent mentioned participating in debates as part of their jobs, and less than one in eight mentioned supporting party manifestos or leaders—another facet of the subservient backbench role institutionalized through chamber-related activities. Members who have not chosen to participate in the new committee system may be expected to emphasize a stronger orientation toward work in the chamber. Indeed, this was precisely the case for 25 percent of those MPs. But the general decline among MPs in describing their jobs as supportive roles for the party was even more evident among non-select committee members; none of them mentioned this as a facet of their jobs. And again, only a few MPs (9.5 percent) stated that waging ideologically oriented campaigns was part of their job. All of these members were Labour MPs, and most of them were not members of the select committees, which are characterized by their consensus, bipartisan approach to politics.

Members were also handed a closed-ended question toward the end of the interviews that asked them to select the role they most wished to play in Parliament. This exercise (shown in Figure 6.H) allowed them to articulate an ideal role, compared with what they actually do or what they find appealing about it. Reflecting a desire to participate more actively in the policy process than their predecessors of a generation before, almost half of the MPs chose "policy influencer" as the role they most wished to play in the House. Support

for this chosen role was much higher among Conservatives (61 percent) than among Labour (39 percent). Having enjoyed eight years of
Tory rule in the House, Conservative MPs were better positioned
than Labour MPs to expect and receive junior ministerial posts, select
committee chairmanships, and Conservative-dominated select committee positions.

Approximately 29 percent of all respondents chose Constituency Representative as the role they most wished to play, which is
consistent with the number of MPs (27 percent) who mentioned
constituency-related duties when describing their jobs. And again,
one sees minimal support for being a Debater or a Supporter of Party
Policies—roles that party leaders would especially like to see their
party followers play in an executive-dominated arena legislature. Although none of the non-select committee MPs mentioned supporting
their respective parties when asked to describe their jobs, one in five
chose this response when presented with three other defined roles.
These members all had senior positions within their respective parliamentary parties—i.e., senior whips, vice-chairman of 1922 committee, chairman of the Parliamentary Labour party—and expected
party loyalty from their colleagues and in turn demonstrated loyalty
to party leaders.

In a follow-up question, members were handed another list of
eight parliamentary duties and asked to rank them in order of importance. The eight possible duties were:

Expressing voters' concerns about the national issues
Dealing with constituents' personal problems
Attending meetings in the constituency
Supporting the party's leadership
Making good public policy
Contributing to debate
Questioning ministers, government officials
Committee work in the House

This question was designed to include all aspects of a member's duties: representation/constituency work, party loyalty, policy making,
chamber and committee work. Once again the policy-making role
elicited the most responses. Forty-two percent of MPs chose this duty
as the most important. And, consistent with previous findings, constituency work followed, with 30 percent indicating "dealing with

constituents' personal problems" as the most important duty. To be sure, only 9 percent ranked "committee work in the House" at the top, but this figure was higher than for any of the other remaining duties. In sharp contrast to those MPs who argued that the proper role for Parliament and its members centered on debate in the chamber, only two members (2.6 percent) felt that "contributing to debate" was their most important duty. Only slightly more support (3.9 percent) was given to "supporting the party's leadership" and "questioning ministers, government officials" in assigning these duties the top ranking.

Members appear to view policy involvement and fulfilling their welfare officer roles for constituents as the two most important duties of their jobs. They do not, however, consider the passive role of supporting their respective party's leadership to be nearly as important, nor do they appear to interpret chamber-oriented activities—debating and questioning—to be their most important duties. These results are misleading, however. While both handling constituents' problems and policy involvement consistently rank high as members' second and third most important duties, "questioning ministers and government officials" was the most-often chosen option as the second and third ranked duty. And there is no contradiction between generally high support for this role and uniformly low support for contributing to debate, although both are usually associated with chamber-related activities. First, members indicated that debates are "by and large a farce," since the outcome of post-debate lobby divisions is generally already known. Their speeches may enter the pages of *Hansard* and an occasional reference found in the press, but their contributions to outcome remain negligible. Both oral and written questions to ministers, on the other hand, necessitate a response, and this remains one of the few avenues available to pry information from the government frontbench. The number of questions to ministers has increased dramatically during the past twenty years.

Second, since the introduction of the current committee system, the questioning of ministers and government officials has become a role performed both on the floor of the House and in the select committees. In fact, committee members take particular pride and pleasure in "grilling ministers," "extracting information," and keeping ministers and officials before committees until they have offered satisfactory responses to members' questions. Of the value in receiving testimony from ministers, Kevin McNamara, former member of the Select Committee on Foreign Affairs and Opposition spokesman for Defence, when interviewed offered the following: "I see that the nature of the committees means that members on it are getting more information given to them by the departments than are members of the Opposition frontbench. I wish I as a frontbench spokesman could get access to the resources they [select committee members] have. I think it is a major error for the Labour party, but for democracy, you are making sure everybody is doing something" (Interview, 2 Feb. 1987).

Alf Dubs added: "I think the average backbencher gets the chance about once every four weeks to ask a question of the Home secretary or relevant minister. On a select committee, a small group of us can have a government minister for an hour, and I can perhaps question him myself for five or seven minutes at a time. So the ability to put government ministers and civil servants under pressure is incomparable" (Interview, 24 March 1987). Rather than being concerned with changing the focus of MPs' jobs in holding government accountable, "chamber-first" members should acknowledge that the focus has not necessarily changed but the forum has.

Role Performance and Role Desire

The evidence presented thus far suggests a gap between what MPs want to do in the House of Commons, and what they are able to do. Making and influencing policy is considered to be their most important duty, they find it the most appealing part of being in politics, and it is the role they most wish to play. But constituency work is overwhelmingly used to describe what they actually do in Parliament. Policy making is a distant second. And while backbenchers increasingly advocate broader participation in shaping national policies, few structural channels are available.

This bifurcation of expressed preferences and emphases on the one hand, and realistic opportunities to respond positively to them on the other, is supported by the number of MPs favoring increased backbench participation in the parliamentary process. Indeed, 70 percent of the members interviewed favored more participation by backbenchers. Reflecting the divergent role orientations of the front- and backbenchers, the former were far less likely to support an expanded role for the latter. Speaking of backbenchers' ability to participate in the policy process, a former Labour home secretary explained: "It is there for those who know how to use it. There are different ways, but you need to learn how to do it" (Interview, 7 July

1987). Another Labour frontbencher concurred: "There is enough. It is a problem of perception. The work load has increased since I came in in 1966. One realizes from being a minister that the only people who change Whitehall is Whitehall. And this is the problem of the backbench; they do not accept the role of cabinet government. A good backbencher can still catch a minister. Select committees are a way of becoming more involved in specific areas, but it is difficult" (Interview, 2 July 1987). These MPs also stressed the chamber-oriented role for members, selecting "contributing to debate" as one the most important duties of their jobs. Moreover, they stated that a successful parliamentary career was defined by getting to the front-bench. By their own definition they were successful, but they had risen to their positions through pursuing a "traditional" backbench role—emphasizing party loyalty and eschewing committee work for debates in the chamber.

While Conservative frontbenchers tended to agree with their Labour counterparts, they were also more likely to stress their party policy committees as a means of allowing backbench participation in the policy process. A Conservative MP stated: "Well, that [backbench participation] works of course through the party committees. . . . There is a close link between them and the secretary of state of the department concerned. So both in terms of tactics and longer-term policies, those committees do have an important input to make (Interview, 2 February 1987). And a minister of state agreed: "Well, I don't see how you can involve them much more than you already do because the governing process is very sensitive to the feelings of the backbenchers. . . . [Do you actively seek out the attitudes of backbench opinion?] Oh yes, oh yes. You have to know what the general body of opinion is so that person [PPS] will go first of all to the opinion-forming backbench committees on your particular area of interest as a government minister, but will also spend a lot of time just chatting to colleagues over coffee, over a beer in the bar" (Interview, 18 Feb. 1987).

Clearly, opportunities do exist for backbenchers to discuss policy proposals with respective party leaders. But discussions are usually informal, not well-attended, and offer an essentially reactive role for backbenchers. Furthermore, ministers' primary concern rests in carrying a substantial number of their party backbenchers in the ensuing division of lobbies on government-proposed policies. It is not to elicit policy proposals or ideas in the formulation stage. In many ways, the relationship and dynamics between ministers and party committees is similar to that of front- and backbenchers in the chamber and ministers and party followers in standing committees. Ministers lead, backbenchers follow. Ministers propose policy initiatives, and backbenchers may oppose, but alternatives and amendments are rarely made and major changes put forth except when backbench revolts threaten passage. Despite ministers' assurances that backbenchers do have adequate means to participate in the policy process and their opinions and advice are given due consideration, Norton points out that in recent years members have proved willing to vote against their own side on more occasions and in greater numbers and with more effect than has been the case since the post-1867 advent of party government (Norton, 1980b).

Backbench dissent is of course one identifiable behavioral manifestation of disaffection with the party leaderships' policy stances. Except for a very few backbenchers who chose to pursue a passive, relatively part-time party-loyal role in the House, virtually all backbench MPs, representing all political parties, expressed a desire for greater participation. Some Conservative PPS's, who are somewhere in limbo between the front- and backbench, were extremely critical of current arrangements. One of them stated, "Government is in essence an autocracy appearing as a democracy through party" (Interview, 23 Feb. 1987). And another charged that the limitations imposed on backbench participation in the House were the root cause for Parliament's "loss of control over the Executive" (Interview, 30 Jan. 1987).

While Labour backbench MPs were equally critical, they were more likely to offer suggestions for increasing backbench participation. Most commented that select committees provided "a good forum for that" but urged stronger agenda-setting and legislation-drafting powers. Liberal and SDP MPs argued for a new constitutional settlement allowing for more backbench (and subsequently third-party) participation. But there was also substantial discussion among all Opposition party members of the perceived flaws in the current parliamentary system. Clare Short, a former member of the Home Affairs Select Committee and currently on Labour's frontbench, echoed the views of many. "I think the British parliamentary system is enormously defective and flawed. I think the Executive is massively powerful; it sets the timetable, it has enormous resources—public relations, press, money. . . . And we have people in this place seeking to rise to the Executive—it isn't a parliament that does a good job of scrutinizing the Executive, and that's its only role. It is all muddled by loyalty to party and aspirations to high office . . . but there is also a total mood that diminishes its role and ability to put a check on the Executive. What we need to see here is an attitudinal change among members of Parliament about what they do here and what Parliament should be doing" (Interview, 27 Jan. 1987).

Frontbench MPs appear to have clear and identifiable perceptions of the existence of meaningful participatory avenues that are available to backbenchers. In contrast, backbenchers do not share this optimism or believe these party-dominate structural channels provide effective input and access to policy formulation. This divergence underscores the authority-hierarchical relationship that exists between frontbenchers and backbenchers. Just as the two frontbenches shared a common interest in hindering previous select committee assertiveness, so too do its members guard their policy-making prerogatives, claiming that backbenchers have sufficient means to participate in the parliamentary process.

The role orientation of the front- and backbenches also reflects the traditional duties and obligations of leaders and followers, respectively. It is not so much that the two groups have differing attitudes about the role of a member of Parliament. Rather, frontbenchers tend to claim the activist, policy-shaping role as their exclusive domain. Broader backbench participation is viewed as an intrusion. Backbenchers by and large also support an activist, policy-shaping role for MPs, but their perception of who should be pursuing this role is a much more inclusive one. In short, they assert that Parliament should provide sufficient means for all its members who wish to lead an active role. Channels for participation must be broadened beyond occasional and perfunctory speeches on the floor of the House and discussions in party committees. As the next chapter highlights in greater detail, members want opportunities for Parliament as an institution to be more actively involved in agenda setting and policy making. They reject the notion of allowing the majority party frontbench, i.e., the government, a monopoly in performing these duties.

Although many legislators have reached the policy-influencing arena by carefully adhering to the norms of party loyalty, members interviewed in my group indicated that maintaining measured degrees of independence and seeking policy-influencing positions are no longer incompatible. Party leaders increasingly rely upon knowledgeable, hard-working MPs with some specialization in particular policy fields, not obsequious supporters. In fact, almost 90 percent of the MPs considered themselves specialists in one or more policy

FIGURE 6.I. CONSEQUENCES OF VOTING AGAINST OR NOT
SUPPORTING ONE'S PARTY

Question: What are the consequences of voting against or abstaining from supporting party leaders'
policy positions?

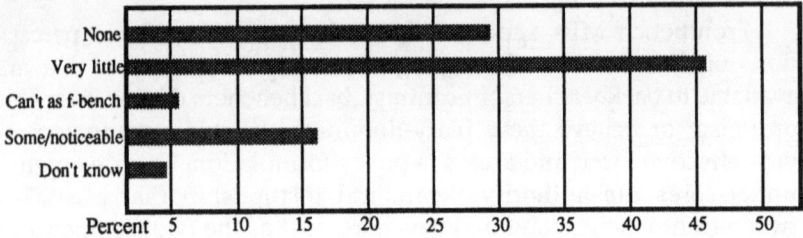

fields. And when asked if conflicts had arisen between their personal
beliefs or constituency interests and party policy, members overwhelmingly indicated in a follow-up question that such conflicts had
indeed arisen. Moreover, despite their desire to be active in influencing policy, members overwhelmingly indicated that there were few if
any consequences in voting against or abstaining from supporting
party leaders' policy positions. (See Figure 6.I).

Finally, although MPs overwhelmingly advocated increased policy influencing roles for themselves, less than a third stated that
acquiring frontbench status necessarily defined a successful parliamentary career. And only 17 percent mentioned party loyalty as a
means to achieve a successful parliamentary career. A senior Labour
MP explained the change in party loyalty this way: "I really do think
there are other means available to pursue a successful career without
going to the frontbench. This place has changed a lot since I came
here in 1945. Members work harder, less deference toward the frontbench. I think this has occurred since 1964, and with each new wave
of intakes you get more dedicated, better educated, better quality
Members. I think in the Labour Party one of the reasons is because
the Constituency Labour Parties are much more demanding. They
expect their Members to be much more aware of constituency problems" (Interview, 25 February 1987).

Both statistical and contextual analysis of MPs responses suggest
members have different role orientations and actual parliamentary
duties. Support for these various roles and duties is not random,
however, and one does not find as many different answers to these
survey questions as there are MPs—as some members expected there
would be—but rather three general conclusions can be drawn. First,

one finds consistently high support for an interest and desire to be involved in policy formulation. Members of Parliament are more likely to mention their constituency related activities than any other task when describing their parliamentary duties, especially backbenchers, but they do not find it the most appealing aspect of their jobs; policy involvement offers the most appeal. Second backbenchers also want far more participation in the parliamentary process, and they overwhelmingly suggest that select committee work is probably the best avenue available to achieve this goal. Frontbenchers, however, protect their policy-shaping monopoly by arguing that backbenchers have sufficient participation through party committees and the floor of the House. Backbenchers disagree. Third, and perhaps most importantly, one detects widespread frustration among backbenchers with that which they want to do as MPs, and that which is allowed them. If MPs do indeed want more participation, more resources, and more maneuverability in Parliament, what then are their attitudes toward Parliament and its role in contemporary national politics? These issues are explored in the following chapter.

7

MPs' Views on
Parliament and Its Role

The individual member of Parliament has a number of career paths available. An MP can be a successful debater, an active committee member, a constituency ombudsman, a frontbench spokesperson, or, if the constituency allows, a "gentleman legislator." With the exception of the latter role, all of these potentially include some policy dimension. One can attempt to influence policy on the floor of the House, scrutinize government policy through select committee service, formulate and articulate party policy on the frontbench, and redress constituents' grievances as well as champion salient issues and microsectional interests of the constituency.

Whatever one might think Parliament's proper role should be in national politics, these routes do exist for its members to pursue. Success in securing one of these roles, especially a frontbench position, and in performing the necessary related tasks, largely depends on the individual. My research indicates that MPs do possess role orientations with corresponding goals, and that to achieve both, they must also adopt the appropriate strategies to secure their desired roles and subsequently satisfy their goals in the House.

But the presence of other mitigating factors—lack of staff and resources to pursue constituency work, limited access to debate for a backbencher, and executive disdain for investigatory committees—intervene to hinder an MP's preferred and ideal role-route. As the preceding chapter illustrated, there is an apparent gap between the roles many members desire to pursue and those that Parliament as an institution allows, or at least renders feasible and likely. It is not surprising that in their interviews several members expressed frustration with their perceived inability to pursue their desired career routes in Parliament. This chapter, then, examines members' attitudes about Parliament's role in influencing national policies and the skills they as MPs require to function effectively in this institution.

Routes in Parliament

Unlike committees in a transformative legislature, such as the U.S. Congress and to some extent the German Bundestag, a committee with legislation-drafting and information-taking powers is rare in the British House of Commons. In fact, MPs use the term "Hybrid Committee" to denote the existence of this seldom-used parliamentary committee. Richard Fenno pointed out that members of Congress seek committee posts that satisfy their goals in order to secure institutional influence or address their particular agendas (Fenno, 1973). But in an arena legislature, correspondingly influential committees are virtually nonexistent. MPs in the House of Commons do have goals, desires, and agendas, but alternative pathways must be pursued to secure those goals, meet desires, and process agendas. Because there is no institutionalized capacity for parliamentary select committees to write or introduce legislation and satisfy their goals in the same manner as congressional committee members, MPs pursue other channels and indeed defend these alternatives, e.g., debate in the chamber.

When I asked members what personal qualities and skills an MP needed to be effective, their responses reflected qualities and skills necessary to pursue particular routes in Parliament. As Table 7.1 illustrates, those qualities and skills that correspond to respective parliamentary pursuits received the most responses except for the necessity of being generally "hard-working." For example, MPs who mentioned verbal and communication skills were generally those who stressed Parliament's debating functions and relied upon those skills as members of their respective frontbenches. For this group of MPs in particular, the chamber was their institutionalized forum and avenue for regular policy criticism and defense. Significantly, too, frontbench MPs asserted that these skills were increasingly important in communicating with the nation through the media. While parliamentary scholars and commentators such as Bagehot have emphasized Parliament's communicative function, many MPs use their formal position as members of the institution to gain valuable access to the electronic media in order "to be heard." They suggested that no

TABLE 7.1. QUALITIES AND SKILLS NEEDED TO BE
EFFECTIVE AS AN MP

Question: What personal qualities and skills does a member of Parliament need
to do an effective job?

Response	All Members of Parliament		Conservative		Labour		Non-Select Committee		Select Committee	
	%	(N-84)	%	(N-41)	%	(N-38)	%	(N-24)	%	(N-60)
Hard-working	48	40	49	20	47	18	29	7	54	33
Communication	38	32	37	15	45	17	42	10	37	22
Interest/sincerity in constituency	27	23	22	9	29	11	17	4	32	19
Instrumental	20	17	29	12	11	4	17	4	22	13
Expertise	14	12	20	8	11	54	13	3	15	9
Variety/combination	8	7	17	7	0	0	17	4	5	3
Carve a role	8	7	7	3	11	4	21	5	3	2
Objectivity	2	2	5	2	0	0	0	0	3	2
Independence	2	2	0	0	5	2	8	2	0	0

one listens in Parliament. As a current minister of state said: "You've got to be an exceedingly good communicator. Communication skills are absolutely essential in this House and particularly in this country today because it is very much making sure you are heard and your voice is heard and that you are approachable. It goes beyond the floor of the House; you are heard in the press and on the television. So you must be good at that and you must not be afraid of communication, because if you are you are lost" (Interview, 18 March 1987).

Other members stressed that being sincere in wanting to assist constituents and "taking a genuine interest" in the affairs of the constituency were necessary qualities to be effective MPs. They were also most likely to present themselves as constituency men and women. Frontbenchers, whose time and energies are necessarily directed toward national and party policies, are less likely to interpret their jobs as oriented toward constituency affairs. Consequently, they are less likely to mention attributes such as "sincerity" and "interest" in constituency work as important in performing effectively. One indication of this is the low ratio (16.7 percent) of non-select committee MPs, many of whom are frontbenchers, who mentioned these qualities. Moreover, several backbenchers who did mention these qualities and who thought of themselves as constituency men and women sought select committee assignments precisely because these posts would assist them in being more effective constituency representatives.

While "expertise" and "specialization" may not usually be considered qualities or skills by social scientists, about 15 percent of the MPs interviewed mentioned these attributes. These responses emanated from frontbench spokesmen, select committee chairmen, and active junior MPs. What they all had in common were their goals to be influential and to be recognized and rewarded for their particular expertise. Specialization, they believed, was a necessary ingredient in securing desired parliamentary posts and enabled them to be effective and influential in these positions. A Conservative chairman of one of the more prestigious select committees asserted: "Well, clearly it is a question of expertise. There are some members who are generalists, but most of them who can make a contribution tend to specialize to a greater or lesser extent. It's very difficult for the House to take any notice of someone who doesn't specialize at all. To that extent, it's probably the select committees that rather brought out that aspect. . . . You've really got to get involved if you are going to do the job properly" (Interview, 2 Feb. 1987).

The least frequent responses were those that did not correspond to institutionally defined career routes. Members who stressed the "jack-of-all-trades" role for MPs mentioned that doing an effective job necessitated a variety of skills and qualities, depending on the particular duties expected of them at a specific time. They were reluctant to view themselves as either debaters, constituency ombudsmen, or committee men and did not pursue any single career route or display specific goals. Their task was to assume any one of a myriad of roles when the need arose. They thought they did them all. Consequently, they did not cultivate certain skills nor assert any personal qualities associated with specific roles that might have made them effective MPs in corresponding career routes.

While some MPs (8 percent) also mentioned that "carving out a role" for oneself led to effectiveness as an MP, they were not necessarily inclined to offer a preferred role nor the skills necessary to achieve it. To them, defining and pursuing any one of a number of alternative career routes would lead to job effectiveness. Like those MPs who suggested that a variety of skills were required to do the variety of tasks incumbent upon an MP, these members also agreed that there were alternative roles to pursue in the House. But, unlike the former group, these MPs emphasized focusing on one particular role. To be effective, one could not be a "jack-of-all-trades" in the House of Commons.

Perceived Importance of Parliament

It is apparent that MPs recognize a number of career routes to pursue in Parliament. One can choose to pursue any one of these routes or a combination thereof because the institution provides at least nominal opportunities and expectations to do so. Moreover, the individual goals and pursuits of the members also translate into collective action of Parliament-as-institution. Parliament may have "declined" in importance as the "Decline of Parliament" literature of the 1960s and 1970s suggested. Parliament, too, may have failed, is failing, or will fail to live up to the expectations placed upon it by many of its commentators and observers. But an institution's influence can only decline if it possesses certain powers and capacities to begin with. It fails to meet others' expectations when it apparently is unable or unwilling to assert its theoretical and formal powers as identified by its critics.

Men and women who stand for Parliament and win do not want to sacrifice their previous careers for admission into an institution incapable of satisfying their individual goals and objectives. Clearly not all members can reach all of their goals and objectives in any legislative institution, but even Parliament provides some opportunities for members' goal satisfaction.

A House of Commons characterized by frontbench elites supported by respective amateur, party loyal, part-time backbenchers, posed no dilemma for party government or the Westminster Model. But serious problems do arise when backbenchers are less likely to value strict party loyalty and to pursue activist, full-time legislative roles. That they can and do pursue such roles also reflects a changing attitude toward Parliament's role in the governing process. Under these circumstances, I expected to find support for an assertive role for Parliament, albeit with the recognized strictures and concomitant frustration imposed by party government and moribund procedures.

I asked members about their attitudes toward Parliament with the following question: "In general, what would you say is the importance and power of Parliament today?" Table 7.2 gives the responses to this open-ended question. With the exception of assisting constituents, the six most frequent responses made explicit references to executive-legislative dynamics. Members generally viewed Parliament's importance in its relation with the executive, not its institution-specific capacities. It is the links with the executive that appear to give Parliament its importance and power, not its autonomous role in the governing process. While the Congressional Model includes a framework for executive-legislative relationships, there is

TABLE 7.2. THE IMPORTANCE AND POWER OF PARLIAMENT

Question: In general, what would you say is the importance and power of Parliament today?

Response	All Members of Parliament		Conservative		Labour		Non-Select Committee		Select Committee	
	%	(N-84)	%	(N-41)	%	(N-38)	%	(N-24)	%	(N-60)
Check executive	45	38	42	21	42	16	21	5	55	33
Debate/challenge	44	37	50	16	50	19	42	10	45	23
Give power to executive	21	18	24	8	24	9	46	11	12	7
Marginal security	17	14	11	9	11	4	29	7	12	7
Constituency aid	14	12	16	6	16	6	21	5	12	7
Behind the scenes	12	10	5	8	5	2	8	2	13	8
Policy for people	11	9	5	5	5	2	0	0	15	9
Educate public	6	5	8	1	8	3	0	0	8	5
Value for money	5	4	5	2	5	2	0	0	7	4

also a considerable domain for unilateral congressional activity. The Westminster Model, in contrast, is predicated upon a close and symbiotic relationship between the executive and the legislature. Consequently, one might expect MPs' attitudes about Parliament to reflect that institution's relationship with its ascendant executive.

Members of Parliament, nevertheless, offered two distinct interpretations of this relationship. Some emphasized Parliament's monitoring role and others stressed its supportive role. These were also mutually exclusive orientations; no one who mentioned checking/pressuring the executive or mounting challenges to the executive also believed that Parliament's importance and power rested on its ability to grant power to the executive.

As shown in Table 7.2, Parliament's assertive constitutional authority received considerably more support than any other. Forty-five percent of MPs interviewed mentioned Parliament's power in checking and pressuring the executive. And almost as many mentioned mounting challenges to the executive through debates. Neither of these functions suggests a passive, supportive role for Parliament, but rather one that is responsive, active, and critical. The adversarial nature of parliamentary politics suggests that the Opposition party will perform these tasks, but my research further indicates that members of all political parties hold these to be important institutional powers. A Conservative PPS stated: "With a very large majority as we now have, it [power and influence] is limited. What we do have is the power to call, to check the executive in a variety of different ways" (Interview, 23 Feb. 1987). A Social Democratic spokesman concurred: "It is its attempt to try to reestablish some control over the executive. It is also important to do this procedurally and control the abuses of one-party government" (Interview, 3 Feb. 1987). And a former Labour home secretary emphasized mounting challenges on the floor of the House: "You can still bring down a minister or prime minister. Ronald Reagan would be out of office by now; Richard Nixon would have fallen much sooner. However, the House made a cock-up over MI5, though; Mrs. Thatcher should never have been able to stand that. But I believe in the adversarial nature and style of this place. This is the style which gets ministers on an issue. I wouldn't want to lose that" (Interview, 7 July 1987).

These remarks are representative of the attitudes expressed by MPs who emphasized fulfilling the constitutional responsibilities of scrutiny and challenge. For them, the formal constitutional obligations and opportunities of Parliament as an institution eclipsed Parliament as a forum-providing arena in which political parties do battle. The floor of the House may not be an effective avenue to produce or alter policy options, but many MPs stress its importance and power in holding individual ministers accountable for their respective departments' policies as well as forcing the government to answer charges in emergency debates. MPs were not suggesting that policy influence was unimportant to them but rather that Parliament's institutional power and importance rested on its ability to curtail unbridled executive power.

Ronald Butt concluded that the power of the House came from its ability to debate the great issues of the day and ultimately to bring down a government (Butt, 1967, 441). During debates on procedural reform, MPs have stressed Parliament's role in scrutinizing, influencing, and publicizing government activity (HCD 75/76, 902:1051; HC 588-I, 1978, vii). And Norton has argued that the central function of the House is scrutiny; its central role is to be a "watchdog" (Norton, 1981a, 75). Butt, however, differs from these other observers by stressing Parliament's essentially reactive role. Its general function, according to Butt, is "to say 'yea' or 'nay' at the end of a process of policy rather than to be associated formally in its production." A reversal of this situation "would be fundamentally to change its nature" (Butt, 1967, 83). Norton, on the other hand, offers a less static interpretation of Parliament's power and importance by emphasizing the fluidity of the Commons (Norton, 47). Lacking a formal, definitive document stipulating the House's functions, Norton asserted, the Commons has evolved and continues to evolve as new functions are added and others are discarded.

Members interviewed did indeed indicate a clear preference for maintaining the constitutional function of holding the executive accountable. And although many of them felt the imposition of party government and limitations of floor debates hampered them in these efforts, in fact they looked to the select committees to fulfill these tasks and subsequently bolster Parliament's power and importance in the governing process. A Labour whip identified Parliament's importance and power this way: "The backbench power. That is why with our select committee system, whatever its problems, it's the first time we have had a system in which backbenchers can become very, very well informed on a particular subject and at the same time oversee the power of the executive. It is important that we keep that system. . . . People will say they will not enter a debate because there are all these expert backbenchers now. That is true, and I think that is good" (Interview 1 April 1987). Other MPs who interpreted Parliament's power and importance in terms of the House's relationship with the executive were less optimistic about the institution's ability to hold the executive publicly accountable. One in five MPs stated that Parliament's power and importance emanated from its role in granting power to the executive. They were frustrated by this relationship because of the lack of any accompanying reciprocity or respect from the executive. One left-wing Labour MP remarked: "Parliament has power and importance solely because it gives to the executive all the power it has to ride rough-shod over the rest of the country. Parliament simply gravitates power to the executive" (Interview, 1 July 1987). And a leader in the Liberal Party made this observation: "Parliament is less important today than it once was, and by once I really mean that period to World War I, because I think people have allowed power to slip more and more into the hands of the executive, and Parliament itself has become more and more of a talking shop. Parliament, if it wanted to, could do something about that. That is why I don't despair of it as an institution" (Interview, 20 Jan. 1987).

But several MPs did "despair of it as an institution." They concurred that Parliament's power and importance relied upon scrutinizing the executive, but were frustrated by Parliament's inability to perform that task adequately. From their perspective, scrutiny of the executive was marginal, and often ineffectual and meaningless. Nevertheless, MPs who served on one of the select committees were far less likely to express this attitude than were those members who had no select committee service. The departmentally related select committees were created primarily to scrutinize the executive. Accordingly, less than 12 percent of select committee members said that Parliament performed only marginal scrutiny over the executive, while almost 30 percent of MPs who had not served on one of the committees shared this view.

Fewer still were the number of MPs who said that Parliament's importance and power emanated from "behind the scenes" activity. This relatively small number of MPs mentioned primarily their ability to speak directly with cabinet ministers as fellow MPs—which they all quickly added was missing in congressional politics—who would assist them in remedying an especially complicated constituency problem with Whitehall. They also mentioned the importance of party policy committees in influencing their respective parties' policy positions. One right-wing Conservative MP offered this analysis: "I think the power is in the party committee systems. When Keith Joseph had a grand scheme to make students pay for their university tuition, that education committee, which is only usually attended by twenty to thirty each week, was suddenly attended by about 180, and Keith Joseph had announced that he had dropped his plan the following day because of this strength of the opposition. The Foreign Affairs Committee is normally attended by about fifteen people, but when we had the Argentinian problem at its height with the Falkland Islands and people had the impression that the Foreign Office had let us down, there was a packed meeting which roasted Lord Carrington, and he resigned the following week. Thirdly, in the 1922 Committee it was poor Leon Brittan who because of the criticisms there, he was forced to resign over the Westland thing. So the backbenchers do have power when they use it and show strength, conviction, and determination. And governments always have to respond to them. So I would say a lot of power of these MPs is done through these party committees" (Interview, 26 March 1967).

Each of these examples is an illustration of a reaction by party members to party policy, however, not a parliamentary initiative to shape and influence the nature of government policy. What is more important is that so few of the members interviewed mentioned the informal, noninstitutionalized, and party dimensions of Parliament's influence and power. Despite the presence of informal norms and party politics, approximately 90 percent of the MPs interviewed mentioned only Parliament's formal, institutional capabilities when highlighting its power and importance.

The remaining responses focused on essentially non-executive/legislative relationships. Members mentioned Parliament's ability to redress constituency grievances, pursue policies important to constituents, educate the public, and seek "value for money" in the administration of government policies. Only MPs who served on select committees mentioned Parliament's power and importance in these latter three areas. These three responses were also the least-often offered and were clearly eclipsed by MPs' larger concerns with achieving executive accountability. Bagehot's emphasis on Parliament's educative function and prior Procedure Committees' emphasis on achieving fiscal economies found little support among MPs.

Executive Power over the House

Although more MPs mentioned the importance and power of monitoring the executive than gave any other response, one cannot conclude that members also thought that Parliament performed this particular task better than any other. Just as there was a large gap between the job-related tasks MPs thought were important to perform and those they were realistically allowed to perform, so too there was a similar gap between what members perceived as Parliament's power and importance and what it did best. When presented with a list of parliamentary tasks, only 6 percent of the MPs selected "monitoring the government's progress and policies" as the task best performed by Parliament. (See Table 7.3.) Only select committee members chose this option. And despite MPs' stated desire to be involved in policy-making, only one in ten—all of them select committee members—stated that Parliament best performed the task of initiating policy.

Chamber-related activities (i.e., debating and ratifying/defeating government-sponsored legislation) were selected by nearly 80 percent of the MPs as the tasks best performed by Parliament. While debating received more support than any other task, many members were quick to point out that, although Parliament as an institution performed this task exceptionally well, debates were generally unimportant in affecting policy outcomes or changes. Debating may be important for contacting a minister, airing Opposition grievances, or championing a personal cause, but it is ineffectual in policy formation.

Clearly, Parliament is an arena legislature. It performs the associated tasks of debating quite well. Its formal and institutional power

TABLE 7.3. TASKS BEST PERFORMED BY PARLIAMENT

Question: Which of the following tasks would you say Parliament performs best?

Response	All Members of Parliament		Conservative		Labour		Non-Select Committee		Select Committee	
	%	(N-84)	%	(N-41)	%	(N-38)	%	(N-24)	%	(N-60)
Debating	44	37	42	16	42	16	35	8	48	29
Ratifying/ defeating Government legislation	35	29	37	14	37	14	58	14	25	15
Initiating policy	10	8	10	4	11	4	0	0	13	8
Monitoring government	6	5	7	3	3	1	0	0	8	5
Aiding constituency	5	4	2	1	8	3	8	2	3	2
Other	1	1	2	1	0	0	0	0	2	1

and influence rest on its ability to mount a challenge and fulfill its constitutional role vis-à-vis the executive on the floor of the House. But the opportunity to maintain consistent, day-to-day scrutiny and policy involvement appears extremely weak. Activity in the chamber is necessary to ratify or defeat proposed legislation, but again this provides the House an essentially reactive role. Moreover, while debates may force governments to defend their policies publicly, institutional influence is usually only noticeable on issues of perceived critical importance or high political "sex appeal", e.g., entry into the EEC, capital punishment, MI5 activities. Salient issues and Question Time do draw large numbers to the chamber, but few members attend the daily, relatively mundane debates.

Balance of Power

Despite the recognition that Parliament does indeed do some things quite well, during testimony to the procedure committees considering parliamentary reform and the accompanying debates, several backbench MPs drew attention to the need to "restore Parliament's power," "redress the imbalance" between the executive and the legislature, and "claw back power it had lost." But were these sentiments shared by other members as well, or were they a reflection of

TABLE 7.4. ATTITUDES TOWARD EXECUTIVE POWER

Question: Do you think the executive has become too powerful vis-à-vis Parliament in recent years?

Response	All Members of Parliament		Conservative		Labour		Non-Select Committee		Select Committee	
	%	(N-84)	%	(N-41)	%	(N-38)	%	(N-24)	%	(N-60)
Yes	76	64	71	29	82	31	71	17	78	47
No	24	20	29	12	18	7	29	7	22	13

the frustrations of a minority of MPs? If members' attitudes toward the balance of power between the two institutions convey an acceptance of the present arrangement, then presumably MPs either are satisfied with their subservient status or perceive no imbalance between the two. I hypothesized, however, that there would be a significant difference between what MPs wanted to do in Parliament and what Parliament as an institution realistically allowed them to do. This turned out to be the case.

MPs could identify functions that gave Parliament power and rendered it important but, given the frustration, dissent, and rebellion identified by Norton coupled with the entrance of policy-interested members, I further presumed that most MPs shared a common perception of a too powerful executive. Immediately after allowing members to discuss the power and importance of Parliament, I asked them, "Do you think the executive has become too powerful vis-à-vis Parliament in recent years?" I wished to avoid any previous discussion of Parliament's limitations and subservience that might color their responses to this question. If anything, MPs might be less likely to think the executive was too powerful having just recited Parliament's power and importance. Nevertheless, more than three-fourths of the MPs said the executive had indeed become too powerful. Table 7.4 gives their responses. Labour MPs were slightly more likely than Conservatives to respond "yes" to this question, as were select committee members compared to non-committee members, but these differences are small. There appears to be widespread recognition in each group that the executive has become too powerful.

Several MPs volunteered details as to what they thought should be done to redress this perceived imbalance. Members who replied "yes" but did not immediately offer any remedies were then

TABLE 7.5. MEANS FOR CHANGING THE EXECUTIVE-LEGISLATIVE BALANCE

Question: What should be done to change the balance between the executive and the legislature?

Response	All Members of Parliament		Conservative		Labour		Non-Select Committee		Select Committee	
	%	(N-84)	%	(N-41)	%	(N-38)	%	(N-24)	%	(N-60)
Select committees	85	55	77	23	90	28	81	13	86	42
Professional members of Parliament	25	16	30	9	23	7	25	4	29	14
Specialize/ scrutiny	14	9	17	5	13	4	13	2	14	7
Freedom of information act	6	4	7	2	3	1	0	0	8	4
Change parliamentary system	6	4	0	0	13	4	13	2	4	2
Don't know	2	1	3	1	0	0	0	0	2	1

TABLE 7.6. MPS' VISION OF A FUTURE PARLIAMENT

Question: How would the Parliament you would like to see a generation from now differ from that of today?

Response	All Members of Parliament		Conservative		Labour		Non-Select Committee		Select Committee	
	%	(N-84)	%	(N-41)	%	(N-38)	%	(N-24)	%	(N-60)
More committee power	49	41	44	18	55	21	54	13	47	28
More policy involved	29	24	22	9	40	15	46	11	22	13
Better resources	27	23	27	11	29	11	13	3	33	20
Better scrutiny	23	19	20	8	29	11	33	8	18	11
Membership changes	19	16	22	9	13	5	17	4	23	14
Efficient/ rationalized procedures	19	16	24	10	13	5	21	5	18	11
New constitutional settlement	13	11	5	2	11	4	4	1	17	10
Less party influence	6	5	7	3	5	2	8	2	5	3
No change	6	5	7	3	5	2	8	2	5	3
Don't know	1	1	2	1	0	0	0	0	2	1

presented with a follow-up question asking them, "What should be done to change this imbalance?" Up to this point in the interview I had only asked questions about members' roles as MPs and the role of Parliament. At no time had I broached the subject of select committees. Nevertheless, 85 percent of those MPs who stated that the executive had indeed become too powerful mentioned the departmentally related select committees as a means to restore the proper balance between the two institutions. (See Table 7.5.)

Members who mentioned the contribution select committees could make in restoring a balance of power between the executive and Parliament were also likely to point out the growth and complexity of modern government and the relatively low access to information and resources available to MPs. A Labour chairperson of one select committee stated: "Departments have grown very strong because of the nature of the complex society in which we live. MPs have gotten increased resources to deal with it and can get much information through select committee work" (Interview, 8 April 1987). A Conservative member of the Public Accounts Committee agreed: "Parliament has lost some power. The machine had taken over, partly because of the complex world in which we live and the institution's inability to cope with scrutiny functions. Select committees are very important here. They are here to stay and are much better than the Estimates and Expenditure Committees" (Interview, 29 April 1987). And a Labour chief whip added: "It has gotten worse since the war. Parliament must understand we vote the government money; the government does not vote us money! There is increasing disquiet on both sides of Parliament. There is a feeling that we cannot speak on the government bureaucracy because we do not have the resources. Select committees are a way to change all this" (Interview, 12 Feb. 1987).

The potential role of select committees in reasserting parliamentary influence also gained considerable support from former and current committee members (Hanson, 1970; Beloff and Peele, 1985; Coombes and Walkland, 1980). What is more surprising, however, is the ratio of non-select committee members (81 percent) who also mentioned select committees as a means to redress the perceived parliamentary-executive imbalance. Moreover, some MPs indicated that the executive had not become more powerful vis-à-vis Parliament precisely because the new select committee system had restored, or was in the process of restoring, the proper balance of power.

Future for Parliament

In addition to the select committees, several members stated that the current legislative-executive imbalance could be altered by a corresponding improvement in the attitudes of MPs toward Parliament and parliamentary service. And some also mentioned the need for members to specialize in particular policy fields and scrutinize the executive far more extensively. Shifting attitudes about one's role to include more active policy involvement, specialization, and legislative scrutiny are all necessary to redress the perceived imbalance as well as to ensure that select committees fulfill the expectations and obligations outlined by the 1978 Procedure Committee Report.

Most of the questions addressed to members required them to express their attitudes and perceptions about Parliament's role as an institution and their roles within it. The creation of the new committee system in 1979 represented a significant change in parliamentary practice and, as members pointed out in interviews, a potential catalyst for change in executive-legislative relations. In its 1978 report, the Procedure Committee repeatedly expressed the wish that parliamentary influence would be strengthened, that MPs would want to participate more actively in parliamentary proceedings, and that select committees would assist in restoring to Parliament power it had lost.

Long-serving members noted the relative change in attitudes and activities of MPs of twenty to thirty years ago compared to more recent entrants. The phrase used most often to describe these new members was "more professional." And Parliament, veteran MPs asserted, had been transformed by the energy and interests of the new recruits. On the one hand, the newest recruits, essentially those entering the House since 1979, were more apt to express frustration with their inability to take on the roles and tasks in Parliament they initially hoped to have. In view of the attitudinal change noted by many veteran MPs and the newer entrants' frustration with the House, all members were asked what further changes they would like to see in Parliament. ("How would the Parliament you would like to see a generation from now differ from that of today?") This question also allowed MPs to focus on reforms they thought to be important and urgent. Table 7.6 summarizes their responses.

Given MPs' stated preferences for increased individual involvement, it is not surprising that the most frequent responses suggest that members want a more active role for Parliament in the policy process and a general restructuring of the legislative-executive relationship. A strengthened select committee system was mentioned more often than any other parliamentary change. One veteran Labour frontbencher said this: "I would like to see more powerful select committees, and I would like to see the members be more assertive against the executive and exercising their traditional and constitutional rights" (Interview, 30 June 1987). And a Conservative MP who had been in Parliament for twenty-eight years added: "I would like to see the select committees take over the powers and process much more. They can only convince others and the government that they should take over more if they have success and are justified in doing so. This is the process they are involved in right now; they are legitimating themselves" (Interview, 18 March 1987).

This increased policy involvement and better scrutiny of the executive—tasks usually associated with select committees—received strong support from Conservative and Labour MPs and from both select committee and non-select committee members. And although only one in eight non-select committee members said they would like to see better supporting resources, a third of select committee members mentioned this. Perhaps most important, an overwhelming majority sought a future legislature actively involved in the legislative process.

Seventy-eight out of eighty-four MPs offered prescriptions that would assist in increasing Parliament's institutional role in the governing process and reduce the governing party's hegemonic authority. Perhaps the former cannot realistically be achieved without the latter; nor is the government frontbench likely to abdicate willingly significant powers and prerogatives to its backbenchers and Opposition MPs.

What does clearly emerge from the interviews, nevertheless, is a consistently high expectation of the catalytic role select committees are to play in the House of Commons. Members assert that Parliament's importance, power, and influence rest on its ability to challenge the executive and hold it accountable. But they express frustration with an institution whose capacities for performing these tasks are eclipsed by its ability to perform well the passive, noncontributory roles these members lament. A substantial majority of MPs stated that the executive had indeed become too strong in disregard of the traditional and constitutional rights of the legislature. That this has been allowed to occur was blamed on the strength of party machines in Parliament, weak backbenchers who secured their personal goals by placating party leaders, and the lack of institutionalized parliamentary mechanisms to allow the House to pursue its traditional and constitutional roles.

Members also asserted, however, that the current executive-legislative imbalance could best be corrected by the new select committees. One can hope for more "professional MPs" or that more members would choose to specialize and scrutinize, but a committee system whose task it is to scrutinize and indeed challenge the executive must also be available and perceived to be worthwhile. It is to this new system that MPs may turn to fulfill their individual goals, pursue their respective role-routes, and increase Parliament's institutional influence. Increasing select committee powers did, after all, receive more "reform-support" than any other reform proposal. The next chapter, then, examines in greater detail the way in which MPs interpret the significance and role of these select committees for themselves and for Parliament.

8

MPs' Attitudes on
1979 Select Committees

The report of the 1977–78 Select Committee on Procedure had high expectations for the new select committees and for the men and women who would choose to serve on them. The previous chapter highlighted the extent to which members of Parliament also hoped these committees would restore a balance of power between the executive and the legislature and serve as a vehicle for members to assume more active and influential roles in the parliamentary process. Select committees, it appears, could potentially assist both in asserting the institution's power and influence and in satisfying members' goals.

This chapter focuses on MPs' attitudes toward select committees, addressing why some members chose committee service and others did not, why some committee members remained on and others left their respective committees. Where applicable, comparisons will be made between those who chose committee service and those who did not. The Procedure Committee in 1978 expressed a desire for a normative subculture to develop among committee members. Comparisons between the two groups, therefore, will highlight the differences and similarities in their attitudes toward select committees.

Why MPs Chose Select Committee Service

Under the norms and rules of party government, backbenchers are expected to play a supporting role for their parties' leaders. Because party leaders are the granters of patronage, the authority rests with them not only to reward MPs with parliamentary and executive posts but also to remove noncooperative members from these positions.

Under this model, members of Parliament, particularly backbenchers, are assumed to share common attitudes and demonstrate similar
behavior about party loyalty and unity that facilitate their appointment to preferred positions wherein individual goals can be satisfied.
Criticism of the positions and policies of one's party leadership undermine an MP's probability of securing a preferred post through the
traditional parliamentary patronage process. Criticism on the floor of
the House, which gains notoriety both in Parliament and in the
press, is met with even more disdain from the party hierarchy.

The rationale for the select committee system, however, is precisely to scrutinize, monitor, criticize, and publicize executive policies. Are members "irrational" in choosing committee service and
still seeking goal satisfaction? Is there an apparent contradiction between criticizing party leaders and seeking patronage positions from
them? The dynamics of the Westminster Model suggest an affirma-
tive response to both questions. My research, in contrast, concludes
that committee membership assists goal satisfaction and, further, that
committee members may criticize party leaders and realistically still
expect patronage positions from them. As such, committee service is
not viewed as an impediment to a future frontbench position.

Like members of other national legislatures, members of Parliament encounter several demands on their limited time, but unlike
legislators in many other industrialized democracies, they have access to comparatively few resources to assist them in meeting these
demands. Clearly, select committee service entails yet another considerable commitment of time and energy from members. Notwithstanding the fact that these committees are unable to process or
introduce legislation as in the U.S. Congress, scores of MPs nevertheless ask to serve on them. Consequently, I asked select committee
members why they chose to become members of their respective
committees. Table 8.1 offers their reasons.

More than half the members interviewed chose to serve on a
committee because as backbenchers they would have more influence
on a select committee than in any other parliamentary forum. They
said they wanted to participate actively in influencing government
policies and that select committee service offered this opportunity.
One Conservative Home Affairs member remarked: "I've had fairly
strong views and attitudes on issues that come under Home Affairs.
Remember that I am on the center-right of my party on a number of
issues—capital punishment, riot control, sentencing—controversies
I've always been in. . . . Once I realized I was not being considered
for a ministerial position in the new government, then the answer
was to look elsewhere for influence. And the select committees pro-

TABLE 8.1. REASONS FOR CHOOSING A PARTICULAR COMMITTEE

Question: Can you tell me why you chose to be on the _____ Committee?

Response	All Members of Parliament		Conservative		Labour	
	%	(N-60)	%	(N-29)	%	(N-26)
More influence on a select committee	53	32	55	16	54	14
Policy interest/ influence	53	32	48	14	58	15
Had expertise	50	30	45	13	62	16
Serve constituency interests	28	17	24	7	31	8
Arena to specialize	20	12	21	6	19	5
Check executive	12	7	3	1	19	5
Post-ministerial role	5	3	3	1	8	2
Had to	5	3	10	3	0	0

vide that" (Interview, 27 Feb. 1987). A Labour MP on Health and Social Services stated: "I was interested in this subject. I did a lot of health work on the local authority; there is more interest and influence here than on the backbench policy committee" (Interview, 5 May 1987). And the Conservative chairman of one committee added: "A select committee I think is where it is starting to be where the real work in Parliament will be done. . . . We had to develop along some lines because the business of government was getting ever more complicated, complex, and technical. And backbenchers as individuals were simply making no impression or influence on it at all. So the only way to redress that was to have a formal structure to do this" (Interview, 23 Feb. 1987).

These three MPs, along with twenty-nine of their committee colleagues, mentioned their desire to influence national policies, and they perceived select committee service as the best means to secure this goal. An equal number of MPs, some of whom are in the above group, mentioned that they chose to serve on a committee because of particular policy interests. These policy interests ranged from developing a national energy policy to providing health care for the elderly to recommending privately run penitentiaries. When one Conservative MP was asked why he chose to be on the Trade and Industry Committee, he replied, "Purely devious purposes. I thought there was a case for a detailed inquiry into Britain's trade deficit with the EEC" (Interview, 26 March 1987). And, indeed, the select committee conducted an inquiry and issued a report on this subject.

Members of Parliament who offered either of the above responses demonstrated a common interest in pursuing an activist role as backbenchers in the policy process. They were less interested in scrutinizing the management and budgets of their respective committees' departments than in influencing the direction and scope of the departments' policies. Select committee service offered active participation in the parliamentary process and a significant departure from the essentially reactive backbench role posited by the Westminster Model.

In 1970, Nevil Johnson examined the development of the nascent select committees from 1966 to 1970. His observations allowed him to conclude that "there are no grounds for believing that for most Members their role as a constituency grievance-man has been modified in favour of that of committee specialist. In short most Members involved in the new committee development are simply endeavoring to superimpose the extra work on to their existing roles as Members of the House" (Johnson, 1970, 240–41). But Johnson's conclusions, at least when compared with the post-1979 committee system, raise two fundamental problems. First, members indicated in interviews that "constituency grievance man" was only one of a handful of roles they wished to pursue. In fact, they wished to pursue a policy-influencing role by a 5–3 margin over a constituency ombudsman role. Nor is there any reason to believe that an MP must give lower priority to constituency demands in order to be a committee specialist, as Johnson suggests. Second, Johnson's claims that MPs are simply trying to take on extra work begs the question. Why would members choose committee service merely for the sake of more work? My research indicates that an overwhelming number of MPs (78 percent) chose select committee service primarily because it was the most effective avenue to achieve the goals they had defined for themselves. They were not merely seeking to add to their parliamentary burdens.

Table 8.1 further shows that half the members interviewed stated they went onto their committees because of the expertise they possessed in their respective fields. Committee service provided them with a more effective forum to use and demonstrate their knowledge. Twenty-eight percent indicated that they joined a committee to serve constituency interests, and 20 percent thought committee service provided the best means to specialize in the House. Members also considered their previously acquired expertise and the opportunity to specialize through committee work compatible with their desire to serve constituency interests. When asked about choosing committee service, one Conservative MP on the Agricultural Committee said: "It was solely for constituency reasons. I have a large greenhouse industry in my constituency, so horticulture was very important to me. I knew nothing about it. But being on this committee would allow me to learn and specialize in this area so important to my constituency" (Interview, 7 April 1987). A Labour MP on the Employment Committee stated: "I had been research officer for the General Municipal Workers Union. I thought I had a lot to bring to this committee and I was interested in it from a broader, constituency point of view, or northern region point of view" (Interview, 5 Feb. 1987).

Members of the Energy Committee and the Employment Committee were especially interested in constituency affairs and the specialist knowledge obtained through committee service. A Labour member of the Energy Committee explained his desire to serve on the committee: "There are two things you can do when you get here. First, you can be overawed by these demigods. Or, second, you can have a go at it. I wanted to get things done. If you want to learn anything, you go onto a select committee, and if you want to look out for interests as I did for my constituency in the energy field, you go onto a select committee" (Interview, 25 Feb. 1987). And one of his Conservative colleagues on the Energy Committee also stressed the constituency and specialization components of committee work. As a Scottish MP, he felt that energy, e.g., North Sea oil, was vital to the Scottish economy. Committee service allowed him to acquire expertise in this field which could be used later to the advantage of his constituents.

Members clearly indicated that they were not eschewing policy influence and specialization for constituency service through committee work. Rather, some select committees offered opportunities for potential policy influence and specialization that were also relevant to constituency-related issues. The Select Committee on the Treasury and Civil Service and the Select Committee on Foreign Affairs offered no opportunities to serve constituency needs, but were important and prestigious policy-oriented committees. Select committees that were more likely to address members' constituency interests were also more likely to have a greater proportion of newer entrants. Not coincidentally, during the initial years of parliamentary tenure, an MP usually spends more time on constituency affairs and grooming the constituency than would be the case after two or three successive election victories.

TABLE 8.2. LINKS BETWEEN COMMITTEE SERVICE AND
CONSTITUENCY ACTIVITY

Question: Does being on this committee have any link to your constituency activity?
(Amended for non-select committee members: Does being on a committee have any links to
a member's constituency activity?)

Response	All Members of Parliament		Conservative		Labour		Non-Select Committee		Select Committee	
	%	(N-84)	%	(N-41)	%	(N-38)	%	(N-24)	%	(N-60)
Yes	61	51	56	23	63	24	71	17	57	34
No	36	30	42	17	32	12	25	6	40	24
Possibly	3	3	2	1	5	2	4	1	3	2

In order to clarify the possible constituency component of committee service, members were also directly asked if select committee service had any link to their constituency activities. Non-select committee MPs were also asked if they thought committee service had any links to committee members' constituency activities. The results are summarized in Table 8.2. Although only 28 percent of committee members indicated that they joined their respective committees for constituency reasons, twice as many members claimed that a link existed between their constituency activities and their committee work. Unfortunately, the sample of non-select committee MPs is relatively small, but there does appear to be a considerable gap between committee members and non-committee members on the perceived association of committee work and constituency activity. Seventy-one percent of non-committee members assumed that such a link did exist, while only 57 percent of committee members claimed such a link. This difference could, of course, be a result of the question itself. Non-committee members may have thought of the potential links one might encounter on Agriculture, Energy, Employment, or Transport and responded affirmatively to the question. And, indeed, members of these committees also claimed constituency-committee links, while Foreign Affairs and the Treasury and Civil Service committee members claimed no such link for themselves.

During several private conversations on this research project, some British academics were skeptical that any MP would seek committee service for constituency reasons or admit any association between the two. They claimed that unlike the American Congress, "pork-barrel politics" is "an alien feature" to British parliamentary life. It is true that select committees do not offer opportunities to draft legislation that protects or promotes members' constituency interests. Nevertheless, members can and do pursue inquiries and issue reports to influence government policies that affect members' constituencies. And they also seek committee assignments whose subject areas are relevant to their constituents in order to learn, gather expertise, and familiarize themselves in these policy fields. Several committee members claimed that this service and expertise allowed them to be more effective representatives and gave them additional competence and respect when pursuing constituency interests on the floor of the House, with a minister, or on a party policy committee. Alf Dubs, a former Labour member of the Home Affairs Committee, stated: "Paradoxically, those people on a select committee are better equipped in terms of the familiarity of the subject matter than frontbench members whose job it is. And of course that is one of the reasons people objected to select committees here, because you build up a small core of MPs. I understand that, but equally you are building up a small core of specialized MPs on any subject there virtually is—housing, MI5, whatever—and you will have a small core of MPs. So if you are going to have specialized MPs, let's have them fully knowledgeable" (Interview, 14 March 1987).

Apparently, too, even the Defence Committee was able to meet some constituency interests. One MP gave an extraordinary account of his committee work and its links with his constituency activity:

I used it [the committee post] quite shamelessly and quite openly to make contacts which would be useful for me in promoting Company A and Company B. And I was very much involved in getting contracts and orders for Company A. It enabled me to obtain information about the various aircraft available, it enabled me to talk to people I would not ordinarily be able to talk to about the strengths and merits about the various aircraft. That in itself enabled me to go back to my own firm—it was not a breach of privilege—it just opened doors for me. I could go back to the chairman of Company A and hear his answers to the queries and come back and promote his particular aircraft. . . . The same thing happened over which firm should be given the order for System X and was able to find out that Trade and Industry was behaving in a way which I did not think was entirely honorable in relation to how they looked at Company B, and [I] was able to counter that. I suppose that can work against me sometimes as well. But in both those cases, it was the first time in decades that Company A actually got an order for an aircraft, and it was certainly the first time in fifteen or twenty years that Company B has had a significant order for a new-built vessel. [Interview, 11 Feb. 1987]

Apparently there are opportunities for "pork-barrel politics" on non-legislation drafting parliamentary select committees. This activity

TABLE 8.3. COMMITTEE MEMBERSHIP AS A STEPPING STONE

Question: Is membership a stepping stone in one's career?

Response	All Members of Parliament		Conservative		Labour		Non-Select Committee		Select Committee	
	%	(N-84)	%	(N-41)	%	(N-38)	%	(N-24)	%	(N-60)
Yes	39	33	42	17	40	15	54	13	34	20
Yes, for others	25	21	20	8	29	11	NA	NA	35	21
Maybe	10	8	10	4	8	3	25	2	10	6
No	26	22	29	12	24	9	4	9	22	13

deviates substantially from the Procedure Committee's intention of creating objective, management-monitoring committees.

For some members of Parliament committees foster specialization in particular policy fields, for others such service provides an avenue to pursue constituency interests or influence policy, and for still others it may satisfy a combination of these goals. But service on a committee may provide other benefits to the individual member's parliamentary career. Party leaders have a shared interest in staffing their respective frontbenches with competent, knowledgeable men and women. Select committees could provide a new training ground for aspiring frontbenchers who have been given a forum to demonstrate their ability to learn a subject well, develop their inquisitive and analytical skills, and suggest new policy initiatives.

Beloff and Peele reached this same conclusion when they reflected on select committee work in the early 1980s. They noted, "Many MPs have found serving on them not merely rewarding in its own right, but a means to political advancement" (Beloff and Peele, 1985, 148). John Golding, former Labour chairman of the Employment Committee, refused a frontbench position in favor of retaining his committee post. He claimed, nevertheless, that other Labour MPs on his committee used their assignments "as an avenue of promotion towards the frontbench" (Golding, 1984, 32). Select committee service, it appears, may bring rewards to backbenchers as well as party leaders.

I asked both committee members and non-committee members if the expertise gained through committee work helped one's political career and if membership might indeed be considered a stepping stone. Table 8.3 offers their views. The responses from these members suggest that committee service is not perceived as an end in itself. An MP can obtain valuable information and expertise, and he can pursue his goals through committee service. But two-thirds of committee members interviewed also believed that committee membership did indeed serve as a stepping stone in either their own or others' parliamentary careers. Conservative and Labour MPs generally held similar attitudes. The largest gap emerged between committee and non-committee members. A majority of non-committee members believed that committee service served as a stepping stone, but this was a substantially smaller proportion (54 percent) than for committee members (69 percent). Furthermore, non-committee members were more divided on this question than committee members and were more likely than committee members to claim that membership was not a stepping stone in an MP's parliamentary career.

Non-committee members who held this latter view were primarily MPs who had been in Parliament for at least fifteen years, had never served on any previous select committees, and had not attained frontbench status. One such Conservative MP remarked: "The young ones would see this, but leaders do not see this. Careers are created by mishap" (Interview, 30 June 1987). And a Labour MP added: "The place to get noticed is still the floor. It is important to watch the new intake here" (Interview, 7 May 1987). Members of the "new intake," however, complained of the lack of opportunities to be noticed on the floor of the House and consistently revealed that they came to Parliament "to get things done," with goals and objectives to pursue. They too chose the relevant career paths in Parliament to meet these goals, which included committee service. Their careers were not "mishaps."

A Conservative chairman of one of the select committees disagreed with the two MPs quoted above: "Several members of the committees have taken on ministerial posts, like Kenneth Baker who is now Secretary of State for Education, Freeman who is now junior minister at Defence. Yes, it does provide something of a stepping stone, particularly in government when you don't have the opportunity to make a name for yourself on the floor of the House in Opposition" (Interview, 2 Feb. 1987). A former member of the Defence Committee who resigned his post to be a Labour whip also disputed the claims that party leaders pay little attention to committee members. He said: "It may not have helped mine, but certainly for others. You find out the quality of the people from their service on the committee and their knowledge, and it is plenty helpful to us in the whip's office. They used to say that being a whip was a route to the frontbench, but I think now that has been superseded by the select committees" (Interview, 1 April 1987).

Several committee members stressed the importance of the "specialist knowledge" and expertise they gathered from committee service. Specialization, they further asserted, also translated into respect from their colleagues. It put them in the limelight on various subjects where they were able to display their knowledge and talents before party leaders. One Environment Committee member relayed an account of gaining recognition outside of Parliament for his expertise and committee service: "We've had debates on acid rain, and in one by-election [Brecon and Radnor] there was a large debate on acid rain. There was a special meeting called and there was a big turnout. As a member of the select committee, I was invited and two other members of the committee to speak as members of their party. It was the first time we ever had to debate publicly our views as developed from a select committee" (Interview, 20 Jan. 1987).

To Stay, Move On, or Never Join?

By the beginning of the 1986–87 parliamentary session, only 30 of the original 148 committee members remained on their respective committees. When these members were asked why they stayed on their committees, 88 percent (N = 22) mentioned the interesting work they engaged in, and an equal number stated that their positions allowed them more influence than would otherwise be possible on the backbench, and in several cases junior ministerial positions. (Obviously, several members mentioned both.) One Labour chair put it this way: "I stayed on because I was chair and our committee has done so much work which has been rewarding and important. It is a real source of power and influence" (Interview, 8 April 1987). Only one committee member claimed he maintained membership because he was unable to get dismissed from his committee; there were no backbenchers from his party in Wales available to replace him on the Welsh Affairs committee.

Clearly, many MPs have left their committee assignments. Gavin Drewry reported that during the 1979–83 Parliament eighty-seven of the members who had been originally appointed ceased to serve on the committees. He observed: "Of these, one died and fifty-three were promoted to ministerial posts or the Opposition frontbench. Various reasons applied to the remaining thirty-three discharges from the committees—change of party, resignation from Parliament, ill health—and disenchantment with the work is mentioned by monitors in only a few cases" (Drewry, 1985, 325). My interview panel of former committee members included those who had served in the 1979–83 and 1983–87 Parliaments. And as Drewry reported that fifty-three committee members (61 percent) in the first Parliament were discharged to accept frontbench positions, a similar ratio (66 percent) of my interview sample reported the same reasons for leaving committee service. (See Table 8.4.)

Although the sub-samples become quite small when controlling for party affiliation, Labour and Conservative MPs left their committees to go to their respective frontbenches in equal proportions. Clare Short, a Labour member of the Home Affairs Committee before moving to the frontbench, described her departure from the committee: "I left because I was appointed to the frontbench. I was getting a little tired of the Home Affairs committee, and if I hadn't been given a position on the frontbench, I would have looked around for a new committee. I don't think I would have just come right off and given up on them. I wouldn't mind sitting on the Treasury Select Committee. Certainly at least that gives you an excellent opportunity to educate yourself" (Interview, 27 Jan. 1987).

I also examined the actual ratios of Conservative and Labour committee members who chose frontbench positions over committee service from 1979 through the most recently published Sessional Returns from 1991. These figures are presented in Tables 8.5, 8.6, and 8.7 and are broken down by year, party, and committee. There is, of course, a time lag involved here; one would expect to find that fewer members who had served on the 1989–90 select committees had been granted frontbench positions in 1989–90 compared to those who had served in the early 1980s. Almost half of the members serving the two years on several of the committees were chosen by party leaders for positions on the government and Opposition frontbenches. The most popular committees for sending its members on to the frontbench were Employment, Environment, Home Affairs, Scottish Affairs, and Treasury and Civil Service. Education reform became a major policy topic during Mrs. Thatcher's second term (1983–87), and it is interesting to note the increased transfer rates from committee service to frontbench status during this time for the Select Committee on Education. And whereas members of the Foreign Affairs and Social Services committees left their posts for the frontbench in only modest numbers for most of the committees' tenure, during 1987–1990 they have had by far the largest ratio of frontbench appointments.

TABLE 8.4. REASONS FOR LEAVING A COMMITTEE

Question: Why did you leave your Committee?

Response	All Members of Parliament		Conservative		Labour	
	%	(N-35)	%	(N-14)	%	(N-17)
Went to frontbench	66	23	71	10	71	12
Sought other post	9	3	0	0	18	3
Took too much time	9	3	17	1	6	1
Disliked inquiries	9	3	14	2	6	1
Boycott/left Parliament	9	3	7	1	0	0

TABLE 8.5. RATIO OF CONSERVATIVE COMMITTEE MEMBERS WHO BECAME FRONTBENCHERS, MAY 1979-NOVEMBER 1990

Select Committee	79/80	80/81	81/82	82/83	83/84	84/85	85/86	86/87	87/88	88/89	89/90
Agriculture	22.2	16.7	10.0	0.0	7.7	8.3	6.3	8.3	6.3	7.7	0.0
Defence	0.0	0.0	7.1	7.7	9.1	9.1	9.1	8.3	9.1	9.1	15.4
Education	0.0	0.0	0.0	0.0	25.0	23.1	23.1	25.0	15.4	15.4	16.7
Employment	0.0	0.0	0.0	9.1	9.1	9.1	14.3	8.3	0.0	0.0	0.0
Energy	16.7	16.7	8.3	7.7	0.0	0.0	7.7	7.7	0.0	0.0	0.0
Environment	15.4	23.1	16.7	0.0	8.3	7.7	7.7	8.3	9.1	9.1	7.1
Foreign Affairs	0.0	0.0	0.0	0.0	8.3	9.1	8.3	0.0	9.1	18.2	15.4
Home Affairs	9.1	7.7	8.3	8.3	0.0	9.1	9.1	15.4	0.0	0.0.	0.0
Scottish Affairs	18.2	16.7	8.3	0.0	0.0	0.0	0.0	0.0	*	*	*
Social Services	23.1	17.7	26.3	18.8	15.4	15.4	7.7	14.3	0.0	0.0	0.0
Trade/Industry	0.0	0.0	10.0	9.9	9.1	7.1	14.3	18.2	16.7	26.7	25.0
Transportation	9.1	8.3	8.3	9.1	0.0	0.0	0.0	0.0	0.0	9.1	9.1
Treasury/Civil Service	18.2	15.4	7.1	0.0	16.7	9.1	8.3	0.0	0.0	0.0	0.0
Welsh Affairs	0.0	0.0	0.0	0.0	0.0	0.0	0.0	0.0	0.0	7.7	9.1

Sources: House of Commons Sessional Returns, 1980-1990.

*Following the 1987 election, the Conservatives did so poorly in Scotland that the party did not have enough members to staff both this committee and all its frontbench posts relating to Scotland. Consequently, this committee was dissolved.

TABLE 8.6. RATIO OF LABOUR COMMITTEE MEMBERS WHO BECAME
FRONTBENCHERS, MAY 1979-NOVEMBER 1990

Select Committee	79/80	80/81	81/82	82/83	83/84	84/85	85/86	86/87	87/88	88/89	89/90
Agriculture	11.1	8.3	0.0	0.0	0.0	0.0	0.0	0.0	0.0	7.7	8.3
Defence	9.1	8.3	0.0	0.0	0.0	0.0	0.0	0.0	9.1	9.1	15.4
Education	0.0	0.0	0.0	0.0	16.7	15.4	23.1	16.7	0.0	7.7	0.0
Employment	44.4	45.5	36.4	27.3	18.2	18.2	21.4	25.0	9.1	7.7	7.7
Energy	8.3	8.3	8.3	7.7	20.0	15.4	23.1	15.4	0.0	0.0	0.0
Environment	30.8	30.8	16.7	8.3	8.3	15.4	7.7	0.0	0.0	9.1	7.1
Foreign Affairs	18.2	15.4	23.1	13.3	0.0	0.0	8.3	0.0	27.3	27.3	23.1
Home Affairs	36.4	38.5	25.0	16.7	20.0	18.2	9.1	7.7	0.0	8.3	8.3
Scottish Affairs	9.1	8.3	8.3	8.3	7.1	0.0	0.0	0.0	*	*	*
Social Services	46.1	41.2	21.1	25.0	7.7	7.7	7.7	14.3	0.0	8.3	0.0
Trade/Industry	10.0	18.2	10.0	9.1	9.1	7.1	0.0	0.0	8.3	13.3	16.7
Transportation	18.2	16.7	8.3	9.1	9.1	0.0	0.0	0.0	16.7	9.1	9.1
Treasury/Civil Service	27.3	30.8	21.4	16.7	8.3	9.1	8.3	8.3	18.2	15.4	7.7
Welsh Affairs	38.5	27.3	30.8	25.0	16.7	18.2	16.7	10.0	0.0	7.7	18.2

Sources: House of Commons Sessional Returns, 1980-1990.

*Following the 1987 election, the Conservatives did so poorly in Scotland that the party did not have
enough members to staff both this committee and all its frontbench posts relating to Scotland.
Consequently, this committee was dissolved.

TABLE 8.7. RATIO OF ALL COMMITTEE MEMBERS WHO BECAME
FRONTBENCHERS, MAY 1979-NOVEMBER 1990

Select Committee	79/80	80/81	81/82	82/83	83/84	84/85	85/86	86/87	87/88	88/89	89/90
Agriculture	33.3	25.0	10.0	0.0	7.7	8.3	6.3	8.3	8.3	15.4	8.3
Defence	9.1	8.3	7.1	7.7	9.1	9.1	9.1	8.3	18.2	18.4	30.8
Education	0.0	0.0	0.0	0.0	41.7	38.5	46.2	41.7	8.3	23.1	16.7
Employment	44.4	45.5	36.4	36.4	27.3	27.3	35.8	33.3	9.1	7.7	7.7
Energy	25.0	25.0	16.7	15.4	20.0	15.4	30.8	23.1	0.0	0.0	0.0
Environment	46.2	53.8	33.3	8.3	16.7	23.1	15.4	8.3	9.1	18.2	14.3
Foreign Affairs	18.2	15.4	23.1	13.3	8.3	9.1	16.7	0.0	36.4	45.5	38.5
Home Affairs	45.5	46.2	33.3	25.0	20.0	27.3	18.2	23.1	0.0	8.3	8.3
Scottish Affairs	27.3	25.0	16.7	8.3	7.1	0.0	0.0	0.0	*	*	*
Social Services	69.2	58.8	47.4	43.8	23.1	23.1	15.4	28.6	0.0	8.3	0.0
Trade/Industry	10.0	18.2	20.0	18.2	18.2	14.3	14.3	18.2	25.0	40.0	41.7
Transportation	27.3	25.0	16.7	18.2	9.1	0.0	0.0	0.0	16.7	18.2	18.2
Treasury/Civil Service	45.5	46.2	28.6	16.7	25.0	18.2	16.7	8.3	18.2	15.4	7.7
Welsh Affairs	38.5	27.3	30.8	25.0	16.7	18.2	16.7	10.0	0.0	15.4	27.3

Sources: House of Commons Sessional Returns, 1980-1990.

*Following the 1987 election, the Conservatives did so poorly in Scotland that the party did not have
enough members to staff both this committee and all its frontbench posts relating to Scotland.
Consequently, this committee was dissolved.

TABLE 8.8. PERCENTAGE OF FRONTBENCHERS WHO HAD SERVED ON
SELECT COMMITTEES, 1980-1990

Year	Labour %	Conservative %	Year	Labour %	Conservative %
1980-81	24	13	1985-86	40	31
1981-82	28	18	1986-87	40	31
1982-83	30	25	1987-88	39	35
1983-84	33	28	1988-89	36	35
1984-85	37	30	1989-90	37	35

Sources: House of Commons Sessional Returns, 1980-1990.

TABLE 8.9. PERCENTAGE OF 1983 FRONTBENCHERS WHO HAD
SERVED ON MONITORING SELECT COMMITTEES, 1968-1979

Year	%	Year	%
1968-69	4.41	1974	9.56
1969-70	2.94	1974-75	13.24
1970-71	6.62	1975-76	13.24
1971-72	8.09	1976-77	11.03
1972-73	5.88	1977-78	11.76
1973-74	11.03	1978-79	9.56

Sources: House of Commons Sessional Returns, 1969-1980.

These figures are, of course, calculated using the total number of persons serving on a committee for a particular year, not the number of committee positions. So, for example, in 1988–89 the Social Services Committee witnessed several members leaving and being replaced. The committee has only eleven posts, but because of that year's high turnover fifteen members of Parliament actually served on the committee that year. Six of the fifteen left for the frontbenches (40 percent), although there is in fact a possible total of eleven seats, for an adjusted ratio of 55 percent. These are extraordinary rates, given the often-repeated assumption that committee service could marginalize an MP in the House or, worse, be a clear impediment to movement up the ministerial ladder. Tables 8.5 and 8.6 also indicate that the Conservatives were initially more reluctant than Labour to seek committee personnel to people the frontbench. The Conservative committee members left their committee posts in greater proportion than their Labour counterparts on only one committee—Agriculture.

The degree to which the government and Opposition sought committee members for leadership positions is further highlighted in Table 8.8. This table demonstrates the percentage of the Conservative and Labour frontbenches who had served previously on one of the departmentally related select committees. Again, it is clear that Labour initially relied more heavily on committee members for front-bench posts than did the Conservatives. From 1980 through 1990, the persistent trend for both parties, however, indicates an increased use of committee members for both government and Opposition front-benches. From the midpoint in Mrs. Thatcher's career as prime minister to the present, the ratio of committee members making up the frontbenches seems to have settled at about a third. From a historical perspective, these rates, too, are extraordinary. While Labour and the Tories in 1990, after three general elections, would choose over a third of their frontbenches from these select committees, I found that in 1983, after three general elections (1974 counted as one because of such low MP turnover from February to October), party leaders chose no more than 13 percent of their frontbenches from persons who had served on any of the comparable monitoring select committees that were the precursors of the 1979 committees. (See Table 8.9.)

Although movement from committee to frontbench has become rather commonplace, transfers from one committee to another are rare; members generally appear content with their original committee assignments, and although some may wish to go to another committee, transfer probability remains low. Several members mentioned that they informed the Committee of Selection of their preferred committee assignments as well as alternates. The preferred committee assignments invariably corresponded with one of the four great departments of state: Treasury, Defence, Foreign Affairs, and Home Affairs. One committee clerk informed me that there were over eighty applications from committee members and non-members for the two vacancies on the Defence Committee in the 1979–83 Parliament (Interview, 25 June 1987; Downs, 1985, 52). The Committee of Selection, moreover, appears to give some preference to distinguished members of the House. For example, Norman St. John-Stevas, who had not been a select committee member and did not have a background in Foreign Affairs, was appointed to the Foreign Affairs Committee in the 1983–84 session. He was, however, a former Leader of the House who had recommended the adoption of most of the 1977–78 Procedure Committee Report and persuaded a reluctant cabinet to introduce this new committee system. Ian Mikardo, a Labour MP first sent to Parliament in 1945 and serving in his last Parliament in 1984, was granted his request to move from the Trade and Industry Committee to the Foreign Affairs Committee.

A few committee members moved to other parliamentary committees or to positions in their parliamentary parties. As one MP explained: "I didn't leave to go immediately to the frontbench [his

TABLE 8.10. ANNUAL TURNOVER RATES FOR SELECT COMMITTEES BY
SESSION, 1979/80-1989/90

Select Committee	79/80	80/81	81/82	82/83	83/84	84/85	85/86	86/87	87/88	88/89	89/90
Agriculture	0	33	11	0	18	10	54	0	9	18	9
Defence	0	9	27	18	0	0	9	9	9	0	18
Education	0	0	11	0	9	15	18	9	9	18	9
Employment	0	22	22	22	0	0	27	9	0	18	18
Energy	10	9	9	18	0	27	18	18	9	9	27
Environment	18	18	64	9	9	18	18	18	0	0	27
Foreign Affairs	0	18	18	36	9	0	9	0	0	0	18
Home Affairs	0	18	18	18	0	9	9	9	0	9	9
Scottish Affairs	0	31	46	15	0	0	8	15	*	*	*
Social Services	11	22	11	22	0	27	36	10	9	36	9
Trade/Industry	0	9	9	9	27	9	18	18	0	9	9
Transportation	0	9	9	0	0	9	9	0	9	0	0
Treasury/Civil Service	0	18	27	0	9	0	9	9	0	18	18
Welsh Affairs	18	0	18	9	9	9	18	0	0	18	10
Sessional Average	4	15	21	13	7	10	19	9	4	11	14

Sources: House of Commons Sessional Returns, 1980-1991.

These turnover rates may differ from those offered by Gavin Drewry in The New Select Committees. He calculated rates on the basis of turnover for a particular committee "slot." For example, if A was replaced by B, who was then replaced by C in one parliamentary session, Drewry counted only one turnover for this hypothetical committee. Consequently, person A's "slot" could be replaced five times in one session but Drewry would only count one turnover. Since there were in fact two new members and two replacements in this example, I counted two turnovers for this session.

The figures for 1983/84 and 1987/88 reflect turnover rates once the committees had been reestablished following the 1983 and 1987 general elections.

*Following the 1987 election, the Conservatives did so poorly in Scotland that the party did not have enough members to staff both this committee and all its frontbench posts relating to Scotland. Consequently, this committee was dissolved.

position when interviewed]. The powers that be wanted me on the Public Accounts Committee. So I did, because I wanted to serve my party the best way I could, and I considered it part of a promotion in my political career" (Interview, 4 Feb. 1987). Turnover rates also varied from committee to committee and from year to year. Table 8.10 gives the turnover rates in membership for each of the committees in each parliamentary session from the committees' creation through 1990.

In both the 1979–83 and 1983–87 Parliaments, the combined average turnover rates increased with each passing session, with one notable exception. During the final session of each Parliament, the trends in turnover rates were reversed and rates dropped below those of the two previous years. Only three committees in the first Parliament increased their turnover rates from the third session to the fourth. And in the second Parliament, only two committees increased their turnover rates from the third to the fourth session. Despite the obvious trend for turnover rates to increase with each passing year in each Parliament, this pattern was reversed during a session when a general election was held.

Electoral concerns may explain this phenomenon. Anticipating a general election in the fourth parliamentary session, party leaders began to assemble their frontbenches during the third session. This maneuver would allow each party to enter the general election campaign with party spokespersons who had been in their positions for at least a year, usually longer. Indeed, many committee members who moved to the frontbench did so during the third session of each Parliament. This third-year turnover of MPs to the frontbenches further highlights the degree to which frontbenches raid select committees for personnel and may be further empirical evidence of MPs' using committee status as a stepping stone in their parliamentary careers.

In the years examined here from the last Parliament (1987–90), there was no sudden decline in the turnover rate for the third session; however, the prime minister was replaced, and politicians and pundits alike were unclear when the next general election would now take place. But in terms of overall committee stability, this last Parliament also witnessed much lower turnover rates overall.

The average annual turnover rate also varied by committee, ranging from 4 percent for the Transportation Committee to 17 percent for the Environment and Social Services committees. Table 8.11 ranks the fourteen select committees based on their average annual turnover rates. These turnover rates suggest a substantial degree of membership stability between committees and over time. Over the eleven-year period covered here, eight of the fourteen committees experienced average turnover rates within a margin of 6 percentage points of one another. In the 1979–83 Parliament, the committees averaged a yearly membership stability ratio of 86 percent. This figure increased slightly in the following Parliament to 89 percent, and increased slightly again for the third Parliament, to 90 percent. Furthermore, only four committees had higher turnover rates in the 1983–87 Parliament than in the 1979–83 Parliament, and only six had higher turnovers from the 1987–90 Parliament than the 1983–87 Parliament. The overall average turnover rate from 1979 to 1990 was only 12 percent. The desire of parliamentary reformers that these committees

TABLE 8.11. AVERAGE TURNOVER RATES FOR SELECT COMMITTEES
BY PERCENT OF MEMBERSHIP, 1979-1990

Committee	11-year average %	1979-83 average %	1983-87 average %	1987-90 average %
Transportation	4	5	5	3
Education	9	3	13	12
Treasury/Civil Service	10	11	7	12
Defence	9	14	5	9
Welsh Affairs	10	11	9	9
Foreign Affairs	10	18	5	6
Home Affairs	10	14	9	10
Trade/Industry	10	7	18	6
Employment	13	17	9	12
Energy	14	12	16	15
Scottish Affairs	*	23	6	*
Agriculture	15	11	22	12
Social Services	17	17	17	18
Environment	17	27	16	9
Committees' Average	12	14	11	10

Sources: House of Commons Sessional Returns, 1980-1991.

*Following the 1987 election, the Conservatives did so poorly in Scotland that the party did not have enough members to staff both this committee and all its frontbench posts relating to Scotland. Consequently, this committee was dissolved.

would have low membership turnover and maintain a high level of continuity from year to year apparently has been borne out. Select committees may indeed be "settling in," as MPs remarked, and if the trend continues they may witness even lower turnover rates in the current Parliament, following the 1992 general election.

Although the select committees may provide an alternative career structure for many members, promotion to the frontbench usually entails more power and influence within the House as well. From a career perspective, committees may not replace the frontbench as a source of influence, but they are the appropriate avenue early in one's career to satisfy the twin goals of involvement and influence, which can be continued and extended subsequently on the frontbench. Because committee membership is incompatible with a position on the frontbench, elevation to the frontbench also necessitates removal from a select committee. Members were asked if most MPs, given a choice between a frontbench position and remaining a

TABLE 8.12. PERCEIVED WILLINGNESS OF OTHER COMMITTEE
MEMBERS TO MOVE TO THE FRONTBENCH

Question: Is it true that almost anyone offered a position on the frontbench would be
willing to relinquish a select committee post?

Response	All Members of Parliament		Conservative		Labour		Non-Select Committee		Select Committee	
	%	(N-84)	%	(N-41)	%	(N-38)	%	(N-24)	%	(N-60)
Yes	96	81	100	41	92	35	92	22	98	59
No	1	1	0	0	3	1	0	0	2	1
Unsure	2	2	0	0	5	2	8	2	0	0

TABLE 8.13. WILLINGNESS OF INTERVIEWED COMMITTEE MEMBER TO
MOVE TO THE FRONTBENCH

Question: Would you be willing to relinquish your select committee assignment for a
position on your frontbench? (Amended for non-select committee members: If you were a
select committee member, would you be willing...?)

Response	All Members of Parliament		Conservative		Labour		Non-Select Committee		Select Committee	
	%	(N-84)	%	(N-41)	%	(N-38)	%	(N-24)	%	(N-60)
Yes	61	51	63	26	61	23	75	18	55	33
No	26	22	29	12	26	10	8	2	33	20
Unsure	13	11	7	3	13	5	17	4	12	7

committee member, would relinquish their select committee posts.
Ninety-six percent believed that most committee members would
choose the frontbench position. (See Table 8.12.) Again, this evidence
suggests that while MPs who adopted an activist role for themselves
initially chose committee service, they would accept a frontbench
post to extend their power and influence in, for example, constituency affairs and/or particular policy domains. All but three of eighty-
four MPs believed most members would be willing to relinquish a
select committee assignment for the frontbench.

But in a follow-up question, I asked each MP if he or she would
be willing to change status in their own case. As Table 8.13 demonstrates, these results are somewhat different. Again party affiliation

TABLE 8.14. REASONS FOR NOT CHOOSING COMMITTEE MEMBERSHIP

Question: Can you tell me why you did not choose to be on a select committee?

Response	All Members of Parliament		Conservative		Labour	
	%	(N-60)	%	(N-29)	%	(N-26)
Other parliamentary/ party post	38	9	17	2	58	7
Unable to be placed	29	7	42	5	17	2
Other committee work	17	4	33	4	0	0
Constituency obligations	8	2	0	0	17	2
Oppose select committees	8	2	8	1	8	1

did not account for any differentiation in members' responses. Whereas all Conservative MPs and nearly all Labour MPs believed most committee members would relinquish their posts, more than a quarter in each party said they themselves would not be willing to abandon their committee assignments for positions on the front-benches. Furthermore, whereas three-fourths of non-committee members thought they would give up their committee posts in this hypothetical scenario, only slightly more than half the committee members were certain they would do the same. Newer entrants were far more likely to give up their committee posts than were those with more than ten years in the House. The latter were especially unin-terested in exchanging their committee posts for junior ministerial positions. Most of these members recognized that the ministerial ba-ton would not be passed to them at this stage of their careers. For the newer/younger cohort, however, committee status was indeed per-ceived as a first rung on the ladder of influence. This was the forum in which to be active, recognized, and rewarded by party leaders. A Conservative committeeman who had just been elected chairman of his committee said: "I would not take a junior job now. I would not be offered one in this administration, but I may be in the next one. It would have to be a pretty senior one for me to give up my power base, as it were. I wish I were in cabinet, but I am not considered one of 'us' [a Thatcherite Tory]. I would not take an undersecretary's job now because it is down in the pecking order from what I've got now. It is very much so a different parliamentary career path rather than just sitting on the backbench" (Interview, 23 Feb. 1987). Another Conservative MP from the Social Services Committee reflected the views of many new entrants who would relinquish their committee posts: "If you want to influence decisions and you are a good administrator and the kind of person you feel safe with in making decisions, then clearly you want to get into the machine. The only way to get into the machine at the moment is to be in government" (Interview, 30 Jan. 1987).

The 1987 general election interrupted the final stages of my research, and consequently several MPs who had agreed to be interviewed either stood down from Parliament or had to cancel appointments due to reelection demands. I was, however, able to interview two dozen non-committee members whose views and attitudes have been included and summarized throughout this project. These members were asked why they did not request to be placed on a select committee. A few were current frontbenchers who were unable to hold both positions and were unlikely to give up those leadership positions to move to a select committee. But their attitudes about Parliament and select committees were equally relevant and were consequently included in my survey. Table 8.14 offers the reasons why these MPs did not join a select committee.

Nearly a third of these members actually wanted to be on a committee; they viewed committees as the appropriate arenas in which to pursue their interests. But the number of positions available is finite, and there were no slots available for them. They were unable to be placed. Most of the remaining MPs in this cohort were unable to pursue committee service because their positions and time commitments lay elsewhere. Only two MPs, one right-wing Conservative and one left-wing Labour, opposed the committees on principle. The Conservative MP stated: "I don't believe in them, except those committees which have something specifically to do with the House itself—PAC, Procedure and the like. I am on the Procedure Committee. The departmental committees don't do anything in relation to the expectations they had. They were founded on a constitutional myth and misconception; those that supported it thought they would emulate the American system, and you can't" (Interview, 30 June 1987). Actually, the Procedure Committee's Report was quite specific that American-style congressional committees were not to be the model for the proposed select committees. The Labour MP added: "I was never on because they just mirror this place. I want to see them more adversarial. I believe in adversarial politics" (Interview, 15 Feb. 1987). On the other hand, frontbench MPs indicated that they would likely request committee posts upon returning to the backbench. Some members, however, also viewed committees as forums primarily for the new entrants. A former home secretary offered this response: "I have been on the frontbench for many years. When I left the frontbench a couple years ago, I decided to spend quite a bit of time pursuing other things that are important to me, and I do that by being active on other committees in the House. If I were a younger man, I think I would go on one of these committees. Younger members like being on the select committees. As the intakes change, the House will change. Local councillors come here and sit on the backbench with nothing to do" (Interview, 7 June 1987).

The former home secretary was correct; younger members do seem to enjoy being on a select committee. They certainly prefer it to sitting on the backbench waiting for an opportunity to speak on the floor of the House or on a standing committee where the proposed government legislation is approved usually without amendments. But committee service also provides opportunities for mid-career MPs who consistently have been passed over for frontbench appointments. It still offers them participatory routes, a degree of policy influence, the means to acquire or use expertise in a given field, and of course a complementary avenue by which to pursue constituency interests.

The decision to choose committee service is not taken lightly. A member of Parliament will be expected to commit a substantial amount of personal and parliamentary time to select committee service. Not all inquiries are equally interesting, nor are the technical aspects easy to grasp. One must weigh the potential benefits of specialization and recognition with the possible risks involved in criticizing party policy. Most members believed that deviation from "the party line" in committee was acceptable to and understood by party leaders.

The Thatcher government, however, had several confrontations with the committees, their reports, and their powers. The prime minister's personal opposition to the new committees was widely acknowledged. Nevertheless, excluding secretaries of state, more than 40 percent of the members of her third government, formed after the 1987 general election, had been active members of the new select committee system. None of the members interviewed—whether Labour, Conservative, Liberal, Social Democrat, or Ulster Unionist, backbench or frontbench, left or right—mentioned that some committee members might be coopted to the frontbench. And, in fact, there are several Conservative committee members who have been much more troublesome and effective in their opposition to current Conservative policies and who have had prior government experience but who have been consistently ignored for promotion to the frontbench. The Thatcher government did not gain a reputation for coopting either committee or non-committee members. John Major's stance on select committees was as unclear as hers on many policy issues until the dissolution of Parliament and the general election campaign in spring 1992, which forced him to enunciate more clearly his government's policy position. He was further hindered by the political reality of being thrust into the post of prime minister near the twilight of a Parliament, with a general election necessarily looming. Moreover, his party lagged Labour in most opinion polls, and he did not welcome further criticisms of his party's policies from parliamentary investigatory committees.

Committee service not only assists in achieving members' goals but apparently may be a stepping stone as well. Despite the numbers who have gone on to frontbench posts, the annual average committee turnover remains low. Clearly, committee service must be rewarding to a majority of the members. In the next chapter I examine the ways in which committee members have found committee service rewarding, how they describe their jobs and tasks as committee members, the qualities and skills they believe are necessary to be effective committee men and women, and the role they believe committees now play in the parliamentary process and their hopes for the future.

9

MPs on Select Committee Roles and Rewards

The previous two chapters highlighted members' attitudes toward Parliament and toward their roles as members of Parliament. They also addressed why these MPs did or did not join a select committee and, if they did join, why they stayed or chose to leave. The duties and tasks of a committee member, however, differ substantially from those associated with the chamber-related activities noted in chapter 6. Committee members need to specialize in a subject area, whereas on the floor of the House an MP may be expected to move adroitly from one subject to another as debate progresses. In debate, an MP's oratorical skills are crucial; in committee they are pointless. Questions raised in chamber serve to score debating points or embarrass the opposition. In committee they are probing, sustained, and usually—but not always—nonconfrontational.

Both committee and chamber-oriented MPs consistently claimed that Parliament played a crucial role in holding the executive accountable for its policies. They differed, however, on the appropriate arena in which this institutional role should be performed. Because the activities in the two arenas are different from one another, I expected to find different attitudes from committee members about their committee jobs and committees' role compared to those associated with the parent chamber.

This chapter, then, addresses the qualities and skills that MPs assume are important to be effective committee members, how members define their committee jobs, and how they perceive the role of select committees in the parliamentary process. Despite the limitations imposed on the power of committees to introduce legislation, to force a government to change policies, or even to ensure that reports are debated by the House, members still choose to serve. Conse-

TABLE 9.1. QUALITIES AND SKILLS NEEDED TO BE AN EFFECTIVE
COMMITTEE MEMBER

Question: What personal qualities and skills should someone have to be an effective select
committee member?

Response	All Members of Parliament		Conservative		Labour		Non-Select Committee		Select Committee	
	%	(N-78)	%	(N-37)	%	(N-36)	%	(N-18)	%	(N-60)
Dedication	65	51	65	24	64	23	50	9	70	42
Master detail	51	40	49	18	53	19	56	10	50	30
Patience	31	24	31	12	28	10	22	4	34	20
Good questioner	28	22	35	13	22	8	11	2	34	20
Reach consensus	13	10	16	6	11	4	17	3	12	7
Independence	3	2	0	0	8	3	11	2	2	1

quently, I examine why members find committee service rewarding,
and whether further involvement in Parliament and access to debates
stem from a member's committee position.

Committee Members' Skills

For an effective committee member, the skills nurtured for use in the
chamber may have little bearing in the more intimate confines of a
committee room. If indeed these arenas operate under different sets
of parliamentary dynamics, the responses of MPs when asked what
qualities and skills are important to be an effective MP should bear
little similarity to those needed to be an effective committee member.
Whereas members stressed the skills associated with different career
routes in the former question, they were forced by the latter to consider those particular skills corresponding to a specific role route.
Table 9.1 summarizes their responses.

These qualities and skills are indeed quite different from those
summarized in Table 7.1. When speaking about the job in Parliament
generally, members did not stress mastering detailed material, toler-
ance and patience, pursuing sustained questioning, or striving for
consensus. None of these are particularly relevant to the chamber,
but they are essential in committee. Earlier scholars who analyzed
Parliament and its members often wrote authoritatively about the
centrality of the chamber and the generalist nature of the members.
On the skills necessary to be an effective MP, Jean Blondel wrote:

"They are Jack-of-all-trades, knowing a little of everything but really nothing in particular. . . . They must be able to grasp quickly the main points of a question with which they are not familiar. Moreover, they must have other talents: they must be able to argue a case in a debate with some cogency, they must be able to retort quickly and see the flaw in the other man's argument" (Blondel, 1965, 131).

These "talents" employed in the thrust and parry of debate received no recognition as important qualities and skills for committee service. Most MPs (85 percent) said that dedication to committee service was an important quality. While Conservative and Labour MPs appear to give proportionately equal support to this particular quality, there is a substantial difference between committee members and non-committee members. Moreover, members stressed dedication as needed for committee work, in contrast to their responses when asked about the necessary skills and qualities to be an effective MP. Those who stressed dedication emphasized the importance of "putting in a full day's work" because the era of part-time, amateur legislators was over. Those who mentioned dedication in response to the select committee question emphasized that one needed to be persistent during the inquiries and maintain attendance. One Labour chairperson remarked: "You must be interested and you must be willing to give up a lot of time elsewhere in the House. It entails a lot of traveling. You must be willing to give up other work" (Interview, 8 April 1987). And a Conservative chairman added: "You must do a lot of preparation and be prepared to do hard work. . . . Our committee has attendance rates three times that of most. . . . People have started to get the idea since 1979 that by working together we turn the whole process into a much more constructive one" (Interview, 23 Feb. 1987).

A corollary to the dedication expected from committee members is the commitment and ability to master the technical and complex issues of successive inquiries. A committee member has access to technical and specialized information unavailable to non-committee backbenchers, and indeed he or she may benefit from this information access merely through sustained committee attendance. But an informal norm of active participation has emerged on the select committees. Members are expected by their committee colleagues to master the detailed testimony, briefs, and memoranda supplied by committee witnesses.

Some members expressed frustration with fellow members who did not meet these expectations. In a few cases, committee members from the slaggard's political party have attempted to have the inactive member dismissed from the committee by appealing to their whips to offer him or her another post or enticement. Mastery of detail and active participation are not expected from backbenchers on the floor of the House, nor are they rewarded in a chamber arena for these pursuits. In the congressional model, the legislature is able to maintain its policy-making role precisely because of the division of labor through committees and subcommittees. The norms of deference, trust, and reciprocity are maintained only when all members and party leaders are secure in the knowledge that all legislators are adequately performing the rigorous work of committee service. Likewise for a select committee, its corporate influence can only be maximized if all its members are committed and dedicated during the complicated technical inquiries they must also pursue.

Approximately one-third of committee members, as opposed to only 11 percent of non-committee members, also stated that the "art of questioning" was an important skill to cultivate. In order to be effective at this task, it is also necessary for a member to become sufficiently prepared in the technical merits of the inquiry. Whereas an MP may be allowed a single question and a follow-up on the floor of the House, where one is expected to think on one's feet and score political points, a member in committee may ask a series of questions and must be prepared to react with several questions as new information or issues arise during oral testimony from a committee witness. As many committee members noted, and any observer of committee hearings will attest, it is an entirely different form of questioning than what takes place in the chamber.

Barristers, in particular, stressed the need to be skilled in questioning. A Labour MP and former barrister on the Welsh Affairs Committee explained it this way: "A barrister's training is I think incredibly important. You develop the cross-examination techniques necessary for a select committee. You learn you can give ministers too much rope and they hang themselves" (Interview, 3 Feb. 1987). A Liberal member of the Treasury and Civil Service Committee who was not a barrister nevertheless agreed: "Since the House is on the adversarial basis, not many MPs, unless they have been lawyers, have calculated the art of questioning, because that is not really how the House of Commons proceeds. I hope the strength of the select committees will be attracting to this place a new breed of member who is versed in the art of questioning. It has been one of the failures of the select committees that far too many of the members of the select committees in my opinion don't realize the questioning importance and tend to throw political sermons to persons they really ought to be probing. And that's going to take time to improve" (Interview, 3 Feb. 1987).

Several committee members did indeed mention that questioning skills needed to be improved, but they also noted that committee members have continued to develop these skills since 1979. Members who first joined their committees in that year mentioned that they and many of their colleagues had had little experience in this type of forum and that probing and questioning during evidence-giving sessions was weak and less effective in these early committee years compared to recent committee inquiries. A Conservative member of the Energy Committee stated: "The ability to get information from people in a public arena is an important skill. My training as a barrister certainly helped. When I first went on, we were each allowed two questions, which meant we asked rather bland, informative type questions, but we could not sustain a line of questioning. But over the course of time, the committee has learned to fulfill this role" (Interview, 25 Feb. 1987).

The two other qualities and skills that members often mentioned were associated with maintaining a nonadversarial, collegial atmosphere on each committee. A third of committee members stressed the importance of being tolerant and patient with fellow members and, at times, with the pace of a particular inquiry. Approximately one in eight committee members mentioned the ability or willingness to strive for consensus in all the committees' proceedings. Members viewed the chamber, not the select committees, as the appropriate arena for partisan and ideological debate.

Committees gained respect and recognition precisely because their proceedings were not guided by party political sentiments nor did they necessarily reflect the attitudes of the majority party members. Those few members who did choose committee work to pursue their parties' or their own political philosophies were soon discouraged with committee service and returned to their pre-committee backbench positions. The message early on to civil servants, ministers, and other members was clear; committees are to be consensual, not adversarial. They are to investigate and to issue recommendations, not to harangue ideologically opposed witnesses and merely repeat the party line. That does not mean, of course, that committee members are not aggressive questioners.

The Role of Select Committees

Members' assessments of the necessary skills and qualities of an effective committee member differed from and presented a more spe-

TABLE 9.2. THE ROLE OF COMMITTEES IN PARLIAMENT

Question: In general, what is the role of these select committees in Parliament?

Response	All Members of Parliament		Conservative		Labour		Non-Select Committee		Select Committee	
	%	(N-84)	%	(N-41)	%	(N-38)	%	(N-24)	%	(N-60)
Monitor executive	81	68	81	33	79	30	83	20	80	48
Bipartisan recommendations	55	46	59	24	50	19	25	6	67	40
Build backbench specialists	17	14	15	6	21	8	17	4	17	10
Supply information	11	9	7	3	16	6	8	2	12	7
Value for money	10	8	10	4	8	3	0	0	13	8
Topical inquires	8	7	7	3	11	4	0	0	12	7
Very limited	8	7	10	4	8	3	29	7	0	0

cific orientation than their assessments of the skills and qualities necessary of an effective member of Parliament. Members may pursue alternative avenues of activity in Parliament that require different skills. As one of the available avenues, committee service necessitates certain arena-specific skills. And just as members perceived chamber-oriented skills to be different from committee skills, I expected members to interpret the role of select committees, as a subunit of the parent chamber, differently from the role of Parliament generally. Members' responses to the role of select committees are summarized in Table 9.2.

When members were asked to assess the power and importance of Parliament, the most frequent response they offered was that it was to check the executive. Similarly, when asked about the role of the select committees, more than 80 percent saw it as to monitor and scrutinize the executive. But Parliament's role in checking the executive was usually defined by mounting challenges and debates on the floor of the House. The government dominates the proceedings and the House's agenda in this adversarial forum, and its policies are rarely influenced through Opposition and backbench speeches.

In committee, however, backbenchers representing all political parties choose the subjects of their inquiries, spend as much time as they believe they need to examine current policies, gain access to more sources of information, and usually produce unanimous, bipartisan policy recommendations to influence government decisions. The role focus of Parliament in general and the select committees specifically are similar, but the style and manner in which they pursue the checking/monitoring role differ substantially. Moreover, there is widespread agreement among Conservative and Labour MPs on the appropriate roles of Parliament and select committees.

Kevin McNamara, a former member of the Foreign Affairs Committee and an Opposition spokesman for Defence when interviewed, stated: "They [the committees] are here to stay. They have achieved a remarkable victory in not allowing Margaret Thatcher to get the changes she wanted after Westland. I want to see them extended. They do the work of looking into options and means of policies. We should know the criteria of policy decisions" (Interview, 18 Nov. 1987). And a long-serving Labour MP added: "They are to monitor, scrutinize government policies. We must claw back power from the executive" (Interview, 25 Feb. 1987).

When members spoke of monitoring the executive through committee service, they indicated that their actions often influenced the government's decision. They were able to be influential, several members claimed, because they produced bipartisan recommendations and authoritative information. Scholars and MPs have suggested that an important role of the committees is the creation of informed public debate and a contribution to the environment of public appraisal and criticism (Price, 1986, 14; Walkland, 1979a, 253). While two-thirds of select committee members noted the importance of bipartisan recommendations, only a quarter of non-committee members mentioned this. Committee members recognized that their consensus approach and varied sources of information were key components in influencing and monitoring government policies.

This nontraditional approach to parliamentary dynamics in the House worked best for MPs in committee. In order to satisfy their goals, meet the Procedure Committee's expectations, and undertake the activities the House entrusted to them, it would be absolutely inappropriate to adopt the norms and dynamics of the chamber. As champions of adversarial politics, non-select committee frontbenchers may have wanted the select committees to adopt another forum that would emphasize the parties' divide. But again committee members regarded this role from the beginning as inconsistent with their views on the role of committees and the role they, as committee members, wished to pursue.

One Conservative committee member who was a former minister remarked: "The power of these select committees is being held in

public and their influence on the public and ministers. But also debated reports help. And based on bipartisan reports in debate, I have
voted against the government. . . . Most importantly, it is fulfilling
one of the traditional roles of Parliament: to monitor the executive. It
brings to the fore matters of national importance—things that don't
otherwise get a chance to get to the fore in such a complicated world"
(Interview, 24 March 1987). And a Labour committee member agreed:
"It is focus of information. You get the public to address themselves
to many new and different issues. It is an attack on the executive's
monopoly of expertise and justifications for policies" (Interview, 4
Feb. 1987). An Opposition spokesman who had not served on a committee also supported these committee members' observations:
"They are a much more effective check on the executive. It gives
higher information process and access for Parliament in general. Outsiders who testify also see Parliament working and dealing with a
problem. This is important for legitimacy" (Interview, 22 June 1987).

   Although most members said they were able to acquire policy
specialization and expertise through their inquiries, only 17 percent
indicated that the role of select committees was specifically to create
backbench specialists. And while the Procedure Committee hoped
that information access would allow committees to examine the cost-
effectiveness ("value for money") of government policies, only 13 percent of committee members interpreted this as a committee's role.
Both committee members and committee clerks stated that committees were far less interested in pursuing expenditure-oriented inquiries than in investigating and recommending policies. Examining the
costs of policies appeared boring and uninteresting to most members. They preferred examining the merits and implications of various policies. Members recognized that they could not actually force
government to alter its policies or adopt all their recommendations.
They did believe, however, that their bipartisan approach to policy
issues, the creation of a corps of knowledgeable and informed MPs,
and their access to various information sources enabled them to monitor the government more effectively and influence the climate of
opinion in which policy decisions were made. Governments would
find it much more difficult to defend policies in the House and in the
press when unanimous, bipartisan House of Commons reports con-
tradicted government policy.

   Party ideologues who left their committees frustrated because
they could not pursue their partisan agendas agreed that select
committees played some role for Parliament and its members. In fact,
every committee member interviewed mentioned some positive role
for these committees. Non-committee members, however, were not

unanimously optimistic in their appraisal of the committees; 29 percent said that select committees played a very small role, or none at all, in Parliament. One Conservative MP, who opposed select committees because he believed they were founded on a constitutional myth, stated: "They are there just to criticize. They can't have real power. They can probe more deeply than on the floor, but it is in a narrow part of the whole concept. It is really just an extension of Question Time, which is pretty worthless" (Interview, 30 June 1987). Another Conservative MP expressed disappointment with the committees because they did not sufficiently assert their political powers: "They are disappointing. I wanted them to keep ministers on their toes. They should be called in three or four times a month. This would allow us to develop a House view on a subject. They have not; they have instead developed a Royal Commission type of inquiry, or else a quick short inquiry. They have missed the middle, admittedly boring, part" (Interview, 30 June 1987).

The Job of a Select Committee Member

During the interviews, select committee members pointed out that they chose committee service in order to influence government policies. From their committee experience they concluded that for members to be effective they needed to be dedicated, tolerant, and consensus-oriented. Furthermore, members should master detailed testimony and the art of sustained and probing questioning. If they cultivated these skills, committee members believed they would achieve their goals of policy influence and would fulfill the select committees' roles summarized in Table 9.2.

When members were asked to describe their jobs as members of select committees, their responses reflected job orientations that would facilitate fulfilling the role expectation of the committees as defined by committee members. But their descriptions of their jobs as MPs (as shown in Table 6.2) again differed from their perceptions about their jobs as committee members. (See Table 9.3.) When committee members described their jobs as MPs, 70 percent mentioned their constituency duties. Despite the links between constituency and committee activities that many members said existed, no one referred to any component of constituency work when describing their roles as committee members. Nor did any committee member mention supporting/advocating party positions and policies. Seventeen percent, however, did mention this role when describing their jobs as

TABLE 9.3. MP'S DESCRIPTIONS OF THEIR JOBS AS
COMMITTEE MEMBERS

Question: How would you describe your job as a member of a select committee?

Response	All Members of Parliament		Conservative		Labour	
	%	(N-60)	%	(N-31)	%	(N-26)
Find truth	57	35	61	19	54	14
Check executive	47	29	39	12	54	14
Advise ministers	31	19	39	12	27	7
Persistent work	27	17	29	9	23	6
Discuss policies	26	16	16	5	35	9
Effective opposition	7	4	3	1	12	3
Redress grievances	3	2	0	0	8	2
Frustrating/boring	3	2	7	2	0	0

MPs. Committee members did not appear to perceive these two traditional backbench roles—constituency ombudsman and party supporter—to be roles MPs pursue as members of select committees.

What committee members did emphasize was "finding the objective truth," as many MPs remarked (i.e., not relying on party-sponsored evidence and analysis) and checking the executive. They maintained that the willingness of committee members to shed party philosophies in committee proceedings allowed committees to produce bipartisan, "objective" recommendations. They further suggested that the bipartisan approach necessarily made their reports objective. This may or may not actually be the case. The Defence Committee, for example, quite easily produces bipartisan, objective reports and recommendations. But its members shared a common attitude about Britain's military role and nuclear status. Labour members who supported the party's then-official position on nuclear disarmament have not been placed on the committee. Consequently, the committee has not had members who differed from the fundamental political consensus on defense policy.

The reports may be bipartisan, but claims of objectivity and of conclusions based on all points of view also seem unjustified. Nevertheless, the bipartisan approach and collegial atmosphere fostered in committee by members willing to scrutinize and criticize party policies does seem to strengthen the legitimacy of ensuing reports and recommendations. One government minister stated: "It is a foolish minister indeed who goes marching up the hill ignoring a bipartisan report from his select committee. He should stop and say, 'Look, they might be on to something here' " (Interview, 18 March 1987).

A common theme expressed when defining each of these roles, whether it was discussing policies, advising ministers, checking the executive, or keeping up to date with all the submitted testimony and memoranda, was the perceived ability to make innovative and proactive contributions through committee service, to influence the policy agenda. A Liberal MP stated: "We are to undertake a thorough investigation of the executive—monitor the government. We bring some authority from Parliament into other issues not being considered—a proactive role which gives Parliament the role and credit for initiating and investigating issues and placing them on the national agendas" (Interview, 29 Feb. 1987). A Conservative committee chairman agreed: "We are working very hard to claw back some of the power we have lost to the executive, and to do so not just reactively, but to do so on issues for which government does not yet have a policy" (Interview, 23 Feb. 1987).

A Labour MP, who emphasized his role advising ministers, also stressed the active, innovative dimensions: "The basic thing is to decide what to recommend to ministers. You get a better report because government doesn't have to take your recommendations. Since you are not forcing them to take a particular view and you set the agenda, you feel more free to bring forth new ideas and fresh approaches and philosophies" (Interview, 25 Feb. 1987).

Benefiting from Committee Service

Apparently committee members do find their committee work rewarding: yearly turnover rates are relatively low, select committees are perceived by their members as important arenas to fulfill their goals of influencing government policies, and these backbenchers maintain that their influence in committee is proactive, not reactive as it is in the chamber. I also asked members directly in what ways, if any, they found committee service rewarding. Only three committee members, all of whom were right-wing Conservatives, stated that they had not found their committee experiences rewarding. (See Table 9.4.) While noting the positive role performed by the committees and acknowledging their usefulness to Parliament, they said they did not receive personal rewards from their committee activities. In fact, they were frustrated and disappointed because they were unable to process their ideological goals.

TABLE 9.4. REWARDS RECEIVED THROUGH COMMITTEE SERVICE

Question: In what ways, if any, would you say select committee membership
is rewarding to you?

Response	All Members of Parliament		Conservative		Labour	
	%	(N-60)	%	(N-29)	%	(N-26)
Expertise/ knowledge/ specialization	85	51	83	24	85	22
Influence policy	32	19	31	9	31	8
Produce good reports	28	17	18	5	46	12
Understand government	12	7	21	6	0	0
None	5	3	10	3	0	0

The most common response to this question indicated considerable member interest in acquiring information in a particular policy
field. Eighty-five percent of committee members interviewed said
they found committee membership rewarding because of the expertise, specialization, or education it gave them. Most members
thought of themselves as policy specialists in one or more areas, and
they also believed that it was important for them to specialize in the
House for career reasons. One Conservative committee member
stated:

It is stimulating. It gives me great knowledge which I can use personally and
in debates. The information you get on a select committee you do not get
down on the floor. Later when we have a debate, I am in familiar territory. I
know the parameters—intellectually, politically—of the subject. On Transport we did "Civil Nuclear Reactors." Now I can read a technical report without any problems, like the "Sizewell Report." The language is clear to me.
And this is one of the things you get. You get to be multi-lingual, which is so
true of all the professions in the modern world, and you have got to be able
to get on the terms with these people. You've got to be able to understand
their jargon. [Interview, 24 March 1987]

A Liberal MP added: "Oh, I think they are too numerous to mention.
First of all it is a marvelous reeducation later in life. I wish personally
I would have been able to go on as a young man. I would very much
like to have seen these in Parliament when I first came in [1966]. I

found without it, Parliament had very little charm for me when I first got here—the adversarial nature seems to me almost entirely outworn" (Interview, 3 Feb. 1987). A new Conservative entrant agreed: "I was getting terribly bored with the backbench. This was a chance to concentrate on a subject and help in the process and role of parliamentary government. It was educational, and I could use this education for input into my own party. It is not the job of an MP to be a generalist" (Interview, 23 Feb. 1987). And a Labour MP who had left committee service for a frontbench position said: "I would fight like Hell to get back on if I returned to the backbench" (Interview, 25 Feb. 1987).

The educative service these committees provided their members was important to them because it increased their likelihood of becoming policy influencers. Without committee membership, their backbench status offered them few opportunities to participate in policy influence or to acquire the knowledge and expertise necessary to evaluate policies and proposals. The only primary cue available to them in making evaluations came from party leaders and whips. Members could not offer reports and recommendations, crossexamine witnesses, or take evidence in this party-directed policy evaluation. What backbenchers could do was to vote "yea" or "nay" at the end of debate.

While members were also rewarded by the influence committee status conferred upon them, they also found the committees' reports rewarding. Almost half of Labour MPs mentioned committee reports, compared with less than one in five Conservatives. For Labour members especially, these reports represented "objective" and independent analysis. These reports, they maintained, contributed to the public body of knowledge available on certain topics. As a result, committee reports offered alternative approaches and recommendations which could not be easily dismissed because of the independent inquiry members undertook and the bipartisan conclusions reached. For Opposition members, this was a useful means to have the government consider many, and adopt some, new policy proposals.

Members' attitudes about the role of select committees, the role they play on them, and the rewards received from committee service suggest that committee members also become more involved in the parliamentary process through committee service. When members of Parliament were asked if committee membership assisted an MP in becoming more involved in the parliamentary process, more than three-fourths of those interviewed thought it did or probably did. (See Table 9.5.) Select committee members in particular were more

TABLE 9.5. PERCEPTIONS OF INCREASED PARLIAMENTARY
INVOLVEMENT THROUGH COMMITTEE MEMBERSHIP

Question: Does a position on a select committee help a member of Parliament become more
involved in the parliamentary process?

Response	All Members of Parliament		Conservative		Labour		Non-Select Committee		Select Committee	
	%	(N-84)	%	(N-41)	%	(N-38)	%	(N-24)	%	(N-60)
Yes, probably	77	65	78	32	74	28	63	15	83	50
No	12	10	15	6	11	4	21	5	8	5
Depends on subject	11	9	7	3	16	6	17	4	8	5

TABLE 9.6. PERCEPTIONS OF INCREASED PARTICIPATION IN DEBATES
THROUGH COMMITTEE MEMBERSHIP

Question: Do committee members have more access to debates due to their membership on
a select committee?

Response	All Members of Parliament		Conservative		Labour		Non-Select Committee		Select Committee	
	%	(N-84)	%	(N-41)	%	(N-38)	%	(N-24)	%	(N-60)
Advantage on special subject	44	37	49	20	40	15	25	6	52	31
More access generally	27	23	24	10	29	11	34	8	25	15
Just a little	14	12	12	5	16	6	29	7	8	5
Debated reports only	14	12	15	6	16	6	13	3	15	9

TABLE 9.7. PERCENTAGE OF BACKBENCH SPEAKERS WHO WERE
COMMITTEE MEMBERS

Year	%	Year	%
1968-69	39.00	1983-84	26.24
1977-78	44.00	1984-85	31.25
1979-80	28.77	1985-86	25.30
1980-81	28.20	1986-87	31.91
1981-82	29.67	1987-88	23.19
1982-83	37.50	1988-89	28.63

Sources: House of Commons Sessional Returns, 1970, 1979-1990; House of
Commons Debates.

likely to state that their positions assisted them in becoming more in-volved in the parliamentary process. Nevertheless, almost two-thirds of non-committee members interviewed also held this view. It seems there is widespread recognition in the House that committee service is a propitious route to pursue for backbenchers interested in in-creased parliamentary participation. One Labour chairperson said: "Oh, very much so, yes. You become an expert. You may not be an expert over the whole range of a report, but you are on certain parts of it. You become more respected in the House and also in debates" (Interview, 8 April 1987).

A Conservative committee member agreed: "We are far more in-volved than what is publicly admitted. Reports often only get luke-warm reception at first, but government does usually follow suit. We usually work as a catalyst. We either help the minister argue a case before the civil service. He can say, 'Hey, a select committee—an in-dependent body—looked at this.' Or it helps with a cabinet argument against colleagues or the chancellor for more money. Reports also in-fluence public opinion and special interests. We are influential within the informed circle of interests. Now the media gives coverage to select committees for comments. We are regarded as informed" (Interview, 19 Nov. 1987). A Conservative MP who had served on a select committee summarized it this way: "Yes probably. You get more influence, more expertise. More boned up on policies. This ex-pertise can in turn be used at different levels: on party backbench committees, sheer reputation in the House, conversation over tea or in the bar. It enables you to talk to ministers and the press" (Inter-view, 12 May 1987).

A current minister of state discussed her attitudes toward select committees as a former committee member and now as a government minister. She explained that her committee experience had taught her the value of committee inquiries and subsequent reports. And as a minister she continued to value the information select committees could provide her and her department. She stated: "The Education Committee just looked at primary education, and quite a lot of the stuff that is in that report is very useful to us and will help us to de-velop our policies. Because they have this ability to go out and look all over the country and in other countries as well, you read that re-port, and that is the collected wisdom they have spent a year looking at primary school education, how it developed in other countries, etc. So we ministers, we read it and in the end (A) we have to make a reply, but (B) we read it because we learn. We don't always agree with everything they come up with, but you can still learn" (Inter-view, 18 March 1987).

When the House of Commons debated the Procedure Committee's recommendations to create this committee system, one of the persistent themes was the effect committee service would entail for the chamber. Opponents of the committees, or "floor-men," argued that attendance on the floor of the House would decline and the level of debate would suffer (Judge, 1986). But neither anticipated result has occurred. In fact, committee members want an increase in the number of reports debated. They also indicated that committee status made them more likely to be called upon in debates than if they were still non-committee backbenchers. Table 9.6 summarizes their views.

MPs did state that committee membership assisted them in getting recognized in debates, but there was disagreement about the conditions under which this access was granted. A majority of committee members claimed their committee service enabled them to be called on during debates on specialized subjects. And whereas 29 percent of non-committee members thought committee service brought only slightly more access to debate, only 8 percent of committee members gave this response. Furthermore, on the floor of the House during a debate, the practice has been established whereby the Speaker will recognize the government minister first, followed by the Opposition spokesperson, and then the relevant select committee chair.

In fact, however, less than a third of backbench members who contributed to debate on substantive motions of committee reports between 1979 and 1989 were members of one of the select committees. (See Table 9.7.) Select committee members constitute roughly 30 percent of backbenchers in the House; it does not appear that the "chamber first" members' fears of select committee members' dominating debates has been borne out by fact. In fact, it appears that the Speaker has taken great care to ensure that committee members do not monopolize parliamentary debates. They may carry greater weight, they may be more informed, they may be more influential cue-givers, but they do not take up more time in the chamber. Interestingly enough, as this table further shows, the experience on the floor of the House during debates germane to Estimates and Expenditure Committee reports was not repeated with the new select committees. Committee members' access to debate in these instances since 1979 has never reached its pre-1979 levels.

The number of reports produced by the departmentally-related select committees and the number of reports debated in the House has also increased since 1979 but has fluctuated considerably, with noticeable declines during election years, when committees and their activities are automatically dissolved along with Parliament. As Table

9.8 demonstrates, the most significant change in the number of committee reports produced rests in the increase of "Special Reports." These reports are generally one of two types: they are either investigations into particularly salient political issues or critiques of the government's responses to previous committee reports and recommendations. In both cases, however, these parliamentary committees have demonstrated their ability and willingness to comment publicly on government policy. These commentaries are then featured regularly in the print media as the views of an "all-party parliamentary committee" or "bi-partisan parliamentary committee."

If committee members find their service rewarding and beneficial to them, and if they also perceive select committees as important tools to facilitate backbench participation and increase institutional influence, then I would expect to see fairly high attendance rates at committee meetings. Indeed, as Table 9.9 demonstrates, attendance rates are high. They are also higher than for similar committees before 1979. Between 1979/80 and 1989/90, the average yearly attendance for all committees ranged from 80 percent to 72 percent. Attendance rates also dropped slightly during election years (1983 and 1987), when members returned to their constituencies more often and spent more time there than in each of the previous three years.

The rates are also considerably higher in comparison to the attendance rates of similar committees prior to the 1979 reforms. Between 1967 and 1969, when select committees were created under the Crossman Reforms, average attendance at the Agriculture Committee was 50 percent, at the Education Committee 66 percent, and at the Science and Technology Committee 70 percent. Average attendance for the Estimates Committee was 36 percent and even lower for its subcommittees (Wiseman, 1970, 214). During the 1979–81 sessions, however, the new Select Committee on Agriculture averaged a 74 percent attendance rate, as did the Select Committee on Education, Science and Art. Over the course of eleven years, Agriculture averaged a 70 percent average attendance rate, and Education averaged 74 percent. As Figure 9.A illustrates, none of the select committees averaged less than 69 percent attendance over the eleven-year period.

Differences in attendance rates also emerge between committees. As an indicator of personal committee appeal, such attendance rates are helpful. Many members said they tried to be assigned to one of the committees associated with the great departments of state—Treasury, Defence, Home Affairs, and Foreign Affairs. Members of these committees further claimed that there were several requests submitted to join the committees whenever a vacancy occurred. Not surpris-

TABLE 9.8. NUMBER OF COMMITTEE REPORTS AND OF REPORTS
DEBATED, 1979-1989

Year	Number of reports	Number of special reports	Number of both: reports and special reports	Number of debates per year on committee reports
1979-80	39	4	43	4
1980-81	56	3	59	4
1981-82	63	1	64	7
1982-83	35	16	51	6
1983-84	52	22	74	15
1984-85	74	18	92	13
1985-86	51	28	79	18
1986-87	49	19	68	4
1987-88	48	26	74	20
1988-89	69	28	97	19

TABLE 9.9. COMMITTEE ATTENDANCE RATES (PERCENTAGES)
1979-1990

Select Committee	79/80	80/81	81/82	82/83	83/84	84/85	85/86	86/87	87/88	88/89	89/90
Agriculture	71	77	78	72	69	58	71	69	68	71	70
Defence	71	31	76	78	69	74	85	73	76	75	70
Education	79	68	72	63	83	77	73	71	75	80	77
Employment	72	67	72	70	81	82	80	76	76	65	71
Energy	76	73	53	69	71	72	64	66	75	68	76
Environment	69	71	82	68	78	75	79	69	73	70	73
Foreign Affairs	81	73	83	87	74	75	70	69	81	73	74
Home Affairs	92	80	75	74	82	78	75	75	73	73	69
Scottish Affairs	87	77	78	68	73	67	61	55	*	*	*
Social Services	79	75	73	77	72	73	61	67	81	76	80
Trade/Industry	85	82	72	70	69	62	69	69	74	74	79
Transportation	73	70	73	65	73	66	73	79	69	70	61
Treasury/Civil Service	92	90	87	85	77	78	68	69	73	75	73
Welsh Affairs	80	75	76	76	86	86	83	70	76	62	66
Sessional Average	80	75	75	73	73	73	72	70	75	72	72

Sources: House of Commons Sessional Returns, 1980-1991.

*Following the 1987 election, the Conservatives did so poorly in Scotland that the party did not have enough members to staff both this committee and all its frontbench posts relating to Scotland. Consequently, this committee was dissolved.

ingly, then, four of the five committees with the highest average attendance rates were these "prestige" committees. And, with the exception of Home Affairs, these committees also conducted more meetings than most of the remaining select committees. The Welsh Committee, for example, which had the second-highest attendance average, averaged only twenty-two meetings a year. Defence and Foreign Affairs each averaged more than forty meetings a year, but attendance was still quite high despite almost double the number of meetings of other committees.

Select Committees in the Future

Select committee members who were interviewed spoke proudly of their committee service and the achievements of their committees. They maintained that the committees had been effective in influencing government policies and had also been instrumental in asserting Parliament's role in the governing process. But committee members also expressed disappointment with the limited powers granted select committees. They certainly found their committee experiences rewarding, but many members wanted to see the committees' powers enhanced. Consequently, members of Parliament were asked in an open-ended question how the select committees they would like to see a generation from now would differ from the current committees. When members were asked a similar question about Parliament's status in the future, half replied they would like to see the role and powers of select committees expanded. And in responding to the future of select committees, 80 percent said they would like to see more power and independence granted to the committees. Members' responses are summarized in Table 9.10.

Labour MPs were more likely than Conservatives to support stronger, more influential select committees, just as Labour was more likely to support a stronger role for select committees in future Parliaments. And although committee members, compared to non-committee members, were slightly more supportive of stronger, more independent committees in the future, two-thirds of non-members also expressed a desire to see stronger committees in the future. Members indicated their desire to see select committees participate more actively in the pre-legislative phase of government policy and/or for committees to be able to guide departmental policy and personnel decisions.

TABLE 9.10. CHANGES DESIRED IN FUTURE COMMITTEES

Question: How would the select committees you would like to see a generation from now differ from those of today?

Response	All Members of Parliament		Conservative		Labour		Non-Select Committee		Select Committee	
	%	(N-84)	%	(N-41)	%	(N-38)	%	(N-24)	%	(N-60)
More power/ independence	49	41	44	18	55	21	54	13	47	28
More resources	27	23	27	11	29	11	13	3	33	20
Better follow-ups	23	19	20	8	29	11	33	8	18	11
Committed members of Parliament	19	16	24	10	13	5	21	5	18	14
None	19	16	24	10	13	5	21	5	18	11
Televised	13	11	5	3	11	4	4	1	17	10

FIGURE 9.A. AVERAGE ATTENDANCE RATE PER SELECT COMMITTEE, 1979-1990

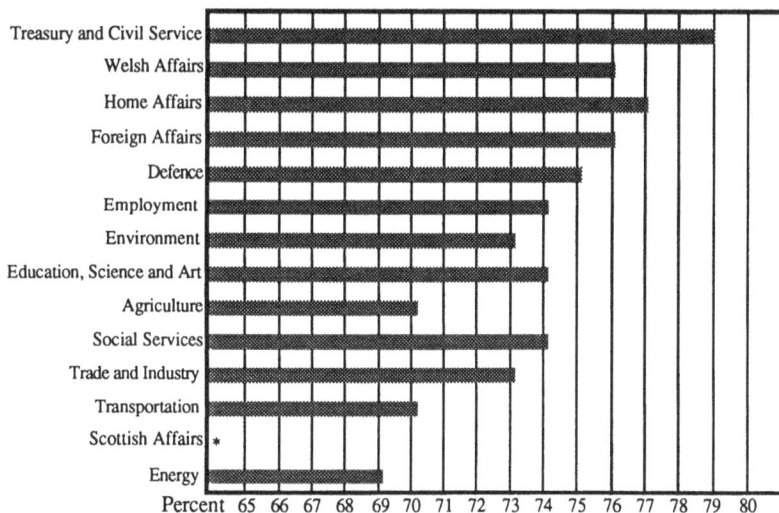

*Did not meet after 1987

Sir Humphrey Atkins, a former Defence Committee chairman and Opposition chief whip in the late 1970s, suggested to the Procedure Committee (1977–78) that select committees could indeed play a useful pre-legislative role. His proposal involved the committal of a bill first to a select committee, which would perform the fact-gathering functions. Subsequently, the bill would be referred to a standing committee which, armed with the select committee's report, would undertake the clause-by-clause consideration of the bill as currently practiced. The Procedure Committee rejected Atkins's proposal on several grounds but primarily because of the anticipated party interference: "If government legislation were regularly referred to specialized select committees, the party leadership would have a natural and proper interest in influencing the proceedings of those committees, and many of the characteristics which select committees now possess would be lost" (HC 588-I, 1978, xv–xvii). Geoffrey Smith, parliamentary correspondent for *Times*, concurred: "If, however, select committees were to be given real power, there is the danger that they might then lose the very qualities that make them attractive: the greater readiness to examine evidence objectively and to consider issues on their merits without conducting every dialogue in terms of the party battle" (Ornstein, 1981, 48).

Committee members interviewed, however, felt that their expertise, knowledge, and bipartisan approach to policy issues were not being effectively utilized under the current arrangements. They objected to the role partisan standing committees played in the scrutiny and evaluation of proposed legislation. They also objected to the inability of select committees to introduce legislation based on committee inquiries and reports. A member of Labour's National Executive Council who had not served on a select committee supported a legislative role for the committees: "I would like to see more hybrid committees where these type of select committees would take all the evidence and also take part in drafting legislation" (Interview, 2 July 1987). Most select committee members were more specific. One Defence Committee member stated: "I'd like to see them as many Europeans committees, as built in to the budgetary process, so the Defence budget would be committed to scrutiny. I would like to see legislation referred to committees. There is more expertise in select committees, not standing committees. We don't currently have the power to reject Ministry of Defence appointments, but I would like to" (Interview, 27 Jan. 1987).

Other committee members emphasized select committees as tools to assert a "House view" on an issue and to regain parliamentary control and influence, which they believed the House had lost. This view was espoused by both Conservative and Labour MPs as well as new entrants and long-serving members. A Conservative elected in 1979 said, "I would like to see them stronger inasmuch as they can be a catalyst in regaining power from the executive" (Interview, 13 May 1987). And a Labour party spokesman first sent to Parliament in 1962 added: "I'd like to see the next generation seeing them as a useful tool for parliamentary control. Parliament can get more involved in the running of the departments and their policies. I would like to see Parliament run more like local government. In the next Parliament you will see more members who have local government experience, and they will be restive" (Interview, 4 Feb. 1987).

The other major response from members reflected a desire to have better resources and more staff available to the select committees. Currently, each committee has one or two clerks who are responsible for administrative details as well as for securing written testimony from witnesses, suggesting lines of questioning to committee members, and writing final reports in consultation with committee chairpersons. Committees also use temporary special advisers who assist them with the technical and complex issues of an inquiry. A few advisers are seconded to a committee for more than one inquiry, but clerks and committee members appear to prefer temporary advisers whose particular background and expertise are compatible with certain inquiries. The exception is the Home Affairs Committee, which does not use specialist advisers in its inquiries. One committee clerk explained that he initiated "political" inquiries and the advisers drafted the initial "technical" reports (Interview, 19 June 1987). The Defence Committee does have one permanent adviser, the audit adviser, who was seconded from the Audit Office. The Scottish Affairs Committee also has one permanent adviser who resides in Scotland and is used exclusively for her comments on the Public Expenditure White Paper.

One Conservative committee member said of committees in the future: "They would be fortified. The clerks would have more infrastructure. The advisers are super, and we could use more of them. I certainly wish these select committees were here when I came into the House. We have tried various schemes in the past, and I think these departmentally related select committees are the way to go" (Interview, 24 March 1987). A committee chairman added: "I would like to see them better staffed. I would like to see the committee system solider and more beefed-up advisers so that those members who need it can be better briefed. I want to train my boys to get used to working in a committee environment and pick up and adopt those kinds of norms" (Interview, 23 Feb. 1987).

Committee members hopeful of increased staffs for their committees may find this particular goal difficult to fulfill. Whereas one-third of committee members wanted to see more staff, only 13 percent of non-committee members interviewed shared this interest. Moreover, several committee members were disquieted with the prospect of large committee staffs. They anticipated that committees would become the products of the staffs and that members would become dependent upon them. Members often supported their claims by noting American congressional committees, which they perceived as being run by large staffs wherein members of Congress knew little about the technical merits and specific arguments of each inquiry. Members of Parliament did not want to abrogate their committee responsibility to staff members. Doing so would make the benefits gained—expertise to be used on the floor, with ministers, in the press, for constituents—a moot point.

Increased staff and resources nevertheless may assist committee members in performing some of the duties and tasks associated with select committee service. More important for the future role of select committees, committee members appear able, and indeed willing, to assert the committees' potential influence through their own initiative. That they are able and willing to pursue actively roles as select committee members is not a function of the size of their staffs. Rather, committee members demonstrate and generally share requisite attitudes about their jobs as committee members and the role select committees should play in the parliamentary process. Members cultivate those skills that are important to undertake effective committee work, dedicate considerable time and energy to committee service, and pursue inquiries and produce reports that may be critical of, or an alternative to, formal party positions. Members have found committee service rewarding, especially through information access and specialization opportunities. They benefit personally and professionally, but they also emphasized that parliamentary government benefits from select committee activity. Select committee service may not be attractive to all members of Parliament, but even non-committee members recognize the role these committees have played in the House and their potential for development. Far from being "wound up" by the government, as was the case twenty years ago, these select committees, with their consistently high attendance rates and low annual turnover, appear to be a prominent feature of the parliamentary landscape that has served both Parliament and its members.

10

Conclusion and Assessment

Observers of British legislative politics have long been aware of the importance of party government in understanding parliamentary politics. But the reliance on "party government" as a convenient variable to explain all legislative dynamics has outlived its usefulness. Loyalty to party leaders is insufficient in explaining why the 1979 select committees were created or why members would seek positions on them. Members' desire to establish and then serve on these select committees is inconsistent with party government, but it is not necessarily inconsistent with parliamentary government. Committee members are not acting "irrationally," nor are they unaware of the many institutional constraints and informal norms that prevent select committees from assuming direct policy-making capacities similar to those of American congressional committees.

One of the problems of analyzing these select committees lies in identifying their significance. Some observers, notably Norman St. John-Stevas and Edward du Cann, have argued that the creation of the new committees has marked a significant challenge to party government and party dominance. On the other hand, David Judge and Philip Norton suggest that the new committee system may evolve into useful channels for backbench frustration and tools for parliamentary assertion. And finally, Richard Rose sees little if any chance of effective challenges to party government being mounted from these committees. Based on my own research and findings, I do not believe that such clear-cut considerations as offered by these various "schools" are acceptable. Rather, it appears that these committees were established as means of countering executive domination, that at times this domination has been challenged, that further challenges to party government and executive domination will continue, and that governments will continue to accept committee recommendations when changing, introducing, or abolishing national policies.

An altered relationship between the legislature and the executive may indeed be a consequence of select committees' activity, but any attempt to assess the impact of the new committees is beset with the problem of multiple objectives. Attempts have been made to disentangle some of the conflicting perceptions of the purpose of select committees. The major objective, according to St. John-Stevas, is "to strengthen the accountability of ministers to the House for the discharge of their responsibilities" (HCD 79/80, 974:1034). Consequently, the aim of the select committees is to scrutinize, monitor, and control the "expenditure, administration and policy of the principal government departments."

A second, and related, function identified for select committees is that of providing the House of Commons and the public at large with factual information derived from the exhaustive, nonpartisan inquiries. This function is concerned partly with the need to secure a greater degree of openness in government, which is a prerequisite for proper executive accountability. It is further concerned with making generally available to the wider interested public volumes of valuable information, much of which, without the powers of committees to send for persons and papers, would remain untapped.

Select committee also have a third and quite separate objective, namely, to influence the development and content of government policy rather than simply to monitor it. The chairman of the Home Affairs Committee, for example, noted in his report to the Liaison Committee: "Our purpose has been . . . to influence ministers in formation of policy" (HC 92, 1982, 52). This view of select committee work is one that has been endorsed by other committee members.

The ways in which one might judge whether or not a specific committee or the committee system has been successful may in turn reflect one's perception of the intended goals. A committee that has monitored a particular department, scrutinized its expenditures, and forced ministers to defend their positions publicly during committee hearings will be judged successful and effective by those who subscribe to a narrow and formal interpretation of Standing Order 9, by which this committee system was created. This same committee would not, however, receive the same plaudits from those who expect the committees actively and persistently to change, block, or formulate policies.

The wording of Standing Order 9 has facilitated alternative interpretations and has ensured that members who strive to influence government policy will find justification for their actions. Previous committees were empowered to consider the expenditure and administration of policies by departments, but the post-1979 era marks the first time that the "policy of the principal government departments" was subject to parliamentary scrutiny. Moreover, committees have moved beyond mere scrutinizing/monitoring functions; select committees have also sought to control and check the executive. These functions have necessitated an active role by committees and committee members and have served to alter the relationship between the executive and members of Parliament. Consequently, committees can also justify their actions when they seek to control and check departmental policies.

The proceedings and activities of the committees are the results of agreements and understandings between committee members. Unlike the parent chamber, committees do not proceed along well-defined or institutionalized rules of procedure. Several committees do not take votes on their reports precisely because members assiduously cultivate compromises and consensus prior to any formal committee decision. One Conservative committee chairman remarked that his committee voted on proposals "only because I've got a communist on the committee and he wants votes" (Interview, 25 Feb. 1987). The way in which committee members perceive their own roles on committees directly affects committee dynamics and proceedings. As Table 9.3 illustrates, members described their committee jobs in terms of "finding the truth," "checking the executive," and "advising ministers." Their responses indicated that challenging the executive's monopoly of information and influencing executive policies are not only possible through committee service but also the proper goals for committees to pursue.

Of course, a persistent problem rests in deciding whether these committees have been effective or are simply outlets with no real influence for frustrated backbenchers. This dilemma is best addressed by establishing the criteria by which the committees should be evaluated. During the interviews, members were asked what criteria they would use to judge the committees' effectiveness. Their responses are presented in Table 10.1. Members indicated that the most appropriate criterion for judging committee effectiveness was the committee's ability to influence policies. This was suggested as the most appropriate criterion by three-fourths of the members interviewed. In fact, this ratio held constant for committee and non-committee members, Labour and Conservative. More important, virtually all committee members indicated that the committees had been effective and successful in achieving policy influence. Only a few MPs, all of whom were non-committee members, accepted this

TABLE 10.1. CRITERIA FOR DETERMINING THE EFFECTIVENESS OF
COMMITTEES

Question: How can one judge whether or not a committee has been "effective"? What
criteria should we use?

Response	All Members of Parliament		Conservative		Labour		Non-Select Committee		Select Committee	
	%	(N-84)	%	(N-41)	%	(N-38)	%	(N-24)	%	(N-60)
Policy influence	75	63	71	29	76	29	75	18	75	45
Quality reports	54	45	49	20	58	22	46	11	57	34
Publicity	29	24	32	13	21	8	13	3	35	21
Educate	19	16	22	9	13	5	17	4	20	12
Value for money	3	2	5	2	0	0	0	0	3	2
Don't know	6	5	2	1	11	4	4	1	7	4

criterion but indicated that committees had not been successful in influencing government policy.

Committee members, on the other hand, were quick to point out
specific examples in which the government's policies had changed
due to committee proceedings and reports, such as repatriation of
the Canadian Constitution. Moreover, committees have played an
important role in prompting new legislation or administrative de-
crees. In these cases, committees were not responding to new government policy proposals but were instead nudging departments to
reevaluate current practices and consider new options, such as post-
natal care.

Norton enunciates the views of many of the select committee
skeptics. He notes that despite the production of reports, there is no
guarantee that the reports will be debated by the House. In fact, very
few reports have been debated. Second, though departments provide
written responses to committee reports, ministers and officials are
under no obligation to take any further action. Third, he maintains
that the committees constitute only one of several "influencers upon"
government: "In the formulation of policy the government will be
influenced by its own political philosophy and, in some cases, by
bodies external to the House of Commons. Select Committees are no
more than proximate actors in the process" (Norton, 1986a, 75).

These are the criticisms most often made about the select committees. Indeed, several members stated they would like to see more
of the committees' reports debated because they view them as authoritative research documents produced outside the normal con-

fines of party politics. The Procedure Committee's report of 1978 recommended that eight days a year be devoted in the chamber to debating the committees' reports. The final recommendations submitted by the government did not, however, include any such provision. A subsequent Procedure Committee report (1981) nevertheless recommended that a number of days be set aside in the chamber for the select committees' review of departmental estimates. Again the government was reluctant to grant the eight days requested, but it did allow three days for such debate. With the exception of Private Members' Bills, this marked the first time in parliamentary history that the right to command time in the chamber was extended beyond the government or the formal Opposition. The decision as to what particular estimates should be debated on these days is made by the Liaison Committee, consisting of the select committee chairpersons.

Some committees have been reluctant to investigate their departments' estimates for a number of reasons. For one, committee members do not wish to repeat the experiences of the previous estimates committee in which inquiries were long and tedious, covering only a narrow part of a department's estimates. Second, conducting an inquiry into departmental estimates necessarily leaves less time for other inquiries which members view as more salient and interesting. Third, the freedom to choose which topics the committees will investigate allows the members to pursue inquiries that focus more precisely on policy recommendations rather than merely reacting to the government's presentation of departmental estimates. Members find their committee work rewarding precisely because their inquiries are interesting, important, and relevant to them. The Treasury and Civil Service Select Committee routinely examines estimates and offers questions and possible areas of interest to other committees based on the annual Expenditure White Paper. Members of the Home Affairs Committee take no interest in examining this facet of their remit, despite the urging from the committee's clerk.

On the other hand, the Select Committee on Foreign Affairs does examine its department's estimates. The committee clerk stated: "As for routine, we do the estimates yearly; committee members realize that policy issues are important here. They do not at all mind this kind of work, and in fact enjoy the estimates work precisely because of the policy dimensions involved" (Interview, 28 May 1987). Committees have, moreover, used the estimates days for general policy debates rather than for discussions of whether the particular estimate is too large or too small. For example, the Trade and Industry Committee initiated a debate in 1985 that was formally on an estimate but actually was used to discuss more general questions about trade with China, a subject comprehensively investigated by the committee. A senior clerk wrote: "However, the system does allow a vigilant select committee to home in on a part of an estimate which it finds disturbing for some reason, take oral and written evidence about it from ministers, civil servants and others, persuade the Liaison Committee that the subject should be discussed, and table an amendment reducing the estimate on one of the estimates days. That is a powerful potential weapon in a parliamentary scrutiny of government policy, but it does not amount to a proper system of thorough scrutiny of each year's estimates by the House of Commons" (Silk, 1987, 175).

While it is also true that ministers and officials are under no obligation to implement the committees' recommendations, they must nevertheless respond to each of them. The committee clerks have established contacts and working relationships with Whitehall officials who act as liaisons between the parliamentary committees and the government departments. These personal relationships appear to assist in reducing the adversarial relationship many members and civil servants initially believed would exist between them. Some committees, such as Defence, have established follow-up procedures whereby they monitor the recommendations formally accepted by the departments. Others, such as Home Affairs, have yet to pursue follow-up inquiries. The clerk to the Defence Committee stated: "We do review recommendations. And a lot of the committee's influence rests here. In MOD [Ministry of Defence], we are known as HCDC (House of Commons Defence Committee), and when we make a recommendation to which the ministry has to respond, they know we will review the status of our recommendations and the nature of the ministry's reply and the degree to which it was followed up and implemented. On the Falklands, we are updating our 1983 report. It has certainly made a difference on how they think and act—and that analysis is from officials in the policy departments at MOD!" (Interview, 12 June 1987). Moreover, in a reply to a parliamentary question in June 1986, the prime minister listed almost 150 select committee recommendations that had been accepted by the government between March 1985 and March 1986 (Silk, 1987, 226).

Select committee members also stressed the quality of the committees' published reports. More than half the committee members stated that committees' "effectiveness" could be judged on the basis of the quality of the written reports. They took particular pride in producing reports that they perceived to be the definitive works on specialized subjects. And the legitimacy of these reports was bolstered by the bipartisan recommendations and the usual unanimity with which they were presented. At the very least committees provided Parliament and the public with an analysis of a current policy problem.

Much of the information gleaned during written and oral testimony was important to interest groups associated with the policy concerns of the departments monitored by the committees. Committee hearings and subsequent reports were often the only means available to interest groups and interested parties to acquire the information they sought from government officials. Given the restrictions placed upon the rights of access to government information, coupled with the secrecy endemic in British government, committees have become an important tool for information gathering by several groups and individuals.

Interest groups follow closely the proceedings of select committees and consider opportunities to present evidence as important means of access to influencing the policy agenda. They ask to give evidence to committees and in turn are often asked to supply the committees with written and oral testimony. The director of Britain's largest lobbying firm indicated that his staff monitors all select committee inquiries and advises his clients to participate in committee inquiries whenever possible. He pointed out that his largest client, British Rail, is "in front of committees all the time." And although the committees have not provided a dramatic shift in the means used to lobby for policy input, they are "an added extra dimension, an additional factor which we believe important to utilize" (Interview, 23 Jan. 1987).

Reports can also be designed for a wider audience than Parliament, the government, or the British public. The Select Committee on the Treasury and Civil Service, for example, conducted an inquiry into international finance which did not receive a government reply because none was expected. The committee clerk noted, "We were just making observations. The real audience was [Federal Reserve Chairman Paul] Volker, the Fed and the Japanese finance minister" (Interview, 4 June 1987). Similarly, the Foreign Affairs committee's report on repatriation of the Canadian constitution influenced the decisions of both the Canadian and the British government. One committee member stated:

Another thing which was very important were the effects we had on the changes in the Constitution in Canada. That all happened because I came in to my desk and found a plain brown envelope. And that plain brown envelope had what then became a very widely read Cabinet document from the French government containing statements about what the British reaction was going to be to the request to transfer the constitution back, in which it said the British government would not object and the government would indeed send it [the constitution] back directly. They were taking us for granted. It seemed to me it was a denial of democracy in Canadian terms for Trudeau to seek to do through the British Parliament what he could not get through his own. And therefore on that basis I persuaded my colleagues to go through with it. There was a lot of Conservatives who did not want to go through with it, but it was the responsibility of the British Parliament. The provinces took their case to the Supreme Court based on our report. [Interview, 2 Feb. 1987]

In order for reports to be more influential, several committees have changed the types of inquiries they will pursue. Follow-up inquiries are indeed important, but so too are inquiries that examine current, topical issues. Most important, committees are avoiding the Royal Commission type of inquiries that plagued the earlier estimates and expenditure committees as well as some of the new select committees during their early years. Both Environment and Agriculture committees, for example, have tried to avoid these long inquiries in recent years. The Agriculture Committee's inquiry into Animal Welfare took a year to complete, and the committee devoted its entire time to that one subject. The Environment Committee also initially pursued long inquiries with which committee members soon grew bored and disinterested. With the naming of a new chairman, however, the committee soon began pursuing shorter, more topical inquiries focusing on "green issues." These included reports on acid rain, London's Green Belt, and radioactive waste. Members find these inquiries more appealing, particularly since they coincide with government reviews in these current and salient policy areas.

In addition to the quality reports produced by these committees, members also measured effectiveness by the publicity received by committee proceedings and reports. Committees are monitored closely by the press, and several journalists, representing the "quality" press, television, and radio are always present when a cabinet minister gives testimony before a committee. Committees also hold their own press conferences to announce reports, recommendations, and, if necessary, confrontations with the government. Reports that are critical of current policies receive considerable attention in the national newspapers. Increasingly, the press seeks out committee members, particularly chairpersons, to comment on new government initiatives. Alternatively, committee chairs will send clear messages to the public and to the government about new proposals by calling publicly for immediate investigations by their committees. When the

Thatcher government, for example, decided to privatize the security forces guarding the Ministry of Defence's munitions storage and production facilities, the Defence Committee chairman immediately called his committee into session and asked for an immediate inquiry. He further notified the press of his grave concern and the committee's activities. The committee's initial skepticism of government policy produced a number of questions during debates in the chamber and attacks from both sides of the aisle. The government was forced to withdraw its proposal within days of its announcement.

Some of the committees' work, however, receives scant attention despite the impact the inquiries and reports may have on shaping, influencing, or changing government policies. Members and clerks of each of the committees could identify specific reports that in some way contributed directly in affecting certain policies. The problem in terms of achieving recognition of the committees' impact was due to the nature of the subjects under investigation. Some simply have low political saliency and engender little widespread public interest or attention. For example, the Thatcher government decided to privatize government vehicle-testing stations. The Transport Committee's report unanimously criticized the government's policy, and eventually the government abandoned its proposals. Although committee members pointed to this report as an example of the committee's success and effectiveness, neither the report nor the government's subsequent actions received publicity. The subject was not "politically sexy," one Conservative committee member observed.

The operation of the select committees also has fostered new relationships with what had been a faceless bureaucracy in Whitehall. I asked members if ministers and civil servants are cooperative with the committees during inquiries. Their responses are summarized in Table 10.2. Over half of the committee members stated that both ministers and civil servants were cooperative, and less than one in four said that neither group were cooperative with the committees. Both committee members and clerks were often quick to add that the relationship between ministers and civil servants on the one hand and committee personnel on the other had also changed significantly since 1979.

In their first few years, committee questioning techniques were admittedly quite weak. Clare Short, a Labour member of the Home Affairs committee, charged that "ministers and civil servants got away with murder, and that's partly the fault of the committee. I think if we were more determined they could have been more cooperative" (Interview, 27 Jan. 1987). A Conservative member of the

TABLE 10.2. PERCEIVED COOPERATION OF MINISTERS AND CIVIL
SERVANTS WITH COMMITTEES

Question: Generally speaking, do you find ministers and civil servants cooperative with
your committee?

Response	All Members of Parliament		Conservative		Labour	
	%	(N-60)	%	(N-27)	%	(N-23)
Both cooperative	56	30	59	39	57	13
Both uncooperative	22	12	26	7	17	4
Depends on issue/personality	11	6	7	2	13	3
Ministers only	9	4	7	2	9	2
Civil servants only	4	2	0	0	4	1

Health and Social Services Committee put it this way: "They were always cooperative in my experience, except where something like
Westland occurred. Perhaps the select committees were being asked,
without really having evolved naturally into this new role, to adopt a
role which was still rather alien to them—that is, much more investigative, prosecutorial role of an American committee rather than the
more studied and objective role which select committees have at
the moment. Normally the secretary of state or minister is ostensibly
perfectly happy to come and talk. He won't necessarily agree with
everything that is said; there were some sharp exchanges on the Employment select committee between Labour chairmen and ministers
and the odd sharp exchange between my Labour chairman [Renee
Short] and the Health minister. But that's to be expected" (Interview,
20 Jan. 1987).

Those committees with low membership turnover rates that continually call upon ministers and officials to testify seem to have
achieved the most cooperation from civil servants and ministers. In
particular, the Defense, Foreign Affairs, and Treasury committees receive considerable cooperation from their departments. The Defense
Committee also gets access to classified and "secret" information precisely because committee members can be trusted not to leak the information. That a parliamentary committee, particularly one staffed
by backbenchers only, should receive classified documents from the
Ministry of Defence marks a fundamental change in the relationship
between the ministry and Parliament. Even during the days of the
estimates and expenditure committees, discussion, let alone scrutiny,

of defense issues was considered off limits and beyond the rights of parliamentary committees. On the other hand committees with high membership turnover and past histories of pursuing Royal Commission type inquiries have not engendered the same degree of cooperation present on the "prestige" committees. One committee clerk remarked:

Well, they [ministers and civil servants] understand that the committee does not have staying power. They are generally cooperative, but they can use delaying tactics. Ministers seem more cooperative; they are in their environment, as it were, whereas senior civil servants clearly do not like this parliamentary innovation. They are in a very much better position to know what could conceivably go wrong and be exposed. This kind of investigation must have created an intense workload, produce some animosity toward testifying given the time involved in just telling them about policies. We have had a few battles over the sending of persons, papers and all that. But what we have done is to lay a trap for them. We start correspondence with the ministry informing them of our needs and we get these letters back informing us that they do not have time right now, or do not have the information or whatever. Essentially they are delaying tactics. Then the chairman goes to the secretary and tells them that the committee is pressing to go public with these correspondence which would be very embarrassing to the ministry. They have fallen for this twice. [Interview, 23 June 1987]

Members of all the committees, both Conservative and Labour, spoke with considerable pride, nevertheless, when recounting the occasions when ministers, and particularly civil servants, have been grilled mercilessly by the committee for showing disdain or contempt toward the committee and its proceedings. But these instances are also growing rarer. Civil servants appear to have altered their initial hostility to committees since 1979, particularly upon realizing that committees provide yet another way to increase leverage for policy initiatives with their ministers. Civil servants also take their sessions with select committees quite seriously. Sir Peter Middleton, permanent secretary to the Treasury, remarked that whereas officials would prepare for one or two hours before giving testimony to one of the previous select committees, civil servants will now often prepare for two to three days. The public forums also have necessitated and produced what he termed "better, more cogent and sensible arguments" (Interview, 6 Feb. 1987).
    In addition to establishing informal liaisons and channels of communication with departmental officials, committee clerks also have actively prodded committee members and chairpersons to pursue

lines of questioning during oral testimony when the witnesses appear evasive or have released important information that the committee members apparently did not notice. Clerks have also actively intervened on the behalf of certain committee interests. For example, one clerk directed a Labour group on one committee to maneuver and install a willing Conservative chairman over the objections of the majority on the Committee who favored another Conservative MP known to be sympathetic to and supportive of the government. These events took place during unusual activities on the part of government whips, who wanted to influence the selection of the committee's new chairman:

The whips were particularly active in the selection of the new chairman. Although he was a Conservative, he was put up by Labour upon the death of his predecessor. Procedurally, whoever takes the chair is in fact the presiding chairman. They came to me and asked what to do about getting around the whips who would be putting up a candidate for the committee. I told them they as a select committee could do whatever they wanted, and I instructed them how to go about it. They were rather surprised at this. They agreed on "X" and grabbed the chair the next time immediately prior to the meeting and moved to have "X" as chairman. Other committee members were still in the hall; they caught the opposition off guard, and the whips and other Conservatives on the committee were none too pleased about it. [Interview, 23 June 1987]

Ten years after the House introduced a new committee system based on the 1977/78 Procedure Committee's recommendations, the Select Committee on Procedure undertook an exhaustive investigation into the "Working of the Select Committee System" (HC 19-I, 1990). Among other things, the 1990 committee examined how the select committees had tackled the 1978 committee's expectation that this new system would monitor the "expenditure, policy and administration" of departments. The committee confirmed what I have suggested above: the record of individual select committees in this area "has been mixed" and "rather patchy" (HC 19-I, 1990, x). Committee members usually found inquiries focusing on the economical use of public funds in annual and supplementary budgetary outlays to be dull and tedious. While disappointed that the committees did not all systematically examine the estimates of their respective departments, the Procedure Committee did note that there were nonetheless reasons to be encouraged: "Whilst undoubtedly the scrutiny of expenditure by departmentally-related Select Committees has left something to be desired, there have also been some very positive results. The total effort devoted to this subject is more sustained and more widely targeted than was possible under the previous Expenditure Committee. There is now more detailed information available to the House about individual spending programmes than ever before—even if there is still room for improvement—and this is a direct result of the new structure of Select Committees" (HC 19-I, 1990, xi).

The committee was further encouraged by individual instances of committees undertaking these admittedly often dry investigations, and it highlighted some notable successes. The Energy Committee, for example, was the first body to alert Parliament and the public to the high and steeply rising cost of compensation for damage arising from coal-mining subsidence. This problem was first noticed during the committee's regular examination of the Energy Department's expenditure plans. The Defence Committee's persistent scrutiny of the Trident missile program highlighted time and cost overruns in the construction program for the warhead. These charges were originally rejected by the Ministry of Defence, but after five successive reports they were grudgingly acknowledged as true. The results of these inquiries and others by the remaining select committees allowed the Procedure Committee to conclude: "It is extremely doubtful whether this sort of information about any of these very substantial spending programmes would have been available to the House, and certainly not in such detail, prior to the establishment of the departmentally-related Select Committees" (HC 19-I, 1990, xii).

The examination of government policy is, by and large, the most important function for these committees to perform; it certainly has the highest profile and the most rewards for committee members. The committees have undertaken a range of investigations criticizing government policies, questioning new initiatives, and proposing their own recommendations. All of these require government responses indicating what action the government will take, and if a committee's recommendations have not been accepted by the government an explanation is expected. Increasingly from 1982 to the present, select committees have chosen not to allow government inaction to proceed unchallenged. When committee recommendations are summarily dismissed, committees now often begin another round of investigations, testimony, and reports.

One of the contributing factors to the committees' legitimating and respected authority is the process of identifying policy, drawing out the assumptions that underlie it, and eliciting explanations of its effectiveness. Bipartisan and unanimous parliamentary reports carry

greater authority than those designed by party loyalists, whose recommendations essentially mirror the priorities and policies of the
majority party. As my survey research suggested, and the witnesses
to the Procedure Committee confirmed, the more a subject of an inquiry passes into territory that is the subject of partisan controversy,
the greater is the likelihood that unanimity within the committee will
be harder to maintain and that any subsequent report will lose its impact (HC 19-I, 1990, xiii). During its first two years, the Environment
Committee concentrated on housing and local government issues,
particularly contentious issues with wide areas of disagreement
among committee members. The committee continually produced
minority and majority reports; the chairman noted that the committee really made little impact. Since then, it has focused on less contentious issues, and the number of Divisions on Reports (instances
where unanimity cannot be achieved and there is at least one dissenting vote) dropped from 159 in the 1979–83 Parliament to 30 in the
1983–87 Parliament.

But that is not to suggest that committees strive for consensus at
the exclusion of politically sensitive issues. As of 1990, reports from
the Employment Committee were virtually all unanimous, despite
the high political content of its inquiries into industrial relations and
trade union issues; the Energy Committee had had only sixteen divisions in its ten years; the Agriculture Committee's reports had all
been unanimous; and of the forty-five Social Services Committee reports, only four had been the subject of a division (HC 19-I, 1990, xii–
xiii). As the ministers I interviewed noted, it is difficult for them to
ignore the unanimous recommendations of a bipartisan select committee, particularly when the minister's own party has a majority on
the committee and in most cases the chairmanship as well.

Very little attention is paid in the Procedure Committee's report
to the select committees' commitment to investigating the administration of government policies. Committees simply very rarely, if
ever, undertake these investigations. This is an ironic turn of events,
as it is precisely this sort of activity that Margaret Thatcher assumed
these parliamentary committees would be pursuing and would
thereby assist the executive in controlling an obstinate and profligate
civil service. Second, the investigation of administration was essentially the only intended purpose of earlier select committees, and a
significant proposal of the 1978 Procedure Committee. Its successor,
however, was little concerned about the lack of inquiries specifically
addressing administration of government policies.

When the Procedure Committee concluded its inquiry after considering views of Select Committee members, the government,

through the Leader of the House and cabinet secretaries, academic observers, House of Commons staff, and unabashed critics (MPs and academics), overwhelmingly pronounced the new system an effective success. In particular, the holding of ministers and officials to account for their policies, actions, and decisions is now carried out by the committees in "a far more rigorous manner than is feasible on the floor of the House," and the approach adopted by the existing committees in questioning witnesses is much more systematic and comprehensive than was the case with the preceding Expenditure Committee (HC 19-I, 1990, lxxviii). In the concluding paragraph of its report, the Procedure Committee asks a number of rhetorical questions as another revealing test of their effectiveness, to imagine the consequences if the 1979 select committee system suddenly ceased to exist. The report concludes: "These questions, and the obvious replies to them, collectively suggest another. Would any government in the foreseeable future be prepared to abolish the system of departmentally-related Select Committees? The fact that this last question virtually answers itself is in many ways the most eloquent testimony to the solid, unspectacular but undeniable achievements of the first decade of the new Committees" (HC 19-I, 1990, lxxxi).

For the members themselves, though, two tiers of MPs, chamber- and committee-oriented, do not appear to have emerged, as many members speculated. What does seem to be evident is a large gap between what members want to do in Parliament and what they can do. Similarly, there exists a gap between what MPs indicate should be the role of Parliament and the role it currently plays. These perceived gaps exist with both committee and non-committee members, indicating that further reforms may be supported by larger numbers of MPs than the minority who have undertaken select committee service.

There now exist, however, two separate sets of skills for members to cultivate to be successful and effective in Parliament. When asked what qualities and skills are necessary to be successful as members of Parliament, MPs stressed characteristics befitting the opportunities and challenges presented by the parent chamber. But the skills they perceived as necessary to be successful in committee reflect the dynamics of an entirely different arena. The committees cannot be considered as microcosms of the larger organization. Committees do not follow the rules and procedures of the House. They do not reflect the adversarial nature of the chamber. Committees do not value members who are not specialists. Committee members do not tolerate colleagues who are not diligent and productive. Committee members do not gain respect or rewards from fellow party members for persistently supporting the party leaders' policies.

Committee assignments, however, do provide benefits to all the actors in Parliament, which may explain why committees have not engendered the persistent hostility from the frontbenches that their actions might otherwise suggest. The private benefits received by committee members are beneficial to other participants in Parliament and to the institution itself. These benefits—expertise, civil servant–MP relationships, in-depth investigations—are benefits potentially shared by all. Consequently, select committees can be viewed as providing the following for Parliament and its members:

1. Opportunities to acquire expertise and specialist knowledge for committee members.

2. Institutionalized avenues to pursue more active roles in the House.

3. Alternative means and display of other necessary skills for promotion to the frontbench. No longer are members necessarily required to play loyal party supporters whose career chances are defined largely by performances in the chamber.

4. More informed debate and discussion in the chamber. Despite the reservations and fears of some members, attendance on the floor of the House has not decreased due to the committees' activities.

5. An enlarged pool of informed personnel for the government and Opposition frontbenches to consider for promotion to a variety of policy areas. Select committees are another training ground for prospective frontbenchers.

6. Another forum for the Opposition to criticize government policies. Reports are increasingly referred to in debate because they are unanimous, bipartisan, and therefore "objective." The reports present a "House view" on a subject which the government cannot easily discredit for representing the views of the minority Opposition.

7. Another forum for third parties whose opportunities presenting their views and influencing the policy are sharply curtailed outside of committee activity.

Enlightenment theorists of the eighteenth century stressed and assumed the centrality of legislatures. The primary role of these institutions in the political affairs of the nation was to make laws, indeed, to legislate. For Locke, Montesquieu, and even Madison, representative bodies were not merely debating chambers; nor were they to function simply as checks on powerful executives. Legislatures were the sole legitimate institution to embody and express popular sovereignty, and as a consequence were the seat of policymaking. The empirical evidence of the nineteenth and twentieth centuries demonstrates that the ability of legislatures to control, or make, national policy is far more limited than these earlier theorists may well have imagined (Dodd, 1981). In conjunction with the constraints on backbenchers imposed by party government, an institution that embraced its role of increasing policy efficiency for the executive, and members who generally accepted the amateur, part-time nature of their jobs, other external variables contributed to the incapacity of legislatures to take an effective role in the policy process, i.e., the growing power of experts and specialists in bureaucracies in information-based societies (Huntington, 1968). The 1977/78 Procedure Committee recognized Parliament's gross inability to deal effectively with the technical and complex world it found itself in. Several committee members echoed this belief.

In the short term, the committees appear to represent a considerable, indeed, a major, change in British legislative politics. A prerequisite for the structural changes that allowed parliamentary assertion was an attitudinal change by MPs. A change in behavior has also been exhibited on the floor of the House, in debate, and in the division of lobbies. Several members remarked that they voted against government proposals precisely because of the contradictory evidence and recommendations contained in committee reports.

The rhetoric of many parliamentary reformers would lead one to believe that a significant transformation of the British House of Commons is under way, the likes of which has not been seen for more than a century. Perhaps they are correct. But like any transformation, the consequences and effects of such a change are only gradual and not immediately noticeable. While the passage of time is the necessary ingredient for examining the change in legislative-executive relationships, the same is not true if closer attention is paid to the attitudes of backbenchers on select committees. The traditional notion of parliamentary subservience due to party government and disinterested, obsequious backbenchers is no longer a valid one. Members of Parliament may not be prepared to establish another "Golden Age" of Parliament, but it is clear that they are less predictable and less willing to be regarded and used as lobby fodder than was the case even twenty years ago.

Appendix A

Questionnaire and Evaluation

I. Open-ended Questions

1. What do you find most appealing about being in politics and government?

2. How would you describe the job of an MP?

3. What personal qualities and skills does an MP need to do an effective job?

4. Do you think there should be more participation by backbenchers in politics and government? If yes, what form?

5. Do you consider yourself a full-time MP? Then you do not have employment outside the House?

6. What makes for a successful parliamentary career in your opinion?

7. Do you consider yourself a "specialist" MP in certain policy areas?

8. Do you consider your primary duty to represent the interests and needs of your constituency, or the party, or what?

9. What percentage of your time is spent on constituency-related activities?

10. What makes an MP a good representative?

11. I want to turn to the inevitable conflict that must sometimes arise between personal belief or constituency interests and party policy. Has this ever arisen for you?

12. What are the consequences of voting against or abstaining from party leaders' policies?

13. In general, what is the importance/power of Parliament?

14. Do you think the executive has become too powerful vis-à-vis Parliament in recent years?

15. If yes, what can be done to change the situation?

16. How would the Parliament you'd like to see a generation from now differ from that of today?

17. Do you think there is more consensus on your select committee than on the floor of the House in general?

18. Why?

19. What makes consensus or cooperation difficult?

20. Can you tell me why you chose to be on the_____ Committee?

21. Did you have any goals you wished to pursue on the committee?

22. Why did you stay on the committee?

23. Why did you leave your committee?

24. Why did you never go on a committee?

25. How would you describe your job as a member of a select committee?

26. What personal qualities or skills must a committee member have to be successful?

27. What are the obligations and responsibilities of a select committee member to party leaders and politicians?

28. In general, what is the role of these select committees in the parliamentary process?

29. Does a position on a select committee help an MP become more involved in the parliamentary process?

30. What is the role of the whips in placing members?

31. Do they have any other contact with your committee?

32. Is it true that almost anyone offered a position on the frontbench would be willing to relinquish his select committee position?

33. Would you?

34. Do you see your political career as being oriented toward the attainment of executive office?

35. Are there other parliamentary career goals for you besides executive office?

36. In what ways would you say that select committee membership is rewarding to you?

37. Will the added expertise help your political career? Is membership a stepping stone?

38. What contributions do committee members make to debates on the floor of the House?

39. Does being on this committee have any link to your constituency activity?

40. How can one judge whether or not a particular committee has been "effective?" What criteria should we use?

41. How would the select committees you'd like to see a generation from now differ from those of today?

42. Generally speaking, are ministers and civil servants cooperative with your committee?

43. Has it ever been suggested that you or members of your committee have ever intruded upon the confidentiality of official advice given to ministers by senior civil servants?

II. Closed-ended Questions

44. Which of the following roles do you most wish to play in the House?

_____ Constituency representative
_____ Debater
_____ Policy Maker
_____ Supporter of party policies
_____ Other (All)

45. Which of the following duties do you consider to be the most important of your job? (Rank from 1 to 8, with 1 being the most important.)

_____ Expressing voters' concerns about the national issues
_____ Dealing with constituents' personal problems
_____ Attending meetings in the constituency
_____ Supporting the party's leadership
_____ Making good public policy
_____ Contributing to debate
_____ Questioning ministers, government officials
_____ Committee work in the House

46. Which of the following tasks is Parliament best at performing?

_____ Initiating public policy
_____ Debating important national issues
_____ Monitoring the governments's progress and policies
_____ Ratifying or defeating government-sponsored legislation
_____ Looking out for your constituency's interests
_____ Other_____

47. Which of the following would you say best describes your constituency?

a. Mostly rural
b. Rural and urban

   c. Rural and suburban
   d. Suburban
   e. Suburban and urban
   f. Mostly urban

48. How would you place yourself on the following ideological spectrum within your own party? Marking 0 indicates the most liberal position, and marking 10 indicates the most conservative position.

0——1——2——3——4——5——6——7——8——9——10
LIBERAL   CONSERVATIVE

III. Interview Evaluation

1. Were there other persons present or within earshot during the interview?

   a. Yes, throughout
   b. Yes, at times
   c. No

2. Estimation of respondent's frankness.

   a. Very frank
   b. Frank
   c. Not very frank
   d. Very evasive

3. Estimate of respondent's cooperativeness throughout the interview.

   a. Very cooperative
   b. Cooperative
   c. Not very cooperative
   d. Very uncooperative

4. General remarks about the interview.

Bibliography

Abbreviations Used:

APSR   *American Political Science Review*
BJPS   *British Journal of Political Science*
CPS   *Comparative Political Studies*
LSQ   *Legislative Studies Quarterly*
PS   *Political Studies*

Primary Sources: Government Documents

Cmnd. 1432. *Control of Public Expenditure*. Plowden Committee. London: HMSO, July 1961.

Cmnd. 4017. *Public Expenditure: A New Presentation*. London: HMSO, April 1969.

Cmnd. 4027. *Ministerial Control of the Nationalised Industries*. London: HMSO, March 1970.

Cmnd. 4507. *Select Committees of the House of Commons*. London: HMSO, March 1970.

Cmnd. 9230. *Report on the Machinery of Government*. London: HMSO, 1918.

HC 19-I. "The Working of the Select Committee System." *Second Report from the Select Committee on Procedure, Session 1989–90*. London: HMSO, 23 Oct. 1990.

HC 24-I. *First Report from the Select Committee on Procedure (Finance), Session 1982–83*. London: HMSO, 11 May 1983.

HC 26-I. "The British Steel Corporation." *First Report from the Select Committee on Nationalised Industries, Session 1977–78*. London: HMSO, 9 Nov. 1977.

HC 28. "Appointment of Sub-committees and Related Matters." *First Special Report from the Estimates Committee, Session 1967–68*. London: HMSO, 29 Nov. 1967.

HC 50. *Return for Session 1982–83*. London: HMSO, 29 July 1983.

HC 62. "Ministers and Civil Servants." *First Report from the Treasury and Civil Service Committee, Session 1986–87*. London: HMSO, 1 Dec. 1986.

HC 79. *Return for Session 1986–87*. London: HMSO, 13 May 1986.

HC 92. "The Select Committee System." *Report of the Liaison Committee*. London: HMSO, 2 Dec. 1982.

HC 92-I. "Civil Servants and Ministers: Duties and Responsibilities." *Seventh Report from the Treasury and Civil Service Committee, Session 1985–86*. London: HMSO, 12 May 1986.

HC 92. *Report from the Select Committee on Procedure: Together with the Proceedings of the Committee, Minutes of Evidence and Appendices*. London: HMSO, 19 Feb. 1959.

HC 92-II. "Annexes, Minutes of Evidence and Appendices." *Seventh Report from the Treasury and Civil Service Committee, Session 1985–86*. London: HMSO, 12 May 1986.

HC 112. *Report from the Select Committee on Procedure*. London: HMSO, 22 March 1966.

HC 118. *First Report from the Select Committee on Procedure (Supply), Session 1980–81*. London: HMSO, 15 July 1981.

HC 127-I. "The British Steel Corporation." *Second Report from the Select Committee on Nationalised Industries, Session 1977–78*. London: HMSO, 15 Dec. 1977.

HC 129. *Report from the Select Committee on Procedure*. London: HMSO, 11 Nov. 1932.

HC 138. *Special Report from the Select Committee on Agriculture, Session 1968–69*. London: HMSO, 12 Feb. 1969.

HC 149. *First Report from the Select Committee on Procedure*. London: HMSO, 26 March 1965.

HC 161. *Report from the Select Committee on Procedure*. London: HMSO, 1931.

HC 172. *Return for Session 1985–86*. London: HMSO, 5 Nov. 1986.

HC 183. *Return for Session 1981–82*. London: HMSO, 3 Feb. 1982.

HC 184. "Minutes of Evidence." *Third Report from the Estimates Committee: Form of Estimates*. London: HMSO, 19 April 1961.

HC 188. "Question Time." *Second Report from the Select Committee on Procedure, 1964–65*. London: HMSO, 14 April 1965.

HC 196. *Return for Session 1983–84*. London: HMSO, 13 Nov. 1984.

HC 217. *Return for Session 1979–80*. London: HMSO, 16 April 1980.

HC 238. "Financial Forecasts of the British Steel Corporation." *Fifth Report from the Select Committee on Nationalised Industries, Session 1977–78*. London: HMSO, 23 Feb. 1978.

HC 241. "Report on Coastal Pollution." *Report from the Science and Technology Committee, Session 1967–68*. London: HMSO, 8 April 1968.

HC 245. *Return for Session 1980–81*. London: HMSO, 4 March 1981.

HC 273. *Report from the Select Committee on Employment*. London: HMSO, 8 April 1968.

HC 282. "Legal Immunities of Trade Unions." *Report from the Select Committee on Employment, Session 1980–81*. London: HMSO, 21 July 1981.

HC 295. *Return for Session 1983–84*. London: HMSO, 13 Nov. 1984.

HC 298. *Special Report from the Select Committee on Nationalised Industries, Session 1967–68.*

HC 303. *Fourth Report from the Select Committee on Procedure.* London: HMSO, 29 July 1965.

HC 307. Standing Order No. 99. *Standing Orders of the House of Commons: Public Business.* London: HMSO, 31 March 1983.

HC 325. *Sixth Report from the Treasury and Civil Service Committee, Session 1980–81.* London: HMSO, 6 July 1981.

HC 371-I. "Ministerial Control of the Nationalised Industries." *Report from the Select Committee on Nationalised Industries, Session 1967–68.* London: HMSO, 24 July 1968.

HC 378-XVII. *First Report of the Agricultural Committee.* London: HMSO, 27 July 1967.

HC 381-XVII. "Report on the U.K. Nuclear Reactor Programme." *Report from the Select Committee on Science and Technology, Session 1966–67.* London: HMSO, 25 Oct. 1967.

HC 393. *Report from the Select Committee on Parliamentary Questions, Session 1971–72.* London: HMSO, 1972.

HC 410. "Scrutiny of Public Expenditure and Administration." *Report from the Select Committee on Procedure, Session 1968–69.* London: HMSO, 23 July 1969.

HC 518. Westland plc: "The Government's Decision-Making." *Fourth Report from the Treasury and Civil Service Committee, Session 1970–71.* London: HMSO, 1985–86.

HC 538. "The Process of Legislation." Second Report from Select Committee on Procedure, Session 1970–71. London: HMSO, 28 July 1971.

HC 539. "Public Bill Procedure, etc." *Sixth Report from the Select Committee on Procedure, Session 1966–67.* London: HMSO, 4 July 1967.

HC 588-I. "Report and Minutes of Proceedings." *First Report from the Select Committee on Procedure, Session 1977–78.* London: HMSO, 17 July 1978.

HC 588-II. "Minutes of Evidence." *First Report from the Select Committee on Procedure, Session 1977–78.* London: HMSO, 17 July 1978.

HC 662. *Second Report from the Select Committee on Assistance for Private Members, Session 1974–75.* London: HMSO, 16 Oct. 1975.

HC Debates (Hansard). Selected years, 1919–20–1980–81. [Cited in the notes as HCD.]

Secondary Sources

Abercrombie, N., and A. Warde. 1988. *Contemporary British Society.* Cambridge: Polity Press.

Allport, Gordon W. 1967. "Attitudes." In Martin Fishbein, ed., *Readings in Attitude Theory and Measurement.* New York: John Wiley.

Alt, James. 1982. *The Politics of Economic Decline.* New York: Cambridge Univ. Press.

Anagnoson, J. Theodore. 1983. "Home Style in New Zealand." *LSQ* (May).
APSA Committee on Political Parties. 1950. "Towards a More Responsible Two-Party System." *APSR* (Sept.).
Arnstein, Walter L. 1976. *Britain Yesterday and Today.* 3rd ed. Lexington, Mass.: D.C. Heath.
Arter, David. 1990. "The Swedish Riksdag: The Case of a Strong Policy-Influencing Assembly." In Philip Norton, ed., *Parliaments in Western Europe.* Portland, Ore.: Frank Cass.
Atkinson, A. B. 1984. "Taxation and Social Security: Reflections on Advising a House of Commons Select Committee." *Policy and Politics* (April).
Aydelotte, William O., ed. 1977. *The History of Parliamentary Behavior.* Princeton: Princeton Univ. Press.
Bagehot, Walter. 1974. "Parliamentary Reform." In Norman St. John-Stevas, ed., *Collected Works of Walter Bagehot.* London: Economist.
Barker, Anthony. 1970. "Parliament and Patience." In Bernard Crick, ed., *The Reform of Parliament,* 2d rev. ed. London: Weidenfeld and Nicolson.
——— , and Michael Rush. 1970. *The Member of Parliament and His Information.* London: Allen and Unwin.
Barnett, Joel. 1982. *Inside the Treasury.* London: Andre Deutsch.
Beer, Samuel H. 1965. *British Politics in the Collectivist Age.* New York: Knopf.
——— . 1969. *Modern British Politics.* London: Faber.
——— . 1980. "British Pressure Groups Revisited: Pluralistic Stagnation from the 50's to the 70's." *Public Administration Bulletin* (April).
——— . 1982. *Britain Against Itself.* London: Faber.
Beith, Alan. 1981. "Prayers Unanswered: A Jaundiced View of the Parliamentary Scrutiny of Statutory Instruments." *Parliamentary Affairs* (Spring).
Beloff, Max, and Gillian Peele. 1985. *The Government of the U.K.: Political Authority in a Changing Society.* 2d ed. London: Weidenfeld and Nicolson.
Benn, Tony. 1979. "Technology's Threat to Parliament." *Guardian* (10 Feb.).
Berrington, Hugh. 1973. *Backbench Opinion in the House of Commons, 1945–55.* Oxford: Pergamon.
——— . 1985. "MPs and Their Constituents in Britain: The History of the Relationship." In Vernon Bogdanor, ed., *Representation of the People? Parliamentarians and Constituents in Western Democracies.* Aldershot: Gower.
Biffen, John. 1984. "The Government's View." In Dermot Englefield, ed., *Commons Select Committees.* Harlow: Longman.
Birch, Anthony. 1964. *Representation and Responsible Government.* London: Allen and Unwin.
——— . 1984. "Overload, Ungovernability, and Delegitimation: The Theories and the British Case." *BJPS* (April).
Black, Gordon. 1970. "A Theory of Professionalization in Politics." *APSR* (Sept.).
——— . 1972. "A Theory of Political Ambition: Career Choice and the Role of Structural Incentives." *APSR* (Sept.).
Blondel, Jean. 1963. *Voters, Parties, and Leaders: The Social Fabric of British Politics.* Middlesex: Penguin Books.

"Blowing Up a Tyranny." *Economist* (5 Nov. 1977).

Bogdanor, Vernon, ed. 1985. *Representation of the People? Parliamentarians and Constituents in Western Democracies*. Aldershot: Gower.

Boyd-Carpenter, J. 1971. "Development of the Select Committee in the British Parliament." *Parliamentarian* (April).

Briggs, Asa. 1982. *Victorian People*. Middlesex: Pelican.

Bruce-Gardyne, Jock, and Nigel Lawson. 1976. *The Power Game*. London: Macmillan.

Buck, Philip. 1963. *Amateurs and Professionals in British Politics, 1918–1979*. Chicago: Univ. of Chicago Press.

Budge, Ian. 1982. "Strategies, Issues, and Votes: British General Elections, 1950–1979." *CPS* (July).

Butler, David. 1958. *The Story of Political Behavior*. London: Hutchinson.

———, and Dennis Kavanagh. 1980. *The British General Election of 1979*. London: Macmillan.

———, and Donald Stokes. 1976. *Political Change in Britain*. New York: St. Martin's.

Butt, Ronald. 1976. *The Power of Parliament*. London: Constable.

Cain, Bruce. 1983. "Blessed Be the Tie that Unbinds: Constituency Work and the Vote Swing in Great Britain." *PS* (March).

———, and John Ferejohn. 1981. "Party Identification in the United States and Great Britain." *CPS* (April).

———, John Ferejohn, and Morris Fiorina. 1979a. "A House Is Not a Home: British MPs in Their Constituencies." *LSQ* (Nov.).

———, John Ferejohn, and Morris Fiorina. 1979b. *The Roots of Legislator Popularity in Great Britain and the United States*. Social Science Working Paper 288. Pasadena: California Institute of Technology.

———, John Ferejohn, and Morris Fiorina. 1983. "The Constituency Component: A Comparison of Service in Great Britain and the United States." *CPS* (April).

———, John Ferejohn, and Morris Fiorina. 1984. "The Constituency Service Basis of the Personal Role for U.S. Representatives and British Members of Parliament." *APSR* (March).

———, John Ferejohn, and Morris Fiorina. 1987. *The Personal Vote*. Cambridge: Harvard Univ. Press.

———, and David B. Ritchie. 1982. "Assessing Constituency Involvement: The Hemel Hempstead Experience." *Parliamentary Affairs* (Winter).

Campion, Lord. 1958. *An Introduction to the Procedure of the House of Commons*. 3d ed. London: Macmillan.

Carstairs, A. M. 1980. *A Short History of Electoral Systems in Western Europe*. Boston: Allen & Unwin.

Change or Decay. London: Conservative Political Centre, 1963.

Chester, D. N. 1970. "Questions in Parliament." In A. H. Hanson and Bernard Crick, eds., *The Commons in Transition*. London: Fontana.

Chubb, Basil. 1952. *The Control of Public Expenditure*. Oxford: Oxford Univ. Press.

Clark, Harold D., et al., eds. 1980. *Parliament, Policy, and Representation*. Toronto: Methuen.

———, and Richard Price. 1980. "Freshman MPs' Job Images: The Effects of Incumbency, Ambition, and Position." *Canadian Journal of Political Science* (Sept.).

———, and Richard Price. 1981. "Parliamentary Experience and Representational Role Orientations in Canada." *LSQ* (Aug.).

Collie, Melissa P. 1984. "Voting Behaviour in Legislatures." *LSQ* (Feb.).

"Committees and Their Powers." Times (19 Feb. 1980).

Conservative Manifesto. London: Conservative Central Office, 1979.

Converse, Philip. 1967. "The Nature and Belief Systems in Mass Publics." In D. E. Apter, ed., *Ideology and Discontent*. New York: Free Press.

Coombes, David. 1966. *The Member of Parliament and the Administration: The Case of the Select Committee on Nationalised Industries*. London: Allen and Unwin.

———, et al. 1976. *The Power of the Purse: The Role of European Parliaments in Budgetary Decisions*. London: Allen & Unwin.

———, and S. A. Walkland, eds. 1980. *Parliaments and Economic Affairs*. London: Heineman/Policy Studies Institute.

Cox, Andrew, and Stephen Kirby. 1986. *Congress, Parliament and Defense*. London: Macmillan.

Crewe, Ivor. 1974. "Do Butler and Stokes Really Explain Political Change in Britain?" *European Journal of Political Research* (March).

———, 1975. "Electoral Reform and the Local MP." In Samuel E. Finer, ed. *Adversary Politics and Electoral Reform*. London: Anthony Wigan.

———, 1985. "MPs and Their Constituents in Britain: How Strong Are the Parties?" In Vernon Bogdanor, ed., *Representation of The People? Parliaments and Constituents in Western Democracies*. Aldershot: Gower.

———, and David Denver, eds. 1985. *Electoral Change in Western Democracies: Patterns and Sources of Electoral Volatility*. New York: St. Martin's.

Crick, Bernard. 1962. *In Defense of Politics*. London: Weidenfeld and Nicolson.

———. 1964. *Reform of Parliament*. London: Weidenfeld and Nicolson.

———. 1965. *Reform of Parliament*. New York: Anchor Books.

———. 1970a. *The Reform of Parliament*. 2d rev. ed. London: Weidenfeld and Nicolson.

———. 1970b. "Whither Parliamentary Reform?" In A. H. Hanson and Bernard Crick, eds., *The Commons in Transition*. London: Fontana.

Crossman, R. H. S. 1976. *The Diaries of a Cabinet Minister*. Vol. 2. London: Hamilton and Cape.

Crowe, Edward W. 1983. "Consensus and Structure in Legislative Norms: Party Discipline in the House of Commons." *Journal of Politics* (Nov.).

Curtice, J., and M. Steed. 1979. "The Analysis of Voting." In David Butler and Dennis Kavanagh, eds., *The British General Election of 1979*. London: Macmillan.

———, and M. Steed. 1982. "Electoral Choice and the Production of Government: The Changing Operation of the Electoral System in the United Kingdom since 1955." *BJPS* (July).

Dalton, Russell S. 1985. "Political Parties and Political Representation: Party Supporters and Party Elites in Nine Nations." *CPS* (Oct.).

Davies, Ann. 1980. *Reformed Select Committees: The First Year.* London: Outer Circle Policy Unit.

"Decline of Parliament, The." *Political Quarterly* (July–Sept.).

Della Sala, Vincent. 1990. "The Italian Parliament in the 1990's: What Reform for What Parliament?" Paper presented at the Annual Meeting of the Midwest Political Science Association, Chicago, Ill., 5–7 April.

Dodd, Lawrence C. "Congress, the Constitution, and the Crisis of Legitimation." In Lawrence C. Dodd and Bruce I. Oppenheimer, eds., *Congress Reconsidered.* 2d ed. Washington, D.C.: Brookings Institution.

Downs, Steven J. 1985. "Select Committees: Experiment and Establishment." In Philip Norton, ed., *Parliament in the 1980's.* Oxford: Basil Blackwood.

Drewry, Gavin. 1985. *The New Select Committees: A Survey of the 1979 Reforms.* Oxford: Clarendon.

Drewry, Robert. 1963. "The MP and His Surgery." *PS* (Oct.).

Du Cann, Edward. 1976. "Reflections on the Control of Public Expenditure in the United Kingdom." *Parliamentarian* (July).

––––––. 1977. *Parliament and the Purse Strings.* London: Conservative Political Centre.

––––––. 1981. "Parliamentary Select Committees and Democracy." *Public Money* (June).

"Duties and Responsibilities of Civil Servants and Ministers, The." *Constitutional Reform* (Summer 1986).

Englefield, Dermot, ed. 1984. Commons Select Committees: *Catalysts for Progress?* Harlow: Longman.

Enzig, Paul. 1959. *The Control of the Purse.* London: Saker and Warburg.

Epstein, Leon D. 1980. "What Happened to the British Party Model?" *APSR* (March).

Eulau, Heinz. 1955. "Committee Selection." In Gerhard Loewenberg, ed., *Handbook of Legislative Research.* Cambridge: Harvard Univ. Press.

––––––. 1978. "Changing Views of Representation." In Heinz Eulau and John C. Wahlke, eds., *The Politics of Representation: Constraints in Theory and Research.* Beverly Hills: Sage Publications.

––––––. 1984. "Legislative Committee Assignments." *LSQ* (Nov.).

––––––, et al. 1959. "The Role of the Representative: Some Empirical Observations on the Theory of Edmund Burke." *APSR* (Sept.).

––––––, and Paul D. Karps. 1977. "The Puzzle of Representation: Specifying Components of Responsiveness." *LSQ* (Aug.).

––––––, and Vera McCluggage. "Standing Committees in Legislatures: Three Decades of Research." *LSQ* (May).

––––––, and John C. Wahlke. 1978. *The Politics of Representation: Constraints in Theory and Research.* Beverly Hills: Sage Publications.

Fairlie, Henry. 1968. *The Life of Politics.* London: Methuen.

Fenno, Richard F, Jr. 1973. *Congressmen in Committees.* Boston: Little, Brown.

———. 1986. "Observation, Context, and Sequence in the Study of Politics." *APSR* (March).

Finer, Samuel E., ed. 1975. *Adversary Politics and Electoral Reform*. London: Wigram.

———. 1980. *The Changing British Party System*. Washington, D.C.: American Enterprise Institute.

———, Hugh Berrington, and D. J. Bartholomew. 1961. *Backbench Opinion in the House of Commons, 1955–59*. New York: Pergamon Press.

Fishbein, Martin, ed. 1967. *Readings in Attitude Theory and Measurement*. New York: John Wiley.

———, and Bertram H. Raven. 1967. "The AB Scales: An Operational Definition of Belief and Attitudes." In Martin Fishbein, ed., *Readings in Attitude Theory and Measurement*. New York: John Wiley.

Fitzgerald, Keith. 1990. "Autonomy and Institutional Will: The Role of Leadership in the French National Assembly." Paper presented at the Annual Meeting of the Midwest Political Science Association, Chicago, Ill., 5–7 April.

Flanagan, S. C. 1982. "Changing Values in Advanced Industrial Society." *CPS* (Jan.).

Flegman, Vilma. 1981. "Government Departments and Select Committees of the House of Commons." Paper presented to the Political Science Association Conference, Hull.

———. 1985. "Civil Servants and the Select Committees of the House of Commons." Paper presented to the workshop on "Relationship between Parliament and the Administration" at the European Group of Public Administration Conference, Leuven, Sept.

Foot, Michael. 1959. *Parliament in Danger*. London: Pall Mall Press.

Frankland, Gene E. 1973. "Cross-National Determinants of Parliamentary Career Advancement: Britain and West Germany." Ph.D. diss., Univ. of Iowa.

Frears, John. 1990. "The French Parliament: Loyal Workhouse, Poor Watchdog." In Philip Norton, ed., *Parliaments in Western Europe*. Portland, Ore.: Frank Cass.

Furlong, Paul. 1990. "Parliament in Italian Politics." In Philip Norton, ed., *Parliaments in Western Europe*. Portland, Ore.: Frank Cass.

George, Bruce, and Michael Woodward. 1984. "The Foreign Affairs Committee and the Patriation of the Canadian Constitution." In Dilys M. Hill, ed., *Parliamentary Select Committees in Action: A Symposium*. Strathchlyde Papers on Government and Politics. Glasgow: Univ. of Strathchlyde.

Gladdish, Ken. 1990. "Parliamentary Activism and Legitimacy in the Netherlands." In Philip Norton, ed., *Parliaments in Western Europe*. Portland, Ore.: Frank Cass.

Golding, John. 1984. "The Chairman's View—II." In Dermot Englefield, ed., *Commons Select Committees*. Harlow: Longman.

Goodhart, Philip. 1960. "What's Really Wrong with the Commons?" *Crossbow* (Spring).

Granada Television. 1973. *The State of the Nation: Parliament.* London: Granada Television Ltd.

Griffith, J. A. G. 1982. "The Constitution and the Commons." In *Parliament and the Executive.* London: Royal Institute of Public Administration.

Guttsman, W. L. 1968. *The British Political Elite.* London: MacGibbon and Kee.

Hailsham, Lord. 1976. "Elective Dictatorship." *Listener* (21 Oct.).

Hale, Leslie. 1966. "The Backbencher." *Parliamentarian* (July).

Halsey, A. 1986. *Change in British Society.* Oxford: Oxford Univ. Press.

Hanson, A. H. 1964. "The Purpose of Parliament." *Parliamentary Affairs* (Summer).

——— . 1970. "The House of Commons and Finance." In A. H. Hanson and Bernard Crick, eds., *The Commons in Transition.* London: Fontana.

——— , and Bernard Crick. 1970. *The Commons in Transition.* London: Fontana.

——— , and Malcolm Walles. 1980. *Governing Britain.* 3d ed. London: Fontana.

——— , and H.V. Wiseman. 1959. "The Use of Committees by the House of Commons." *Public Law* (Autumn).

——— , and H.V. Wiseman. 1961. *Parliament at Work.* London: Fontana.

Harrop, M. 1982. "The Changing British Electorate." *Political Quarterly* (Oct.–Dec.).

Heatherington, Alastair. 1980. "The Pips Are Beginning to Squeak in the Treasury." *Listener* (14 Aug.).

Hedlund, Ronald D. 1984. "Organizational Attributes of Legislatures: Structures, Rules, Norms, Resources." *LSQ* (Feb.).

Hennessy, Peter. 1980a. "New Committees Make an Impressive Start." *Times* (25 March).

——— . 1980b. "Pips Are Beginning to Squeak as Treasury Faces the Demands of Committee, Former Chief Says." *Times* (13 Aug.).

——— . 1980c. "Whitehall Men Told What Not to Disclose." *Times* (22 May).

——— . 1980d. "Why the Leader Is Walking the Tightrope." *Times* (6 Aug.).

——— . 1984. "League Table for the Watchdogs." *Times* (10 Jan.).

Hill, Andrew, and Anthony Whichelow. 1964. *What's Wrong with Parliament?* London: Penguin Books.

Hogg, Quintin. 1969. *New Charter.* London: Conservative Political Centre.

Hollis, Christopher. 1949. *Can Parliament Survive?* London: Hollis and Carter.

"How MPs Have Kept Their Zeal for Reform." *Times* (6 June 1966).

Huntington, Samuel P. 1968. *Political Order in Changing Societies.* New Haven: Yale Univ. Press.

Inglehart, Ronald. 1977. *The Silent Revolution: Changing Values and Political Styles among Western Publics.* Princeton: Princeton Univ. Press.

——— . 1983. "The Persistence of Materialist and Post-Materialist Value Orientations." *European Journal of Political Research* (March).

"Is the House of Commons Too Big to Work Properly?" *Times* (12 Sept. 1977).

Jackson, Robert. 1968. *Rebels and Whips.* New York: Macmillan.

Jennings, Bruce, and Daniel Callahan. 1985. *Representation and Responsibility: Exploring Legislative Ethics.* New York: Plenum.

Jennings, Ivor. 1934. *Parliamentary Reform*. London: Victor Gollancz.

———. 1939. *Parliament*. Cambridge: Cambridge Univ. Press.

Jewell, Malcolm E. 1983. "Legislator-Constituency Relations and the Representative Process." *LSQ* (Aug.).

———, and Samuel C. Patterson. 1979. "Editors' Introduction: Toward a New Model of Legislative Representation." *LSQ* (Aug.).

Jogerst, Michael A. 1991. "Backbenchers and Select Committees in the British House of Commons: Can Parliament Offer Useful Roles for the Frustrated?" *European Journal of Political Research* (Spring).

Johnson, Nevil. 1966. *Parliament and Administration*. London: Allen and Unwin.

———. 1970. "Select Committees as Tools of Parliamentary Reform." In A. H. Hanson and Bernard Crick, eds., *The Commons in Transition*. London: Fontana.

———. 1984. "An Academic's View." In Dermot Englefield, ed., *Commons Select Committees*. Harlow: Longman.

Jowell, Jeffrey, and Dawn Oliver. 1985. *The Changing Contribution*. Oxford: Clarendon Press.

Judge, David. 1981. *Backbench Specialization in the House of Commons*. London: Heinemann.

———. 1982. "Ministerial Responsibility." *House Magazine* (26 Nov.).

———. 1983. *The Politics of Parliamentary Reform*. Rutherford, N. J.: Fairleigh Dickinson Univ. Press.

———. 1986. *Parliament and the Public*. 2d ed. New York: Longman.

Katz, Richard S. 1986. "Party Government: A Rationalistic Conception." In Francis G. Castles and Rudolf Wilderman, eds., *Visions and Realities of Party Government*. New York: de Gruyter.

Kelley, J., I. McAllister, and A. Mughan. 1983. *The Changing Electoral Salience of Class in England, 1964–79*. Working Papers in Sociology. Canberra: Australian National Univ.

Kerr, David. 1969. "The Changing Role of the Backbencher." *Parliamentarian* (July).

Kimber, Richard, and Jeremy Richardson. 1968. "Specialization and Parliamentary Standing Committees." *PS* (Feb.).

King, Anthony. 1974. *British Members of Parliament: A Self-Portrait*. London: Macmillan.

———. 1976a. "Modes of Executive-Legislative Relations: Great Britain, France, and West Germany." *LSQ* (Feb.).

———. 1976b. "The Problem of Overload." In Anthony King, ed., *Why Is Britain Becoming Harder to Govern?* London: BBC.

———. 1981. "The Rise of the Career Politician in Britain—And Its Consequences." *BJPS* (July).

Kirkpatrick, Evron. 1971. "Towards a More Responsible Two-Party System: Political Science, Policy Science or Pseudo-Science." *APSR* (Dec.).

Koester, Robert. 1968. "Standing Committees in the British House of Commons." *Parliamentarian* (April).

Kornberg, Allan, ed. 1973. *Legislatures in Comparative Perspective*. New York: McKay.

Lankester, R. S. 1981. "The Remodelled Select Committee System of the House of Commons." *Contemporary Review* (Jan.).

Laski, Harold. 1938. *Parliamentary Government in England*. London: Allen and Unwin.

Lees, John D., and Malcolm Shaw. 1979. *Committees in Legislatures: A Comparative Analysis*. Durham, N.C.: Duke Univ. Press.

Leison, Richard. 1973. "Comparative Legislative Institutionalization: A Theoretical Exploration." In Allen Kornberg, ed., *Legislatures in Comparative Perspective*. New York: McKay.

Leonard, Dick, and Valentine Herman, eds. 1972. *The Backbencher and Parliament*. London: St. Martin's.

Leonardi, Robert, Raffaella Nanetti, and Gianfranco Pasquino. "Institutionalization of Parliament and Parliamentarization of Parties in Italy." *LSQ* (Feb.).

Lloyd, Ian. 1984. "The Chairman's View—I." In Dermot Englefield, ed., *Commons Select Committees*. Harlow: Longman.

Lowenberg, Gerhard, ed. *Modern Parliaments: Change or Decline?* Chicago: Aldine-Atherton.

Loewenberg, Gerhard, and Chong Lim Kim. 1978. "Comparing the Representativeness of Parliaments." *LSQ* (Feb.).

——— , et al. 1985. *Handbook of Legislative Research*. Cambridge: Harvard Univ. Press.

——— , et al. 1952. *Parliament: A Survey*. London: Allen and Unwin.

Lowell, A. Lawrence. 1924. *The Governance of England*. New York: Macmillan.

Lynskey, J. J. 1970. "The Role of the British Backbencher in the Modification of Government Policy." *Western Political Quarterly* (June).

MacKenzie, Kenneth. 1950. *The English Parliament*. Harmondsworth: Penguin.

McKenzie, Roger. 1964. *British Political Parties*. 3d ed. London: Heinemann.

Mackintosh, John P. 1968a. *The British Cabinet*. 2d ed. London: Methuen.

——— . 1968b. "The Failure of a Reform." *New Society* (28 Nov.).

——— . 1969. "Dwindling Hopes of Commons Reform." *Times* (13 March).

——— . 1970a. *The Influence of the Backbencher, Now and a Hundred Years Ago*. Manchester: Manchester Statistical Society.

——— . 1970b. *Specialist Committees in the House of Commons: Have They Failed?* Waverly Paper No. 1. Edinburgh: Univ. of Edinburgh.

——— . 1971. "Reform of the House of Commons: The Case for Specialization." In Gerhard Loewenberg, ed., *Modern Parliaments: Change or Decline?* Chicago: Adine-Atheron.

——— . 1977. *The Government and Politics of Britain*. 4th ed. London: Hutchinson.

——— . 1978. *People and Parliament*. Aldershot: Saxon House.

Marsh, A. 1975. "The 'Silent Revolution,' Value Priorities, and the Quality of Life in Britain." *APSR* (March).

Marsh, D. 1983. "Dr. Norton's Parliament." *Public Administration Bulletin* (April).

Marsh, Ian. 1986. *Policy Making in a Three Party System.* London: Methuen.

Marsh, James W. 1983. *The Value of the Constituency Member of Parliament.* Hull Papers in Politics, no. 211. Hull: Univ. of Hull.

———. 1985. "Representational Changes: The Constituency MP." In Philip Norton, ed., *Parliament in the 1980's.* Oxford: Basil Blackwood.

Matthews, Donald R. 1984. "Legislative Recruitment and Legislative Careers." *LSQ* (Nov.).

Mellors, Colin. 1978. *The British MP: A Socio-Economic Study of the House of Commons.* Farnborough: Saxon House.

Members of the Study of Parliament Group. 1976. "Specialist Committees in the British Parliament: The Experience of a Decade." *Political and Economic Planning* (Spring).

Mezey, Michael L. 1979. *Comparative Legislatures.* Durham, N.C.: Duke Univ. Press.

Mikardo, Ian. 1970. "The Select Committee on Nationalised Industries." In Alfred Morris, ed., *The Growth of Parliamentary Scrutiny by Committee.* Oxford: Pergamon.

Miller, W. L. 1977. *Electoral Dynamics in Britain since 1918.* London: Macmillan.

Mishler, William. 1978. "Nominating Attractive Candidates for Parliament: Recruitment to the Canadian House of Commons." *LSQ* (Nov.).

———. 1983. "Scotching Nationalism in the British Parliament: Crosscutting Cleavages among MPs." *LSQ* (Feb.).

Morrell, F. 1977. *From the Electors of Bristol.* Nottingham: Spokesman Books.

Morris, Alfred, ed. 1970. *The Growth of Parliamentary Scrutiny by Committee.* Oxford: Pergamon.

Mughan, A. 1978. "Electoral Change in Britain: The Campaign Reassessed." *BJPS* (April).

Munroe, Ronald. 1977. "The Member of Parliament as Representative: The View from the Constituency." *PS* (Dec.).

"Mutiny on the Benches." *Times Literary Supplement* (12 March 1976).

Neale, J. E. 1949. *The Elizabethan House of Commons.* London: Jonathan Cape.

Neave, Airey. 1968. *Control by Committee.* London: Conservative Political Centre.

"New Departmental Select Committee Structures, The." *Factsheet*, No. 6. House of Commons, Public Information Office, 11 Feb. 1980.

Norton, Philip. 1975. *Dissension in the House of Commons: Intra-Party Dissent in the House of Commons' Division Lobbies, 1945–74.* London: Macmillan.

———. 1976. "Dissent in Committee: Intra-party Dissent in Commons's Standing Committees, 1959–74." *Parliamentarian* (Aug.).

———. 1977. "Private Legislation and the Influence of the Backbench MP." *Parliamentary Affairs* (Autumn).

———. 1978a. *Conservative Dissidents: Dissent within the Parliamentary Conservative Party, 1970–74.* London: Temple Smith.

———. 1978b. *The House of Commons in the 1970's: Three Views on Reform.* Hull Papers in Politics, no. 3. Hull: Univ. of Hull, 1978.

———. 1980a. "The Changing Face of the British House of Commons in the 1970's." *LSQ* (Aug.).

———. 1980b. *Dissension in the House of Commons, 1974–1979.* Oxford: Clarendon.

———. 1981a. *The Commons in Perspective.* Oxford: Martin Robertson.

———. 1981b. "The House of Commons and the Constitution." *Parliamentary Affairs* (Summer).

———. 1982a. *The Constitution in Flux.* Oxford: Martin Robertson.

———. 1982b. "Dear Minister . . . : An Analysis of MPs'Correspondence with Ministers." *Parliamentary Affairs* (Winter).

———. 1983a. "Parliament and Policy in Great Britain." Paper presented to the Annual Meeting of the American Political Science Association, Sept.

———. 1983b. "Party Committees in the House of Commons." *Parliamentary Affairs* (Winter).

———. 1984. "Parliament and Policy in Britain: The House of Commons as a Policy Influencer." *Teaching Politics* (May).

———, ed. 1985. *Parliament in the 1980's.* Oxford: Basil Blackwood.

———. 1986a. "Committees in the House of Commons." *Social Studies Review* (Jan.).

———. 1986b. "Independence, Scrutiny, and Rationalisation: A Decade of Change in the House of Commons." *Teaching Politics* (Jan.).

———, ed. 1990. *Parliaments in Western Europe.* Portland, Ore.: Frank Cass.

Oliver, Dawn, and Rodney Austin. 1987. "Political and Constitutional Aspects of the Westland Affair." *Parliamentary Affairs* (Spring).

Olson, David M. 1980. *The Legislative Process: A Comparative Approach.* New York: Harper & Row.

Oppenheimer, Bruce I. 1985. "Legislative Influence on Policy and Budgets." In Gerhard Loewenberg, ed., *Handbook of Legislative Research.* Cambridge: Harvard Univ. Press.

Ornstein, Norman J., ed. 1981. *The Role of the Legislature in Western Democracies.* Washington, D.C.: American Enterprise Institute.

Parliament and Government in Our Industrial Society. 1963. London: Conservative Political Centre.

"Parliament Prepares to Seize Power." *Economist* (24 Feb. 1979).

"Parliamentary Development." *Parliamentary Affairs* (Summer 1980).

Partington, Martin. 1970. "Parliamentary Committees: Recent Developments." *Parliamentary Affairs* (Autumn).

Pasquino, Gianfranco. 1986. "The Impact of Institutions on Party Government: Tentative Hypotheses." In Francis G. Castles and Rudolf Wildenmann, eds., *Visions and Realities of Party Government.* New York: de Gruyter.

Patterson, Samuel. 1973. "The British House of Commons as a Focus for Political Research." *BJPS* (July).

Pedersen, Mogens N. 1984. "Research on European Parliaments: A Review Article on Scholarly and Institutional Variety." *LSQ* (Aug.).

Pooke, K. P. 1979. "The Powers of Select Committees of the House of Commons to Send for Persons, Papers and Records." *Parliamentary Affairs* (Summer).

Popham, G. T., and D. Greengrass. 1970. "The Role and Functions of the Select Committee on Agriculture." *Public Administration* (Autumn).

Price, Christopher. 1986. Review of *The New Select Committees*, ed. Gavin Drewry. *Public Administration* (Spring).

Pring, David. 1982. "Backbench Power Lives Again." *Economist* (14 Aug.).

———. 1983. "The New Select Committee System at Westminster." *Parliamentarian* (April).

———. 1984. "The Clerks' View." In Dermot Englefield, ed., *Commons Select Committees*. Harlow: Longman.

Punnett, R. M. 1973. *Front Bench Opposition: The Role of the Leader of the Opposition, the Shadow Cabinet and Shadow Government in British Politics.* London: Heinemann.

Putnam, Robert D. 1973. *The Beliefs of Politicians: Ideology, Conflict and Democracy in Britain and Italy.* London: Yale Univ. Press.

———. 1976. *The Comparative Study of Political Elites.* Englewood Cliffs, N.J.: Prentice-Hall.

Raison, Timothy. 1978. *Power in Parliament.* Oxford: Basil Blackwell.

Ranney, Austin. 1965. *Pathways to Parliament: Candidate Selection in Britain.* Madison: Univ. of Wisconsin.

Rasmussen, Jorgen. 1971. "Government and Intra-Party Opposition." *PS* (March).

Redlich, Josef. 1908. *Procedure of the House of Commons.* Vol. 1. London: Constable.

Rees-Mogg, William. 1965. *Liberty in 1964.* London: Conservative Political Centre.

Reid, Gordon. 1966. *The Politics of Financial Control.* London: Hutchinson.

Rhodes, Gerald. 1975. *Committees of Inquiry.* London: Allen and Unwin.

Richards, Peter. 1972. *The Backbenchers.* London: Faber & Faber.

Richardson, J. J., and A. G. Jordan. 1979. *Governing under Pressure.* London: Martin Robertson.

Robinson, Ann. 1978. *Parliament and Public Spending: The Expenditure Committee of the House of Commons, 1970–76.* London: Heinemann.

Robson, William A. 1964. "The Reform of Government." *Political Quarterly* (July–Sept.).

Rose, Paul. 1981. *Backbencher's Dilemma.* London: Frederick Muller.

Rose, Richard. 1981. "British MPs: A Bite as Well as a Bark?" Paper presented for conference on the Role of Parliamentarians in Contemporary Democracies, Madrid, 15–16 Dec.

Roth, Andrew, et al. 1981. *The Business Background of MPs.* London: Parliamentary Profiles.

Rush, Michael. 1969. *The Selection of Parliamentary Candidates*. London: Nelson.
————. 1977. "The Members of Parliament." In S.A. Walkland and Michael Ryle, eds., *The Commons in the 70's*. London: Fontana.
————. 1982. "Parliamentary Committees and Parliamentary Government: The British and Canadian Experience." *Journal of Commonwealth and Parliamentary Politics* (July).
————. 1986. *Parliament and the Public*. 2d ed. New York: Longman.
————, and Malcolm Shaw. 1974. *The House of Commons Services and Facilities*. London: Allen and Unwin.
Ryle, Michael. 1965. "Committees of the House of Commons." *Political Quarterly* (July–Oct.).
————. 1977. "The Commons in the Seventies—A General Survey." In S. A. Walkland and Michael Ryle, eds., *The Commons in the 70's*. London: Fontana.
————. 1981. "The Legislative Staff of the British House of Commons." *LSQ* (Nov.).
Saalfeld, Thomas. 1990. "The West German Bundestag after 40 Years: The Role of Parliament in a 'Party Democracy.' " In Philip Norton, ed., *Parliaments in Western Europe*. Portland, Ore.: Frank Cass.
St. John-Stevas, Norman. 1982. "Government by Discussion." In J. R. Nethercote, ed. *Parliament and Bureaucracy*. Sydney: Hale and Iremonger.
Schwarz, John E. 1981. "Attempting to Assert the Commons' Power: Labour Members in the House of Commons, 1974–79." *Comparative Politics* (Oct.).
————. 1980. "Exploring a New Role in Policy Making: The British House of Commons in the 1970's." *APSR* (March).
————. 1978. "The Commons Bites Back." *Financial Times* (2 June).
————, Barton Fenmore, and Thomas J. Volgy. 1980. "Liberal and Conservative Voting in the House of Representatives: A National Model of Representation." *BJPS* (July).
"Scrutiny by the Commons." *Times* (4 Aug. 1978).
Searing, Donald D. 1982. "Rules of the Game in Britain: Can the Politicians be Trusted?" *APSR* (June).
Self, Peter. 1985. *Political Theories of Modern Government, Its Role and Reform*. London: Allen & Unwin.
Shell, Donald R. 1970. "Specialist Select Committees." *Parliamentary Affairs* (Autumn).
Silk, Paul. 1987. *How Parliament Works*. New York: Longman.
Smith, Geoffrey. 1979. *Westminster Reform: Learning from Congress*. Thames Essay no. 20. London: Trade Policy Research Centre.
————. 1980. "The Younger Men that Mrs. Thatcher Must Convince of Her Strategy." *Times* (21 March).
————. 1982. "Where Do MPs Go When They're Not on Stage?" *Times* (5 June).
Smith, Steven S. 1986. "The Central Concepts in Fenno's Committee Studies." *LSQ* (Feb.).

Stacey, Frank. 1975. *British Government: Years of Reform, 1966–1975.* Oxford: Oxford Univ. Press.

Strauss, G.R. 1972. "The Influence of the Backbench: A Labour View." *The Backbench and Parliament,* ed. Dick Leonard and Valentine Herman. London: St. Martin's.

Studlar, Donald. 1978. "Policy Voting in Britain: The Coloured Immigration Issue in the 1964, 1966, and 1970 General Elections." *APSR* (March).

Study of Parliament Group. 1965. "Reforming the Commons." *Political and Economic Planning* (Oct.).

Suleiman, Ezra N. 1986. *Parliaments and Parliamentarians in Democratic Politics.* New York: Holmes and Meier.

Swinhoe, Kenneth. 1971. "A Study of Opinion about the Reform of the House of Commons Procedure, 1945–68." Ph.D. thesis, Univ. of Leeds.

"Three Dozen Parliamentary Reforms by One Dozen Parliamentary Socialists." *Socialist Commentary* (July 1964).

Trethowan, I. 1967. "Mr. Crossman Is Offering Backbenchers a Deal." *Times* (16 March).

Wahlke, John C. 1971. "Policy Demands and System Support: The Role of the Represented." *BJPS* (July).

Walkland, S. A. 1962. "The Form of Parliamentary Estimates." *Yorkshire Bulletin of Economic and Social Research* (Nov.).

——— . 1968. *The Legislative Process in Great Britain.* London: Allen and Unwin.

——— . 1977. "Whither the Commons?" In S. A. Walkland and Michael Ryle, eds., *The Commons in the Seventies.* London: Fontana.

——— . 1979a. "Committees in the British House of Commons." In John Lees and Malcolm Shaw, eds., *Committees in Legislatures: A Comparative Analysis.* Durham, N.C.: Duke Univ. Press.

——— , ed. 1979b. *The House of Commons in the Twentieth Century.* Oxford: Oxford Univ. Press.

——— . 1985. "Forward." In Gavin Drewry, ed., *The New Select Committees: A Study of the 1979 Reforms.* Oxford: Clarendon Press.

——— , and Michael Ryle, eds. 1977. *The Commons in the Seventies.* London: Fontana.

——— , and Michael Ryle, eds. 1981. *The Commons Today.* London: Fontana.

"Watchdog Body Barks On." *Times* (13 March 1969).

Willey, Frederick. 1974. *The Honourable Member.* London: Sheldon Press.

Williams, R. 1968, "The Select Committee on Science and Technology." *Public Administration* (Autumn).

Wiseman, H. V. 1970. "The New Specialized Committees." In A.H. Hanson and Bernard Crick, eds., *The Commons in Transition.* London: Fontana.

Index

www.ingramcontent.com/pod-product-compliance
Lightning Source LLC
Chambersburg PA
CBHW020607270326
41927CB00005B/220